JAMIE MADROX WAS BORN WITH THE ABILITY TO CREATE E[illegible] HIMSELF WHENEVER THERE IS PHYSICAL IMPACT UPON HIS BODY. HE CAN THEN ABSORB THESE DUPLICATES THROUGH CONTACT, TAKING THEIR MEMORIES AND SKILLS. HE'S WALKED MANY PATHS, BUT ONLY ONE JOURNEY AS...

MULTIPLE MAN

IT ALL MAKES SENSE IN THE END

WRITER MATTHEW ROSENBERG

ARTIST ANDY MacDONALD

COLOR ARTIST TAMRA BONVILLAIN

LETTERER VC's TRAVIS LANHAM

COVER ART MARCOS MARTIN

ASSISTANT EDITOR CHRIS ROBINSON

EDITORS CHRISTINA HARRINGTON & JORDAN D. WHITE

COLLECTION EDITOR JENNIFER GRÜNWALD ••• ASSISTANT EDITOR CAITLIN O'CONNELL

ASSOCIATE MANAGING EDITOR KATERI WOODY ••• EDITOR, SPECIAL PROJECTS MARK D. BEAZLEY

VP PRODUCTION & SPECIAL PROJECTS JEFF YOUNGQUIST ••• SVP PRINT, SALES & MARKETING DAVID GABRIEL

BOOK DESIGNER JAY BOWEN

EDITOR IN CHIEF C.B. CEBULSKI ••• CHIEF CREATIVE OFFICER JOE QUESADA

PRESIDENT DAN BUCKLEY ••• EXECUTIVE PRODUCER ALAN FINE

MULTIPLE MAN: IT ALL MAKES SENSE IN THE END. Contains material originally published in magazine form as MULTIPLE MAN #1-5. First printing 2018. ISBN 978-1-302-91297-0. Published by MARVEL WORLDWIDE, INC., a subsidiary of MARVEL ENTERTAINMENT, LLC. OFFICE OF PUBLICATION: 135 West 50th Street, New York, NY 10020. **Printed in Canada.** DAN BUCKLEY, President, Marvel Entertainment; JOHN NEE, Publisher; JOE QUESADA, Chief Creative Officer; TOM BREVOORT, SVP of Publishing; DAVID BOGART, SVP of Business Affairs & Operations, Publishing & Partnership; DAVID GABRIEL, SVP of Sales & Marketing, Publishing; JEFF YOUNGQUIST, VP of Production & Special Projects; DAN CARR, Executive Director of Publishing Technology; ALEX MORALES, Director of Publishing Operations; DAN EDINGTON, Managing Editor; SUSAN CRESPI, Production Manager; STAN LEE, Chairman Emeritus. For information regarding advertising in Marvel Comics or on Marvel.com, please contact Vit DeBellis, Custom Solutions & Integrated Advertising Manager, at vdebellis@marvel.com. For Marvel subscription inquiries, please call 888-511-5480. **Manufactured between 10/26/2018 and 11/27/2018 by SOLISCO PRINTERS, SCOTT, QC, CANADA.**

10 9 8 7 6 5 4 3 2 1

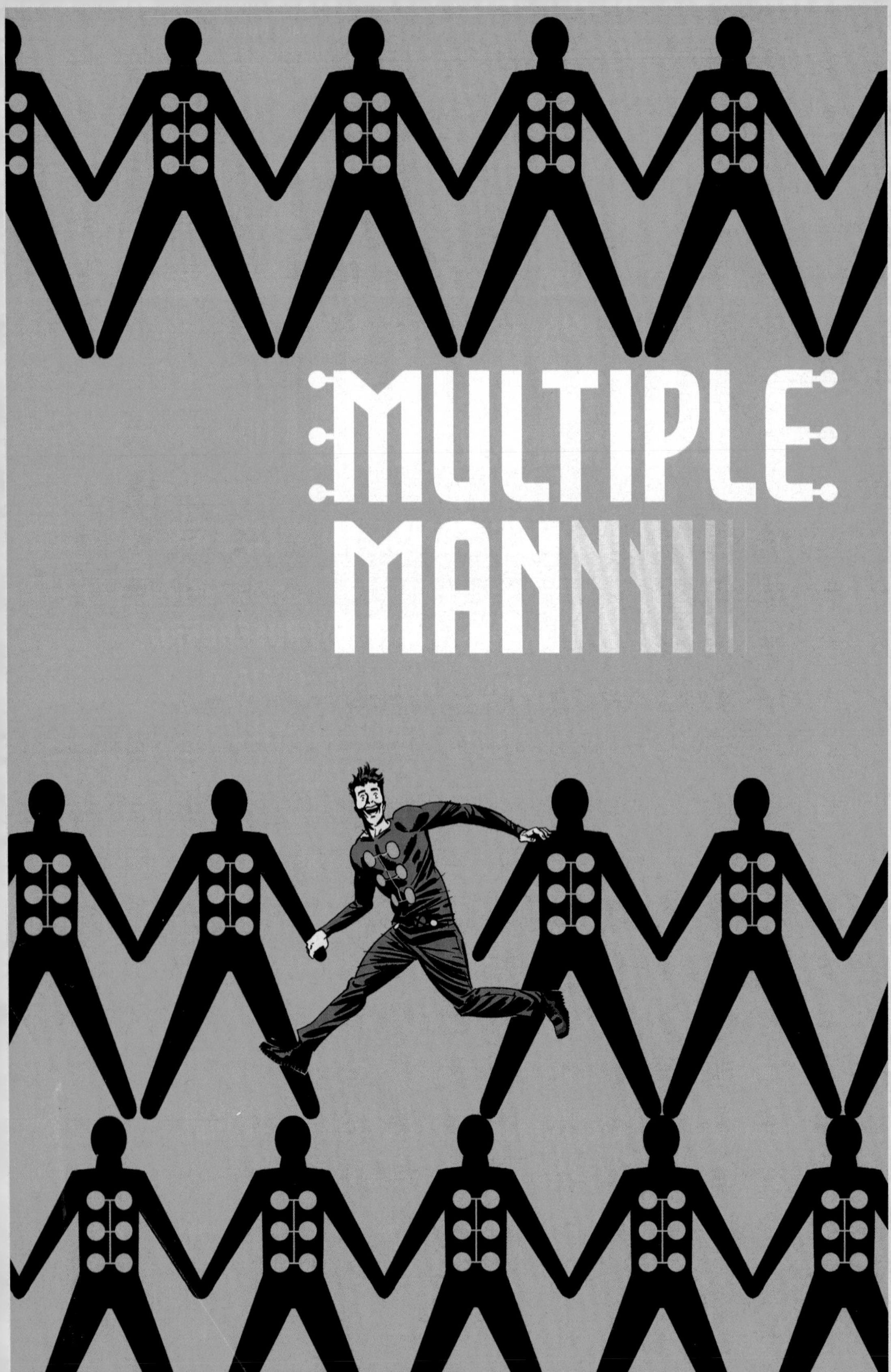
MULTIPLE
MAN

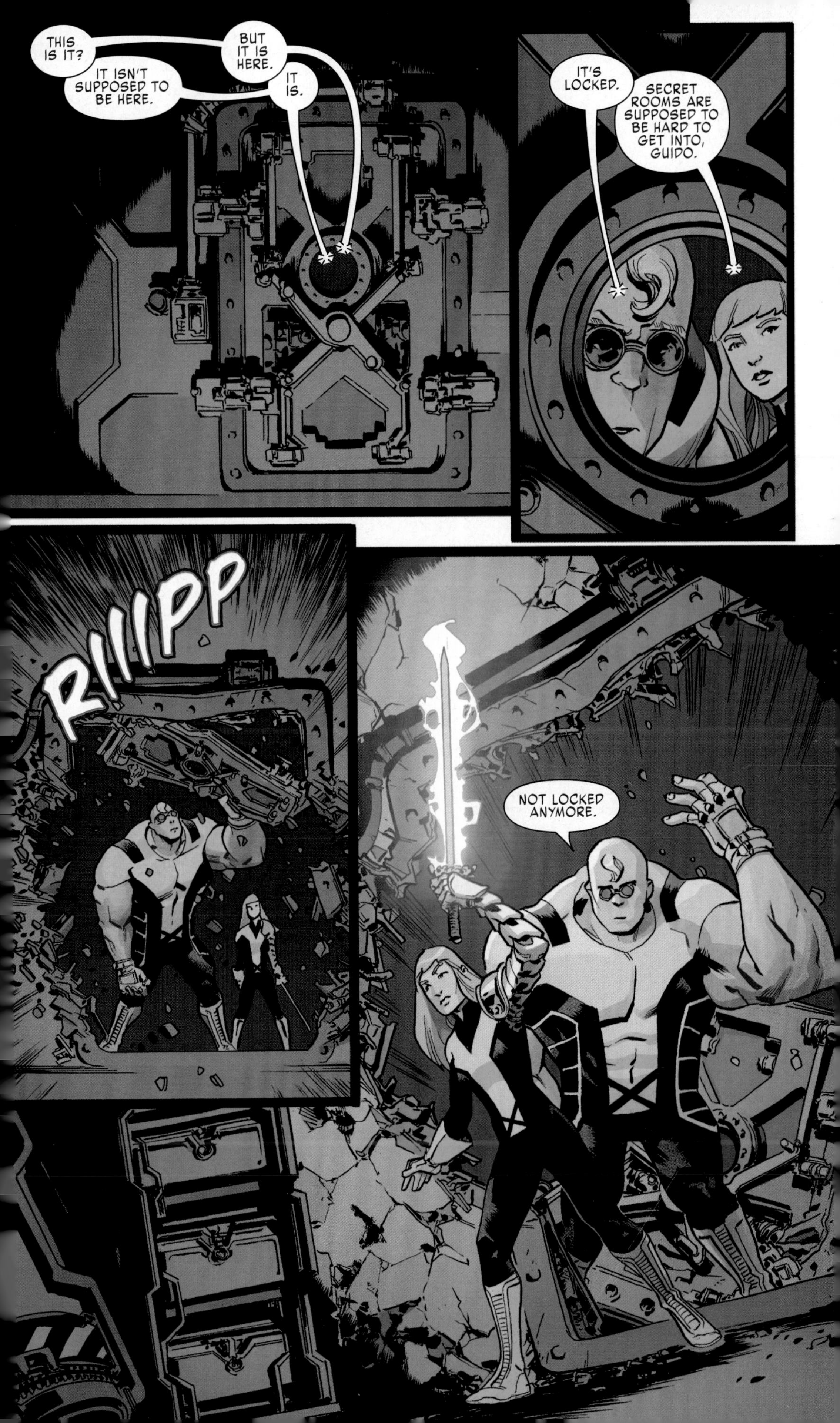
THIS IS IT?
IT ISN'T SUPPOSED TO BE HERE.
BUT IT IS HERE.
IT IS.
IT'S LOCKED.
SECRET ROOMS ARE SUPPOSED TO BE HARD TO GET INTO, GUIDO.
RIIIPP
NOT LOCKED ANYMORE.

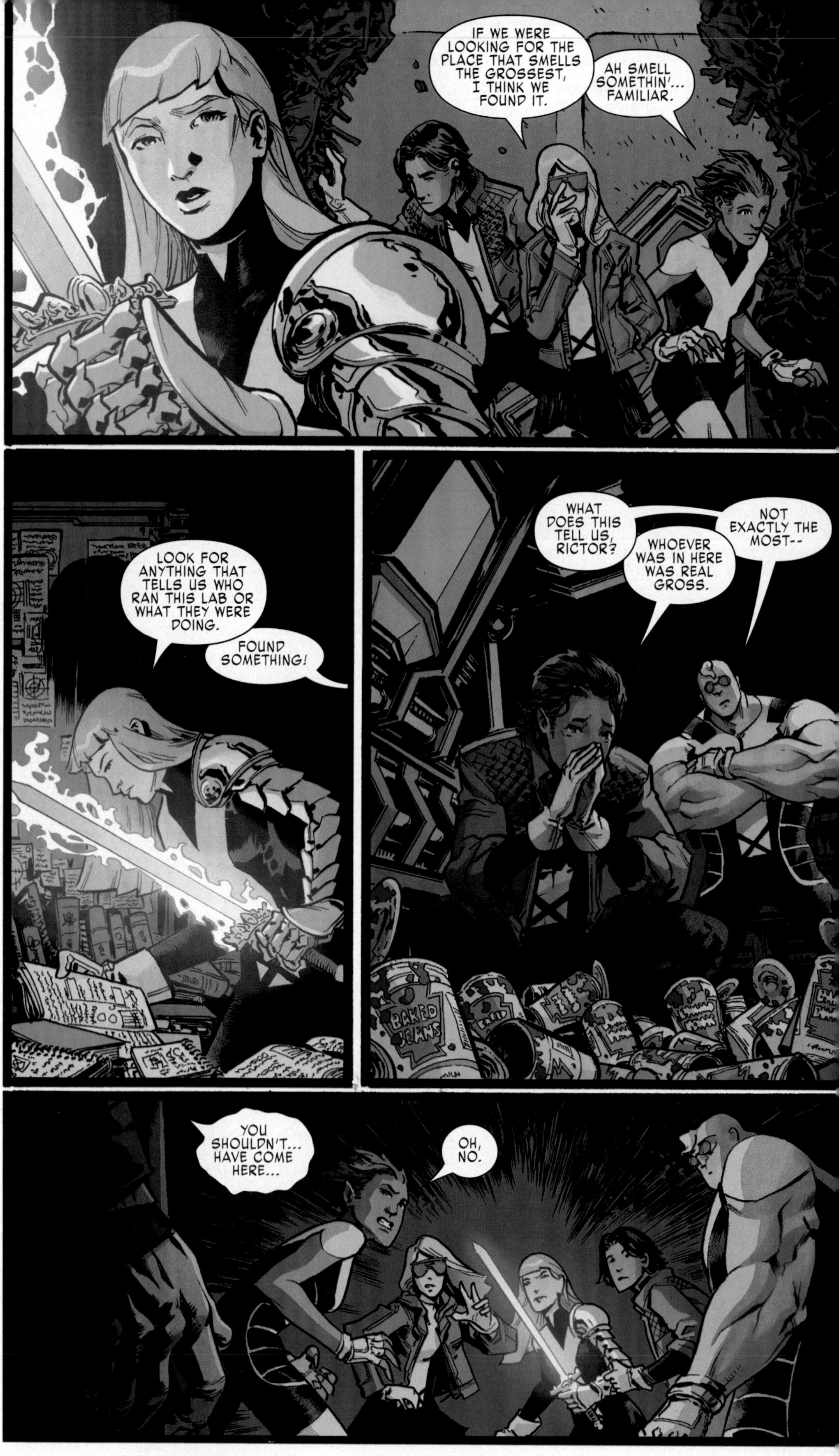
IF WE WERE LOOKING FOR THE PLACE THAT SMELLS THE GROSSEST, I THINK WE FOUND IT.
AH SMELL SOMETHIN'... FAMILIAR.
LOOK FOR ANYTHING THAT TELLS US WHO RAN THIS LAB OR WHAT THEY WERE DOING.
FOUND SOMETHING!
WHAT DOES THIS TELL US, RICTOR?
WHOEVER WAS IN HERE WAS REAL GROSS.
NOT EXACTLY THE MOST--
BAKED BEANS
YOU SHOULDN'T... HAVE COME HERE...
OH, NO.

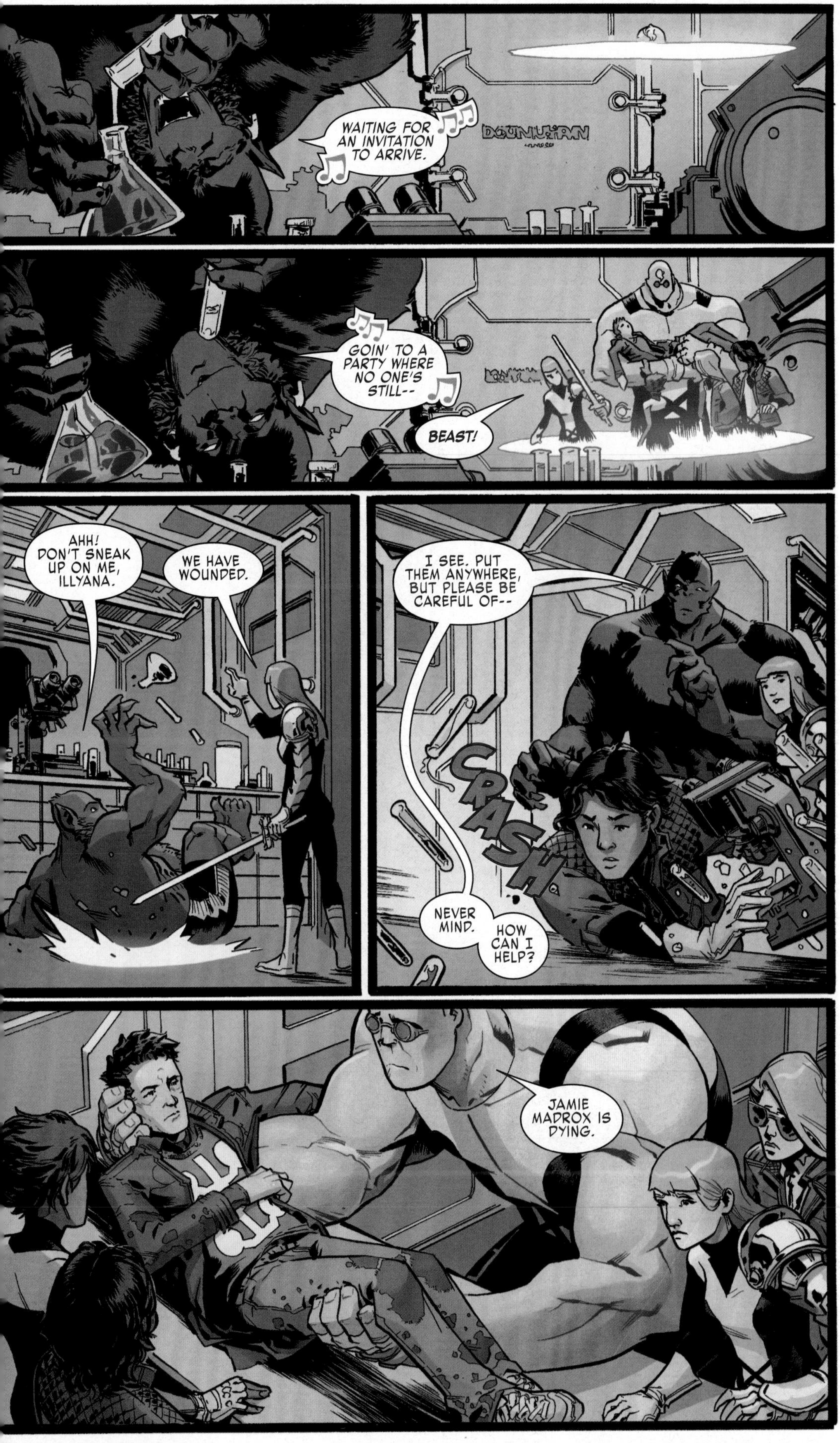
WAITING FOR AN INVITATION TO ARRIVE.
GOIN' TO A PARTY WHERE NO ONE'S STILL--
BEAST!
AHH! DON'T SNEAK UP ON ME, ILLYANA.
WE HAVE WOUNDED.
I SEE. PUT THEM ANYWHERE, BUT PLEASE BE CAREFUL OF--
CRASH
NEVER MIND.
HOW CAN I HELP?
JAMIE MADROX IS DYING.

LEMME GET THIS STRAIGHT. JAMIE MADROX WAS EXPOSED TO THE TERRIGEN MISTS AND DIED.

CORRECT.

AND ALL OF HIS DUPES DIED WITH HIM.

CORRECT AGAIN.

BUT HERE HE IS.

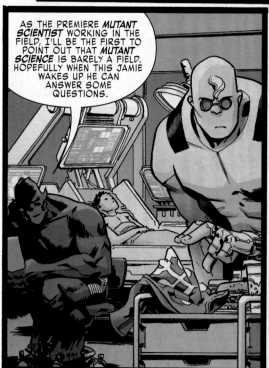

AS THE PREMIERE *MUTANT SCIENTIST* WORKING IN THE FIELD, I'LL BE THE FIRST TO POINT OUT THAT *MUTANT SCIENCE* IS BARELY A FIELD. HOPEFULLY WHEN THIS JAMIE WAKES UP HE CAN ANSWER SOME QUESTIONS.

IF HE WAKES UP.

ARE YOU TALKING ABOUT ME?

OH, JAMIE! EXCELLENT.

HUNGRY?

THAT'S NOT ADVISABLE IN--

THANKS!

I GUESS I DIED, RIGHT?

I'M AFRAID SO.

THAT SUCKS.

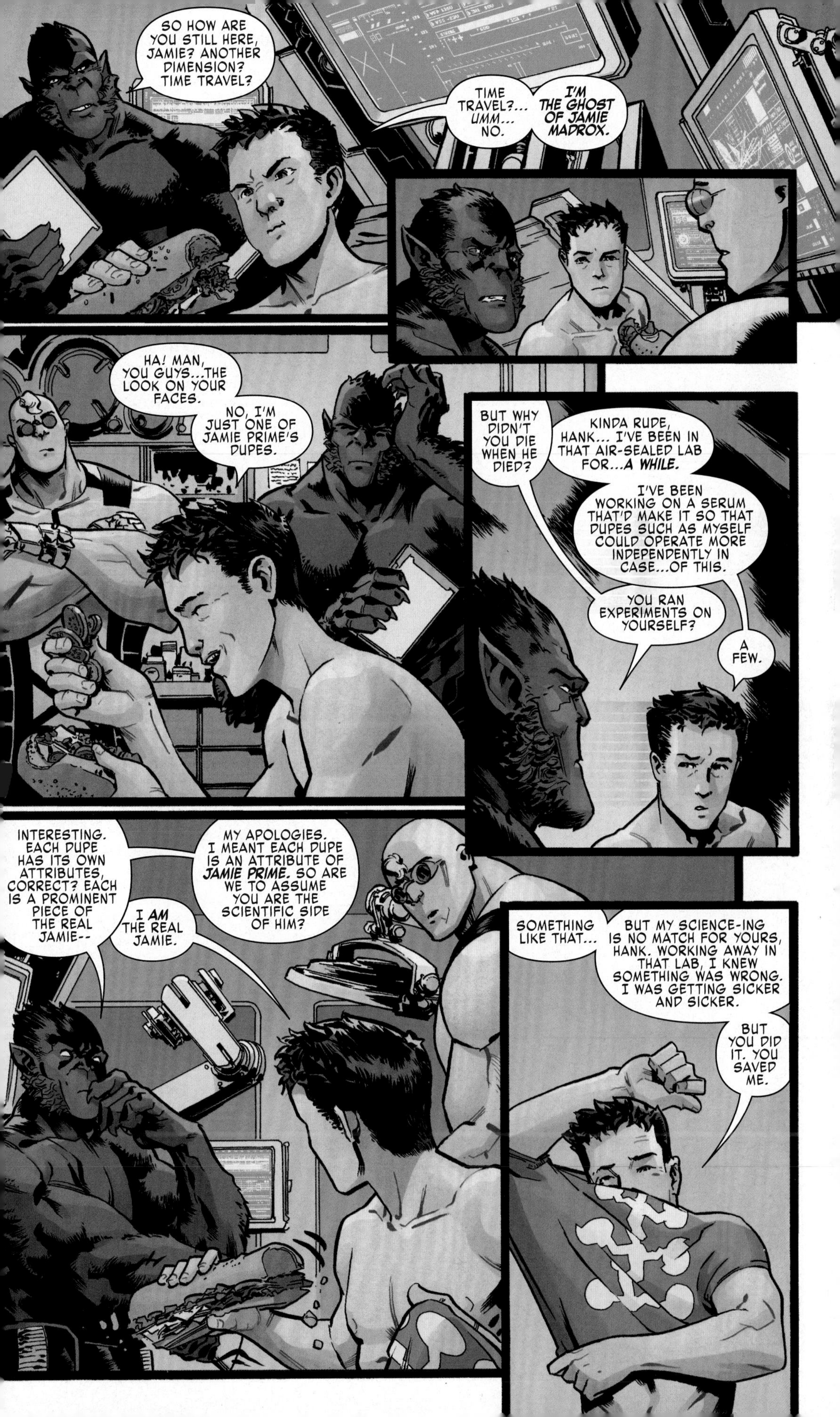
SO HOW ARE YOU STILL HERE, JAMIE? ANOTHER DIMENSION? TIME TRAVEL?
TIME TRAVEL?... UMM... NO.
I'M THE GHOST OF JAMIE MADROX.
HA! MAN, YOU GUYS...THE LOOK ON YOUR FACES.
NO, I'M JUST ONE OF JAMIE PRIME'S DUPES.
BUT WHY DIDN'T YOU DIE WHEN HE DIED?
KINDA RUDE, HANK... I'VE BEEN IN THAT AIR-SEALED LAB FOR...A WHILE.
I'VE BEEN WORKING ON A SERUM THAT'D MAKE IT SO THAT DUPES SUCH AS MYSELF COULD OPERATE MORE INDEPENDENTLY IN CASE...OF THIS.
YOU RAN EXPERIMENTS ON YOURSELF?
A FEW.
INTERESTING. EACH DUPE HAS ITS OWN ATTRIBUTES, CORRECT? EACH IS A PROMINENT PIECE OF THE REAL JAMIE--
I AM THE REAL JAMIE.
MY APOLOGIES. I MEANT EACH DUPE IS AN ATTRIBUTE OF JAMIE PRIME. SO ARE WE TO ASSUME YOU ARE THE SCIENTIFIC SIDE OF HIM?
SOMETHING LIKE THAT...
BUT MY SCIENCE-ING IS NO MATCH FOR YOURS, HANK. WORKING AWAY IN THAT LAB, I KNEW SOMETHING WAS WRONG. I WAS GETTING SICKER AND SICKER.
BUT YOU DID IT. YOU SAVED ME.

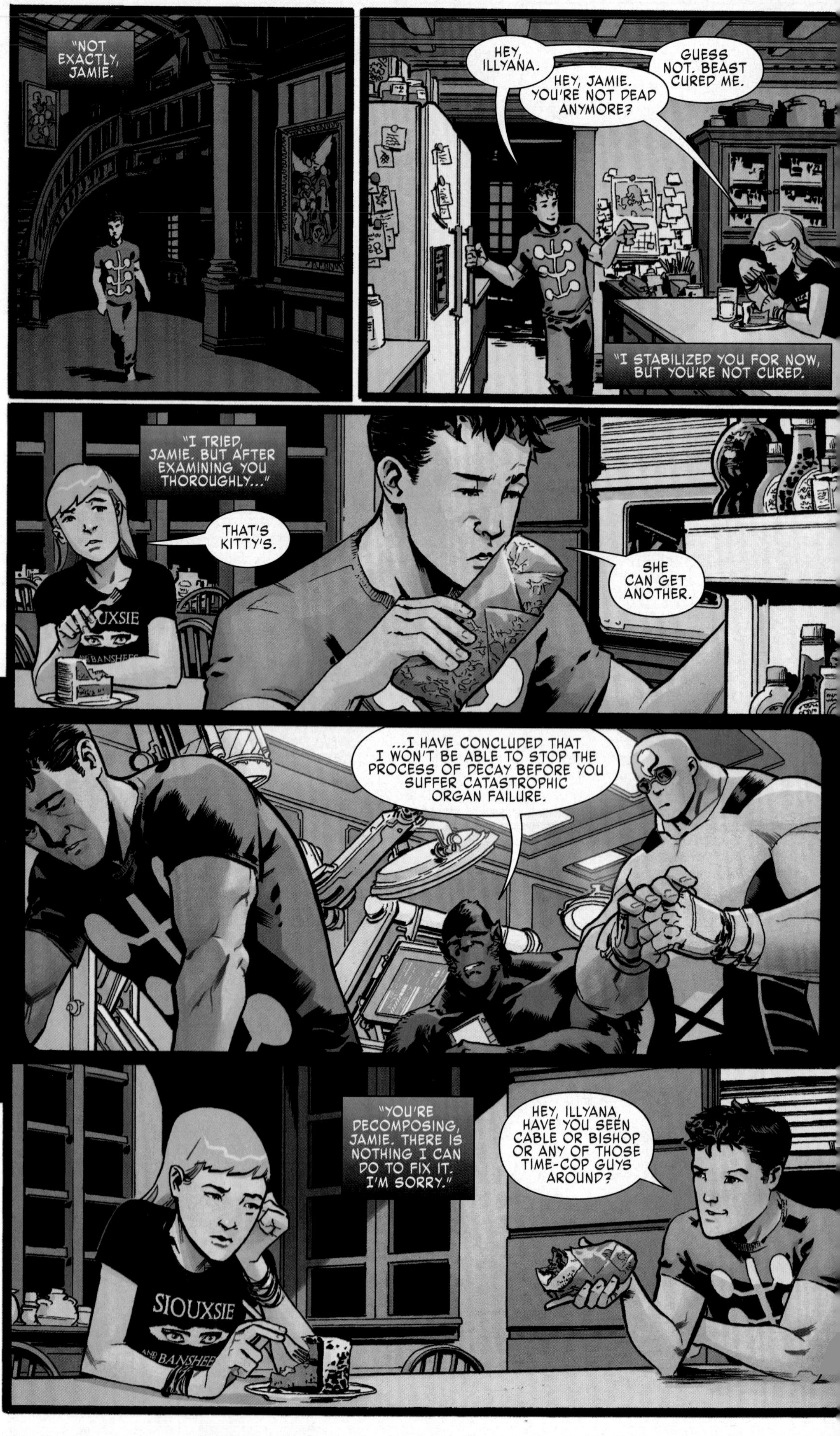

"NOT EXACTLY, JAMIE.
HEY, ILLYANA.
HEY, JAMIE. YOU'RE NOT DEAD ANYMORE?
GUESS NOT. BEAST CURED ME.
"I STABILIZED YOU FOR NOW, BUT YOU'RE NOT CURED.
"I TRIED, JAMIE. BUT AFTER EXAMINING YOU THOROUGHLY..."
THAT'S KITTY'S.
SHE CAN GET ANOTHER.
SIOUXSIE AND THE BANSHEES
...I HAVE CONCLUDED THAT I WON'T BE ABLE TO STOP THE PROCESS OF DECAY BEFORE YOU SUFFER CATASTROPHIC ORGAN FAILURE.
"YOU'RE DECOMPOSING, JAMIE. THERE IS NOTHING I CAN DO TO FIX IT. I'M SORRY."
HEY, ILLYANA, HAVE YOU SEEN CABLE OR BISHOP OR ANY OF THOSE TIME-COP GUYS AROUND?
SIOUXSIE AND THE BANSHEES

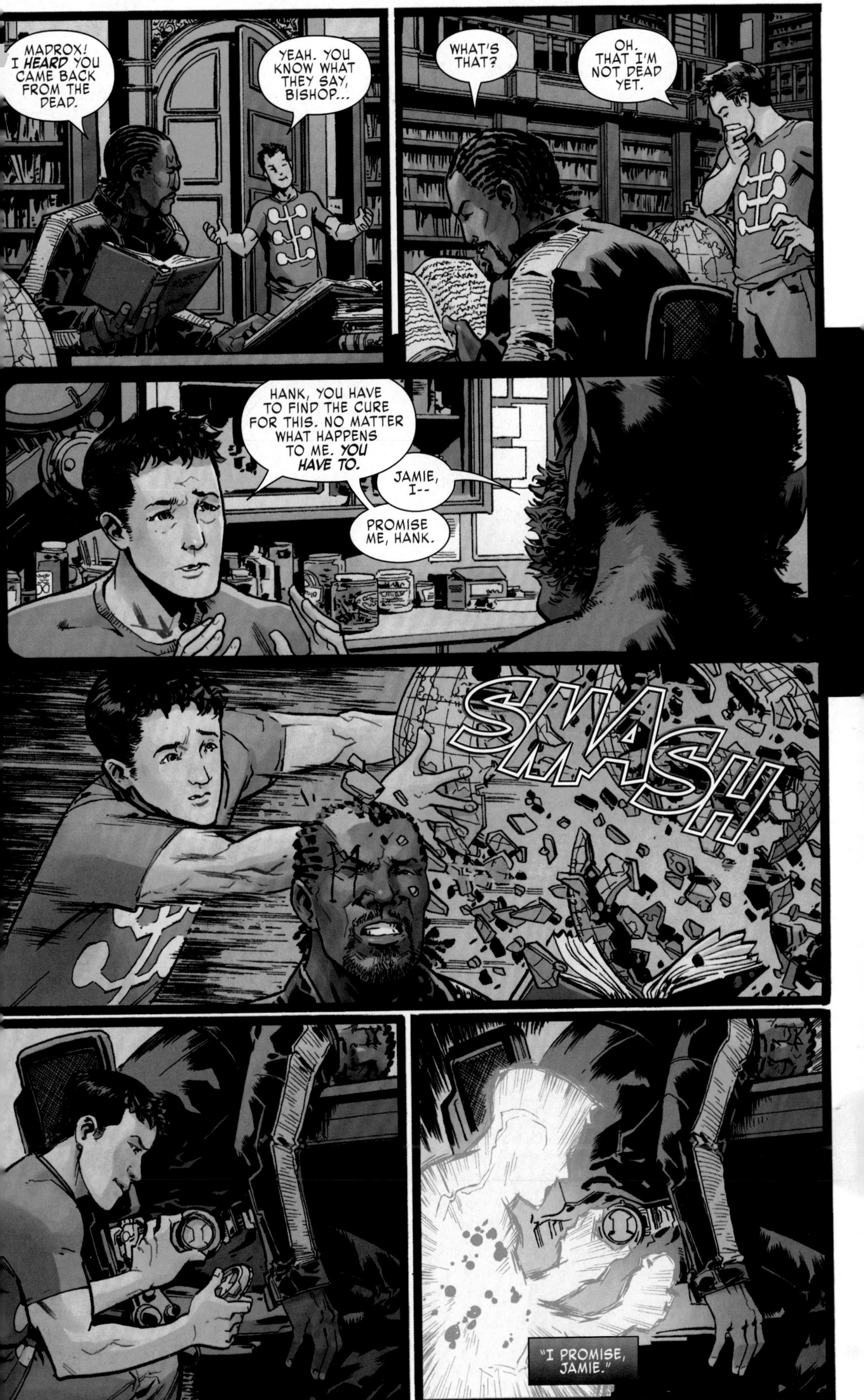

MADROX! I HEARD YOU CAME BACK FROM THE DEAD.
YEAH. YOU KNOW WHAT THEY SAY, BISHOP...
WHAT'S THAT?
OH. THAT I'M NOT DEAD YET.
HANK, YOU HAVE TO FIND THE CURE FOR THIS. NO MATTER WHAT HAPPENS TO ME. YOU HAVE TO.
JAMIE, I--
PROMISE ME, HANK.
SMASH
"I PROMISE, JAMIE."

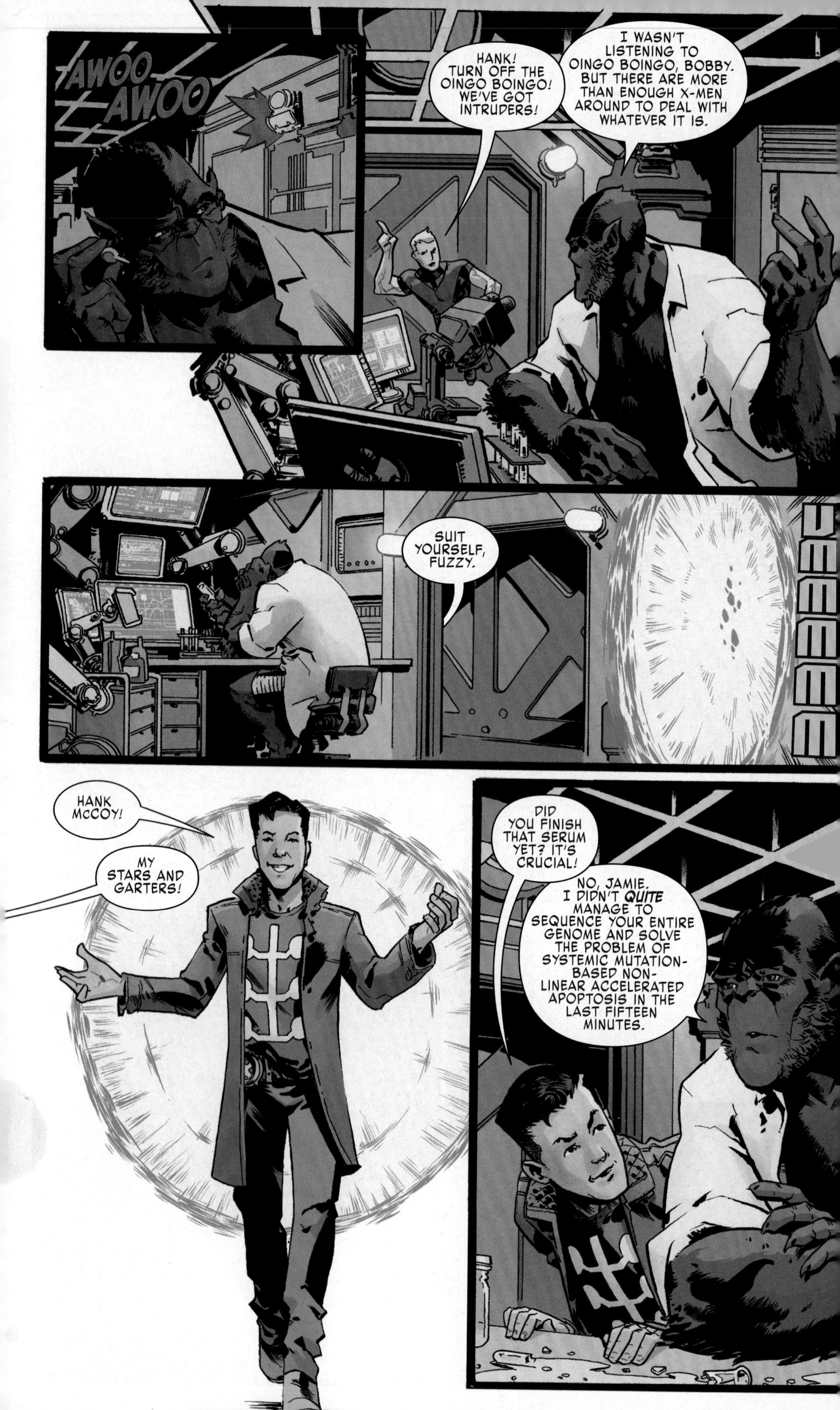
AWOO AWOO
HANK! TURN OFF THE OINGO BOINGO! WE'VE GOT INTRUDERS!
I WASN'T LISTENING TO OINGO BOINGO, BOBBY. BUT THERE ARE MORE THAN ENOUGH X-MEN AROUND TO DEAL WITH WHATEVER IT IS.
SUIT YOURSELF, FUZZY.
VMMMMM
HANK McCOY!
MY STARS AND GARTERS!
DID YOU FINISH THAT SERUM YET? IT'S CRUCIAL!
NO, JAMIE. I DIDN'T QUITE MANAGE TO SEQUENCE YOUR ENTIRE GENOME AND SOLVE THE PROBLEM OF SYSTEMIC MUTATION-BASED NON-LINEAR ACCELERATED APOPTOSIS IN THE LAST FIFTEEN MINUTES.

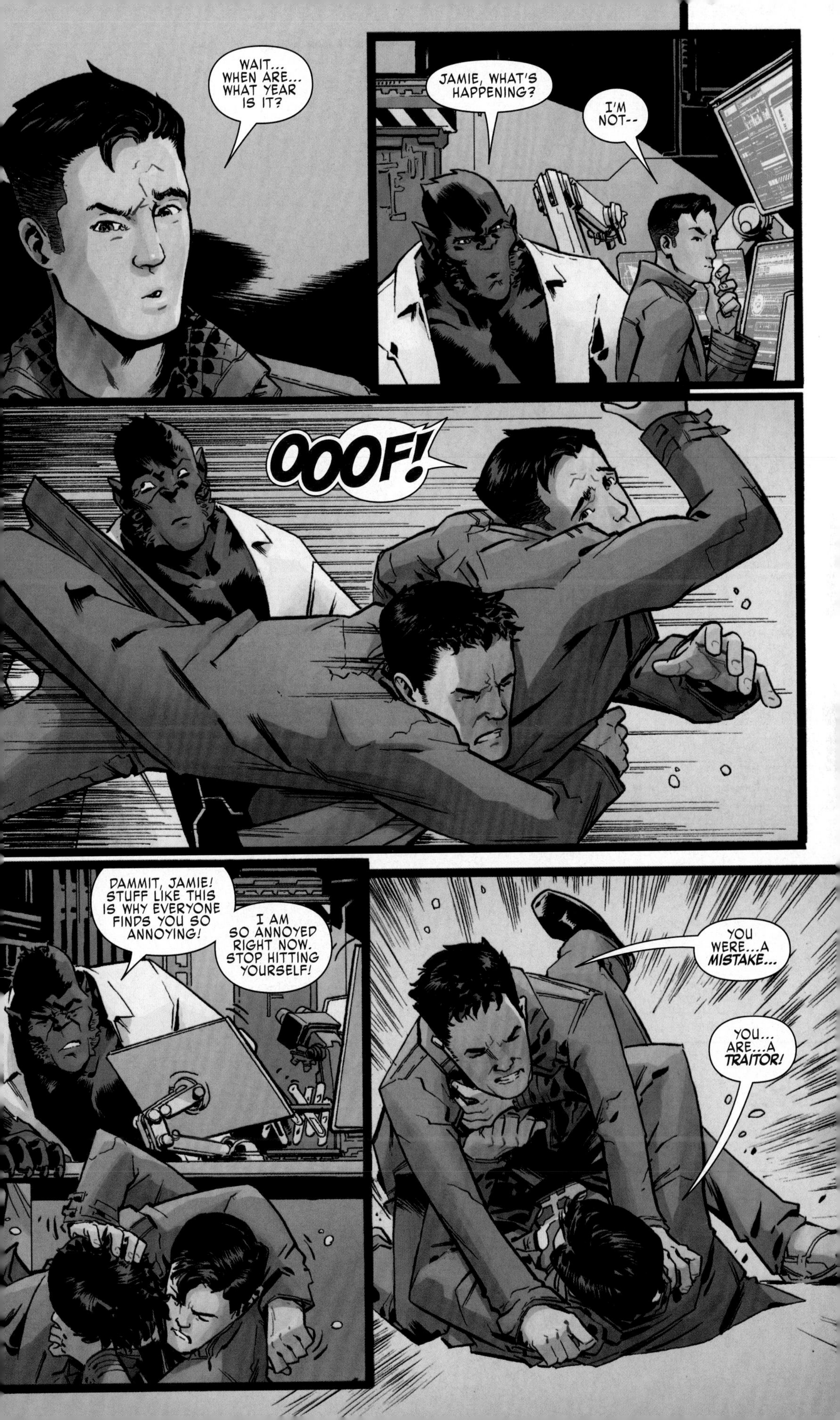
WAIT... WHEN ARE... WHAT YEAR IS IT?
JAMIE, WHAT'S HAPPENING?
I'M NOT--
OOOF!
DAMMIT, JAMIE! STUFF LIKE THIS IS WHY EVERYONE FINDS YOU SO ANNOYING!
I AM SO ANNOYED RIGHT NOW. STOP HITTING YOURSELF!
YOU WERE...A MISTAKE...
YOU... ARE...A TRAITOR!

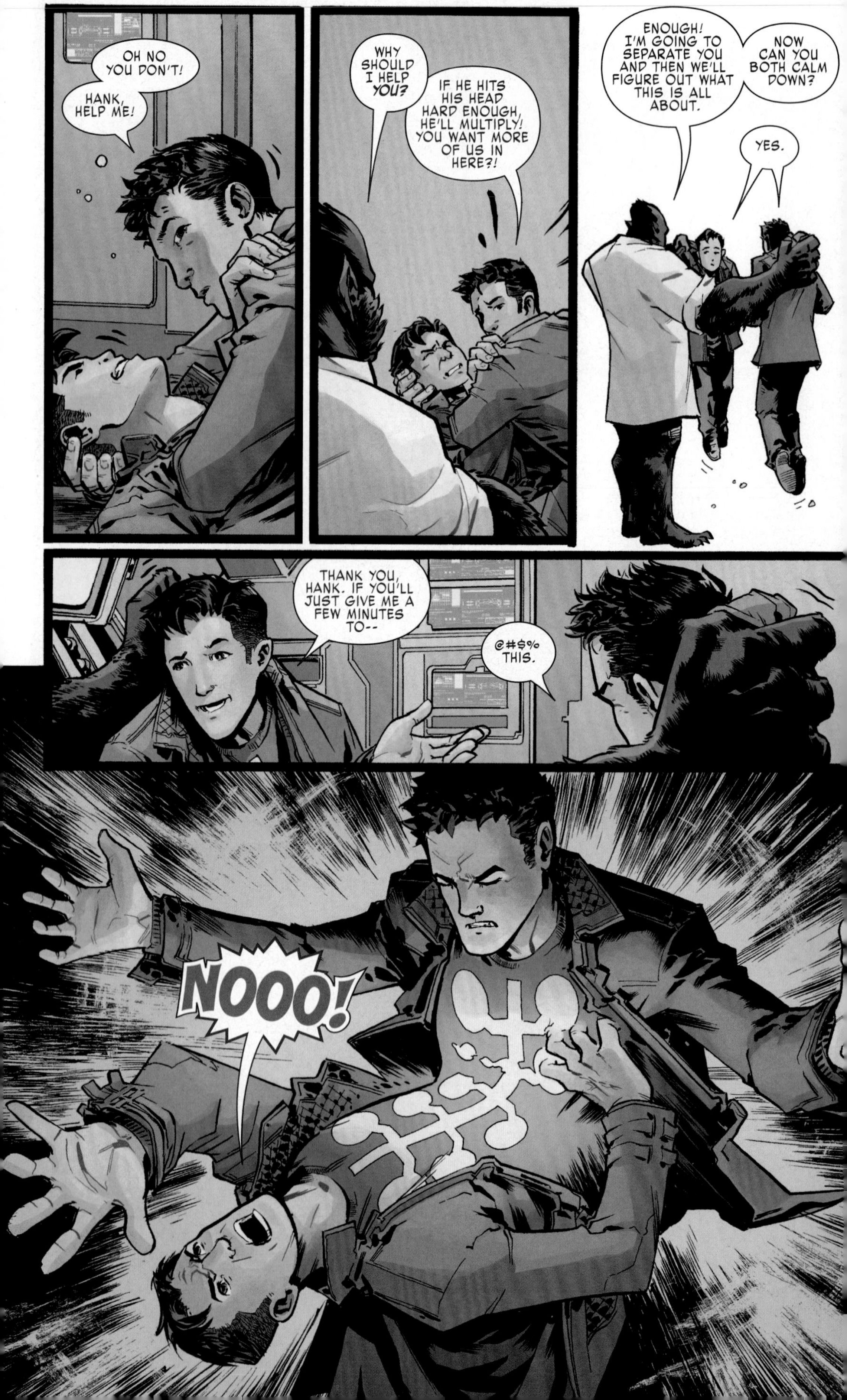

OH NO YOU DON'T!
HANK, HELP ME!
WHY SHOULD I HELP *YOU?*
IF HE HITS HIS HEAD HARD ENOUGH, HE'LL MULTIPLY! YOU WANT MORE OF US IN HERE?!
!
ENOUGH! I'M GOING TO SEPARATE YOU AND THEN WE'LL FIGURE OUT WHAT THIS IS ALL ABOUT.
NOW CAN YOU BOTH CALM DOWN?
YES.
THANK YOU, HANK. IF YOU'LL JUST GIVE ME A FEW MINUTES TO--
@#$% THIS.
NOOO!

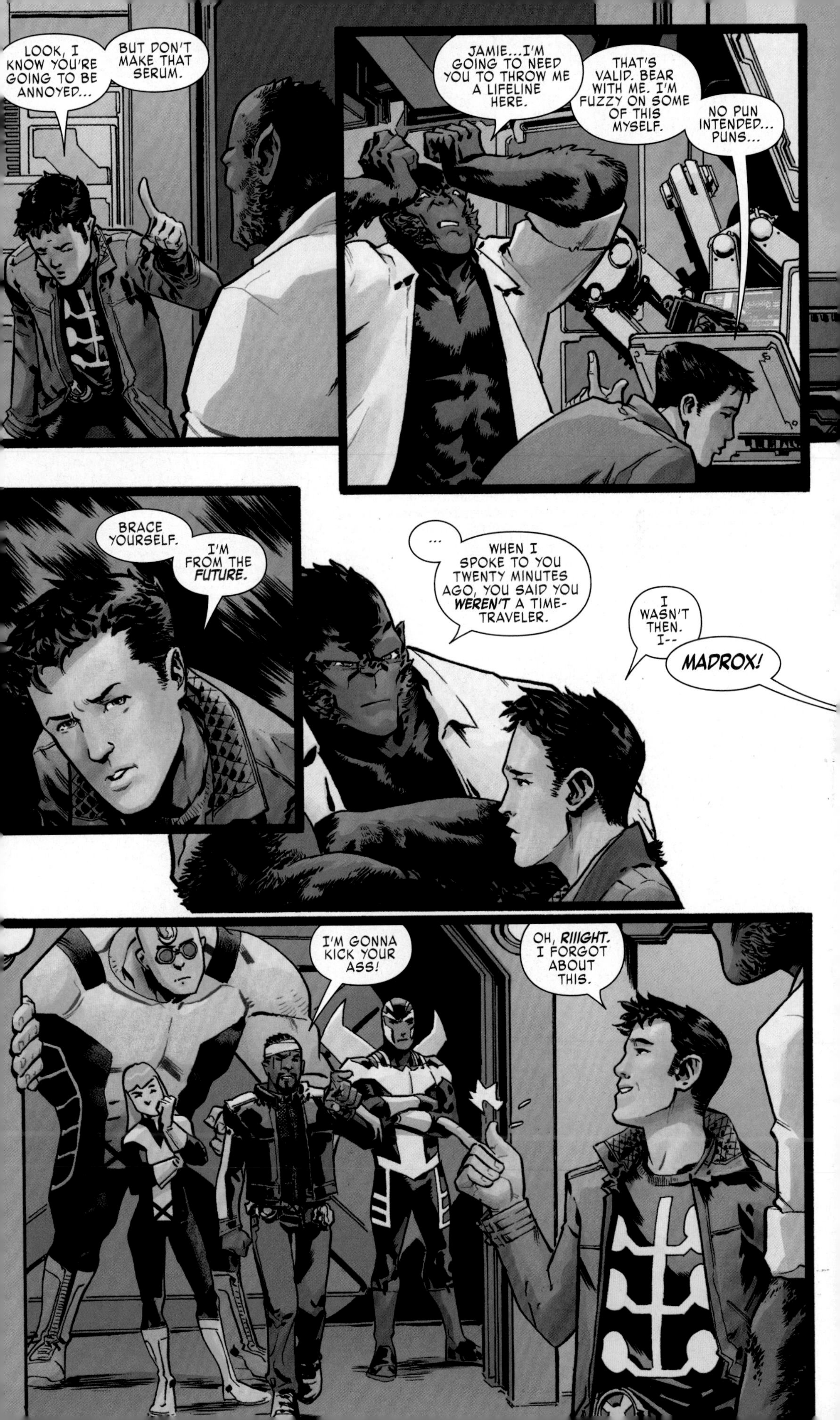
LOOK, I KNOW YOU'RE GOING TO BE ANNOYED...
BUT DON'T MAKE THAT SERUM.
JAMIE...I'M GOING TO NEED YOU TO THROW ME A LIFELINE HERE.
THAT'S VALID. BEAR WITH ME. I'M FUZZY ON SOME OF THIS MYSELF.
NO PUN INTENDED... PUNS...
BRACE YOURSELF.
I'M FROM THE FUTURE.
...
WHEN I SPOKE TO YOU TWENTY MINUTES AGO, YOU SAID YOU WEREN'T A TIME-TRAVELER.
I WASN'T THEN. I--
MADROX!
I'M GONNA KICK YOUR ASS!
OH, RIIIGHT. I FORGOT ABOUT THIS.

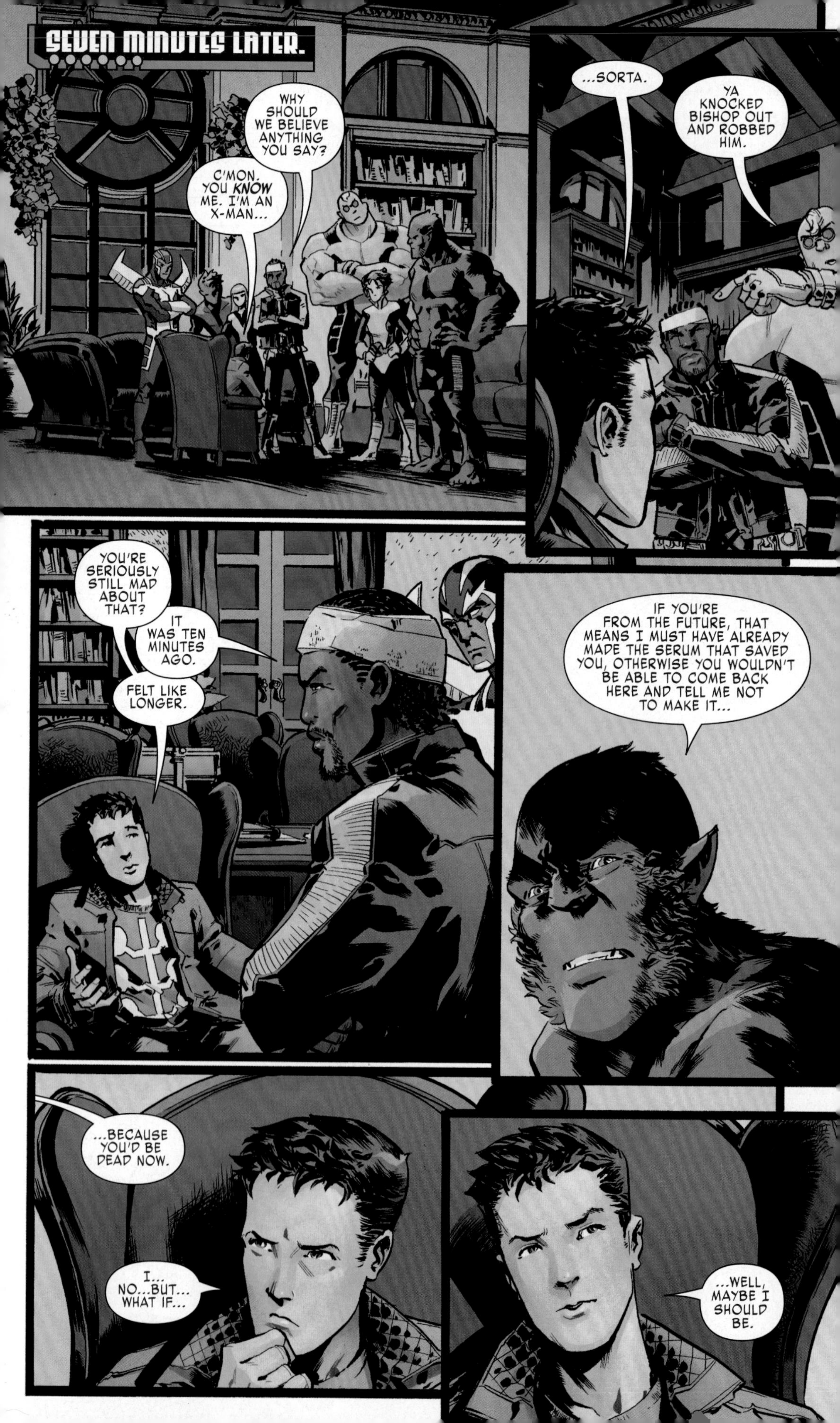
SEVEN MINUTES LATER.
WHY SHOULD WE BELIEVE ANYTHING YOU SAY?
C'MON. YOU KNOW ME. I'M AN X-MAN...
...SORTA.
YA KNOCKED BISHOP OUT AND ROBBED HIM.
YOU'RE SERIOUSLY STILL MAD ABOUT THAT?
IT WAS TEN MINUTES AGO.
FELT LIKE LONGER.
IF YOU'RE FROM THE FUTURE, THAT MEANS I MUST HAVE ALREADY MADE THE SERUM THAT SAVED YOU, OTHERWISE YOU WOULDN'T BE ABLE TO COME BACK HERE AND TELL ME NOT TO MAKE IT...
...BECAUSE YOU'D BE DEAD NOW.
I... NO...BUT... WHAT IF...
...WELL, MAYBE I SHOULD BE.

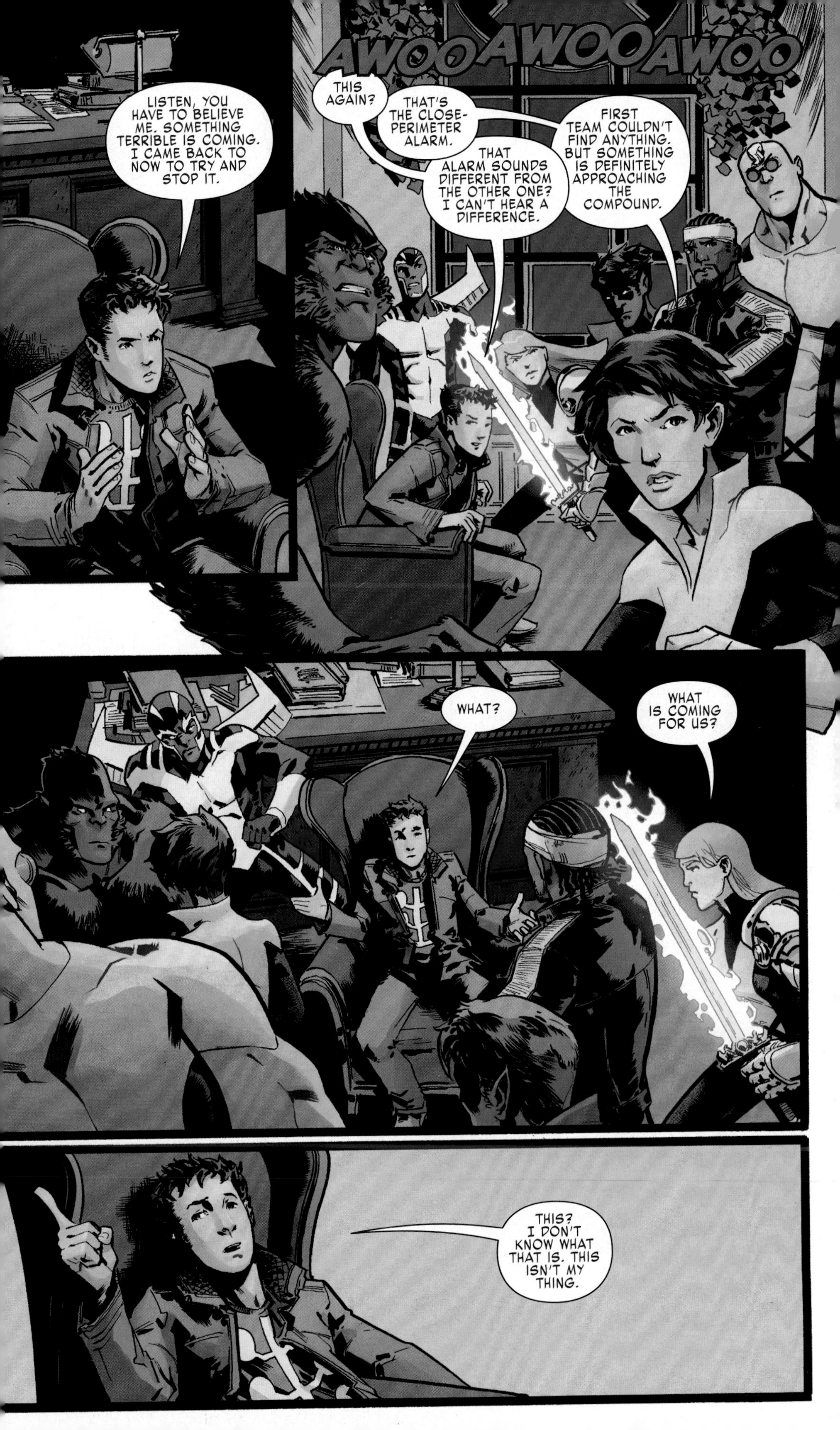
LISTEN, YOU HAVE TO BELIEVE ME. SOMETHING TERRIBLE IS COMING. I CAME BACK TO NOW TO TRY AND STOP IT.
AWOOAWOOAWOO
THIS AGAIN?
THAT'S THE CLOSE-PERIMETER ALARM.
THAT ALARM SOUNDS DIFFERENT FROM THE OTHER ONE? I CAN'T HEAR A DIFFERENCE.
FIRST TEAM COULDN'T FIND ANYTHING. BUT SOMETHING IS DEFINITELY APPROACHING THE COMPOUND.
WHAT?
WHAT IS COMING FOR US?
THIS? I DON'T KNOW WHAT THAT IS. THIS ISN'T MY THING.

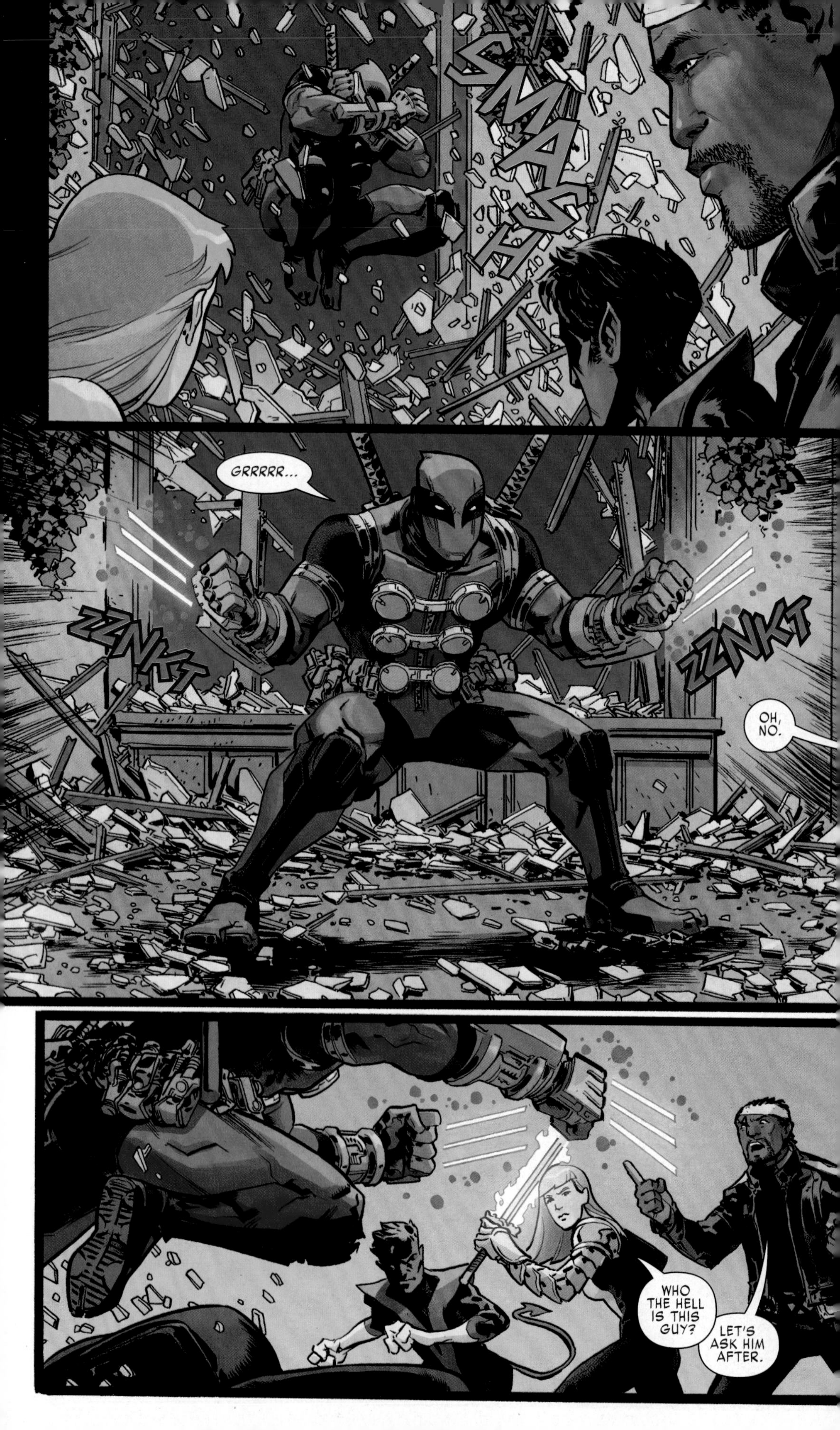
SMASH
GRRRRR...
ZZNKT
ZZNKT
OH, NO.
WHO THE HELL IS THIS GUY?
LET'S ASK HIM AFTER.

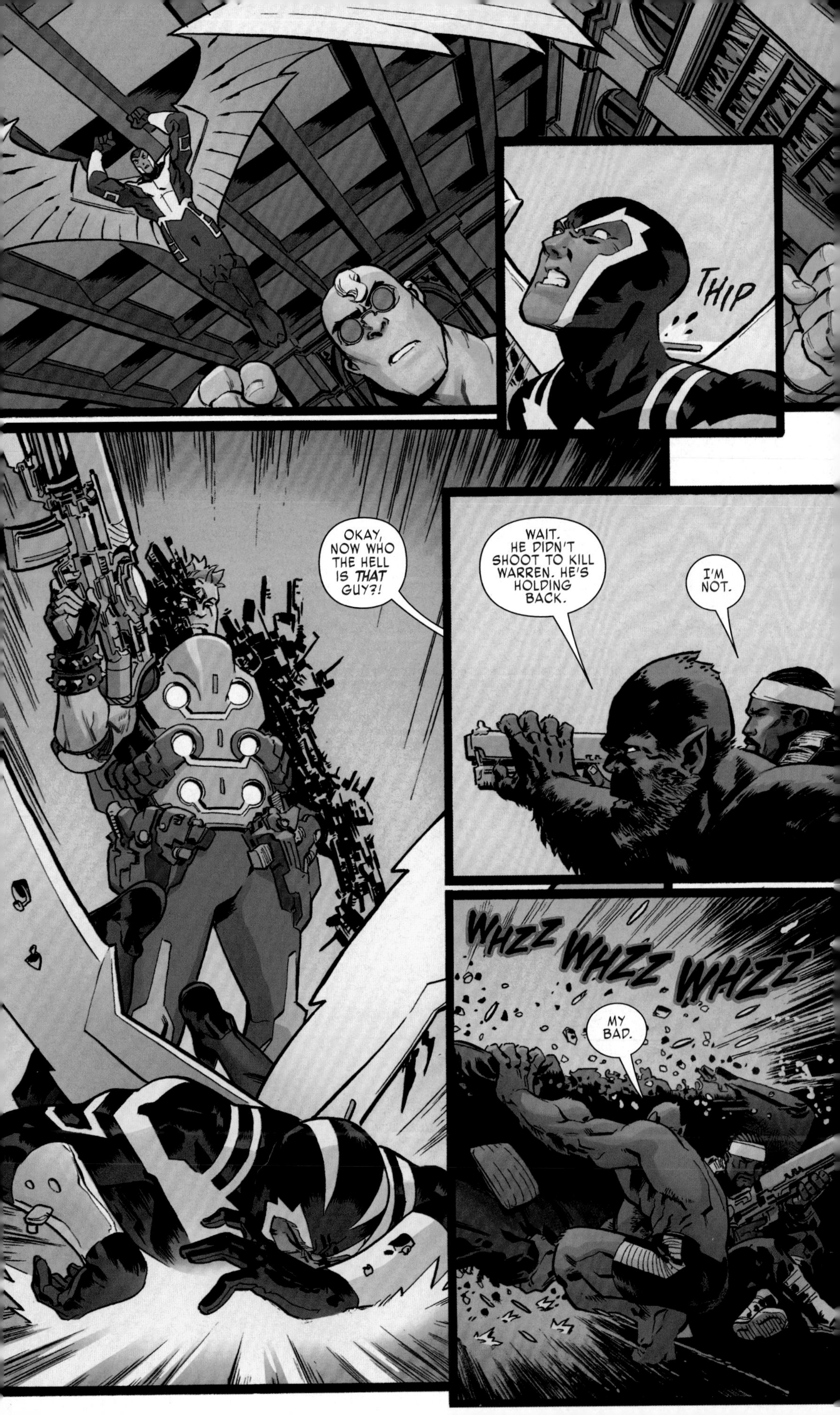
THIP
OKAY, NOW WHO THE HELL IS *THAT* GUY?!
WAIT. HE DIDN'T SHOOT TO KILL WARREN. HE'S HOLDING BACK.
I'M NOT.
WHZZ WHZZ WHZZ
MY BAD.

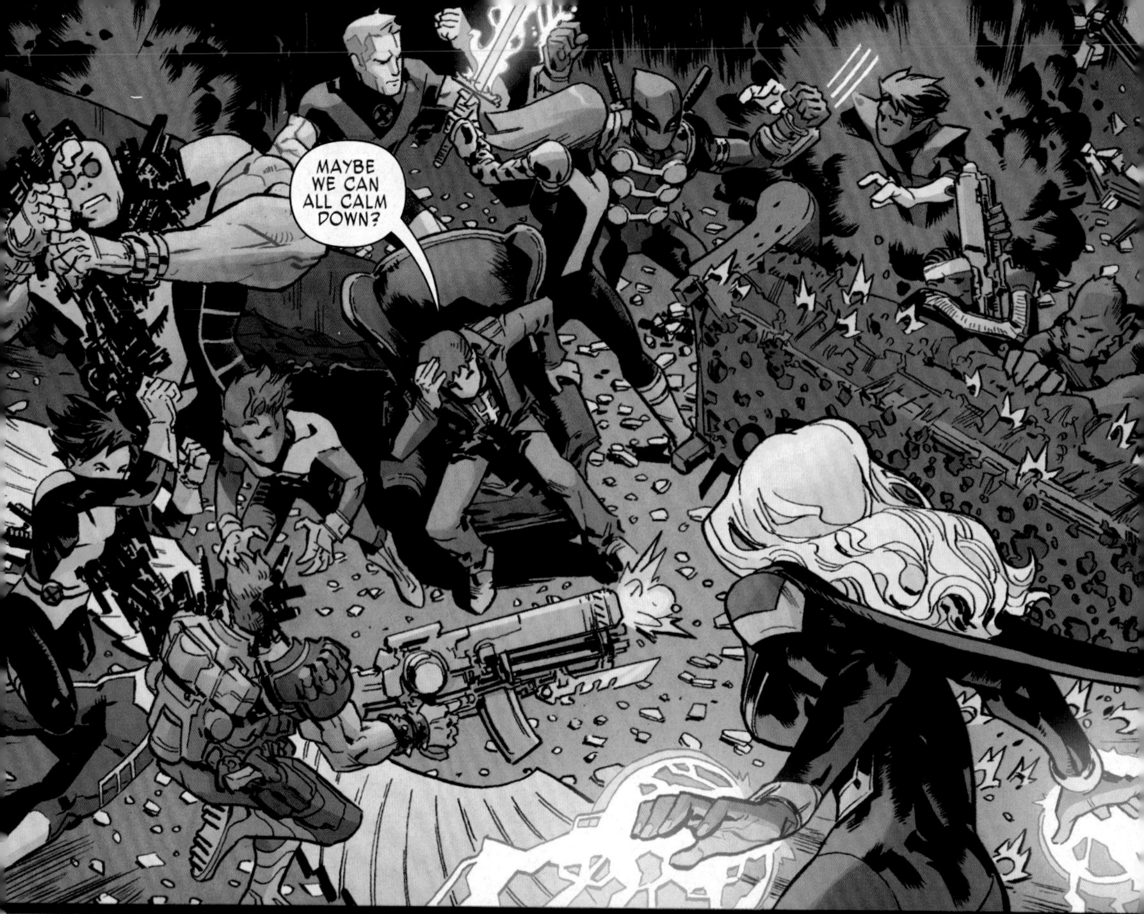
MAYBE WE CAN ALL CALM DOWN?

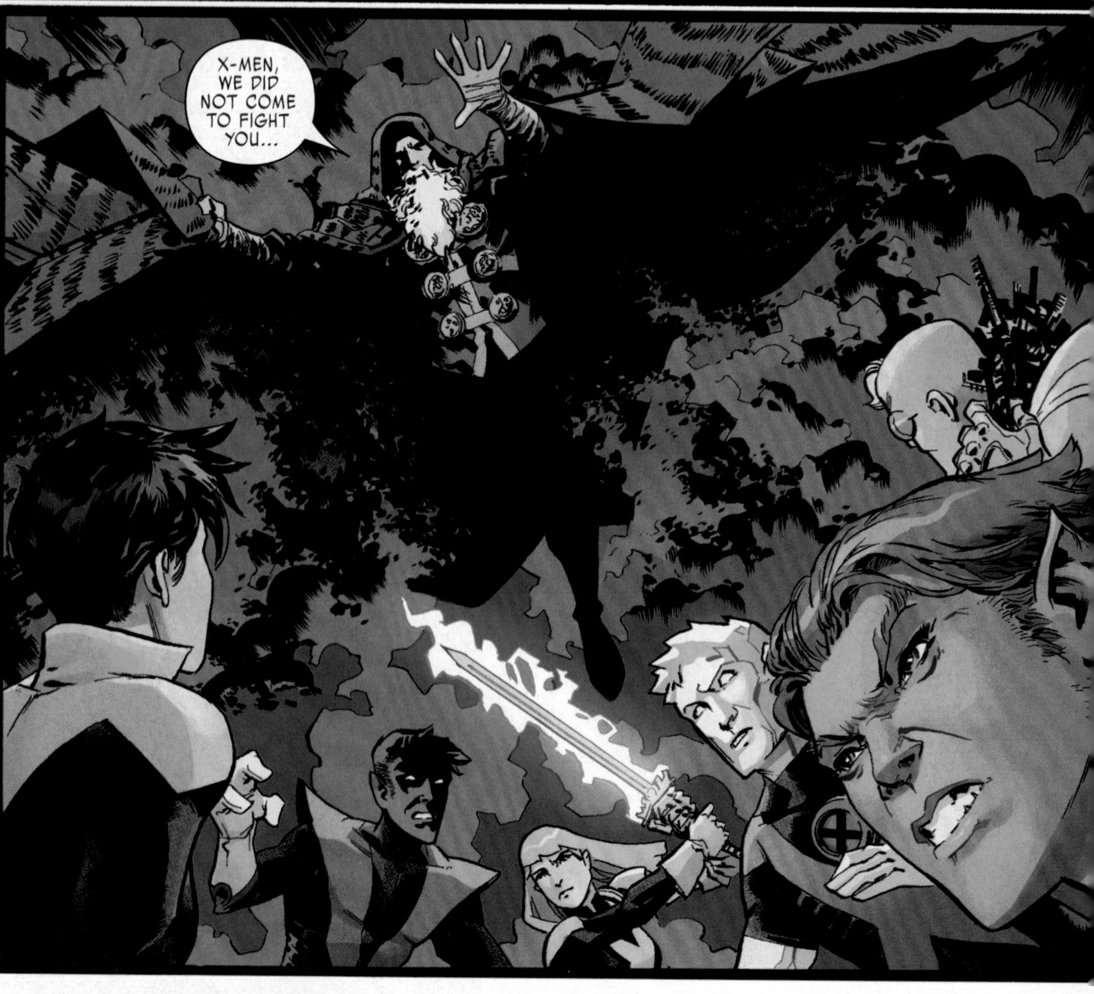
X-MEN, WE DID NOT COME TO FIGHT YOU...

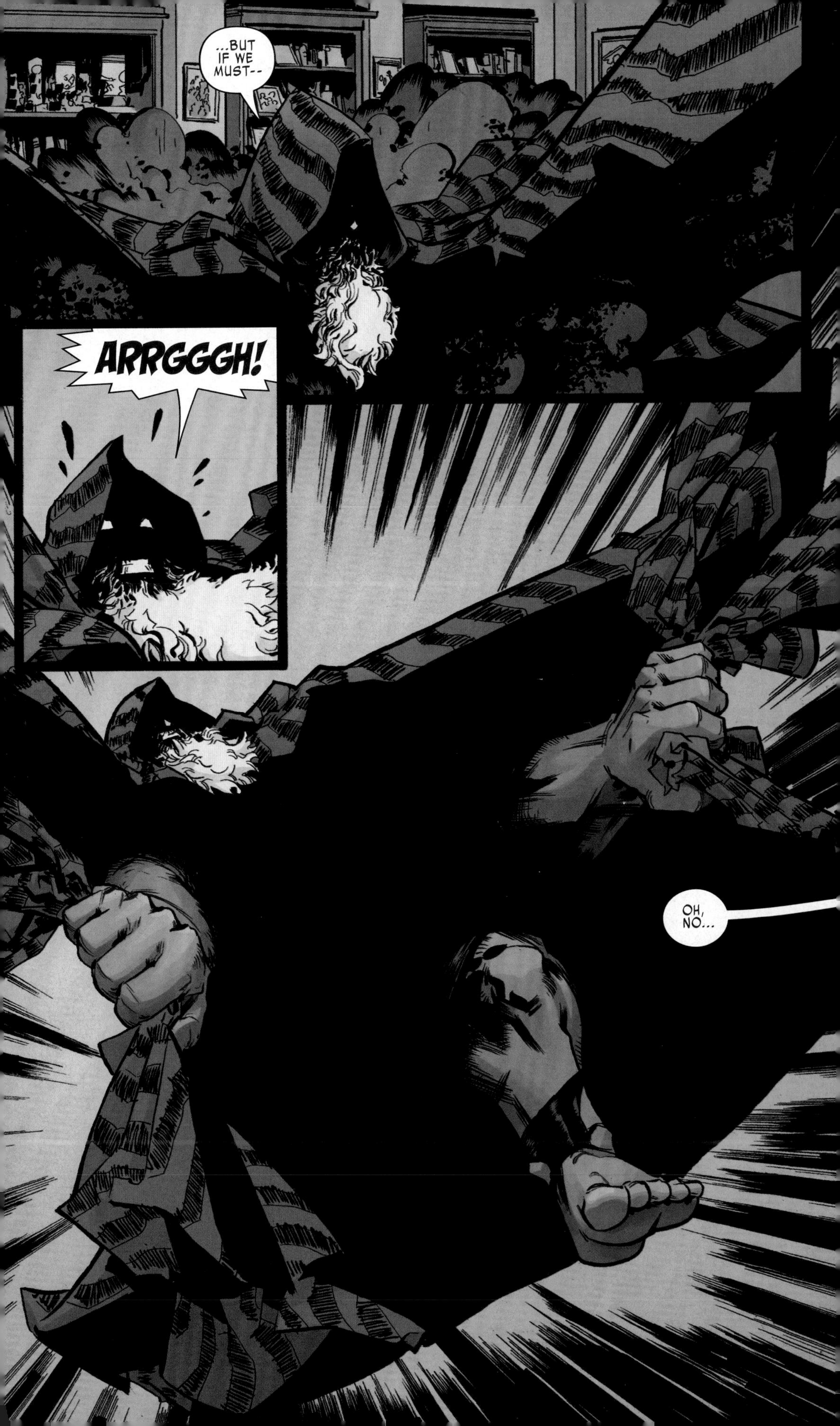
...BUT IF WE MUST--
ARRGGGH!
OH, NO...

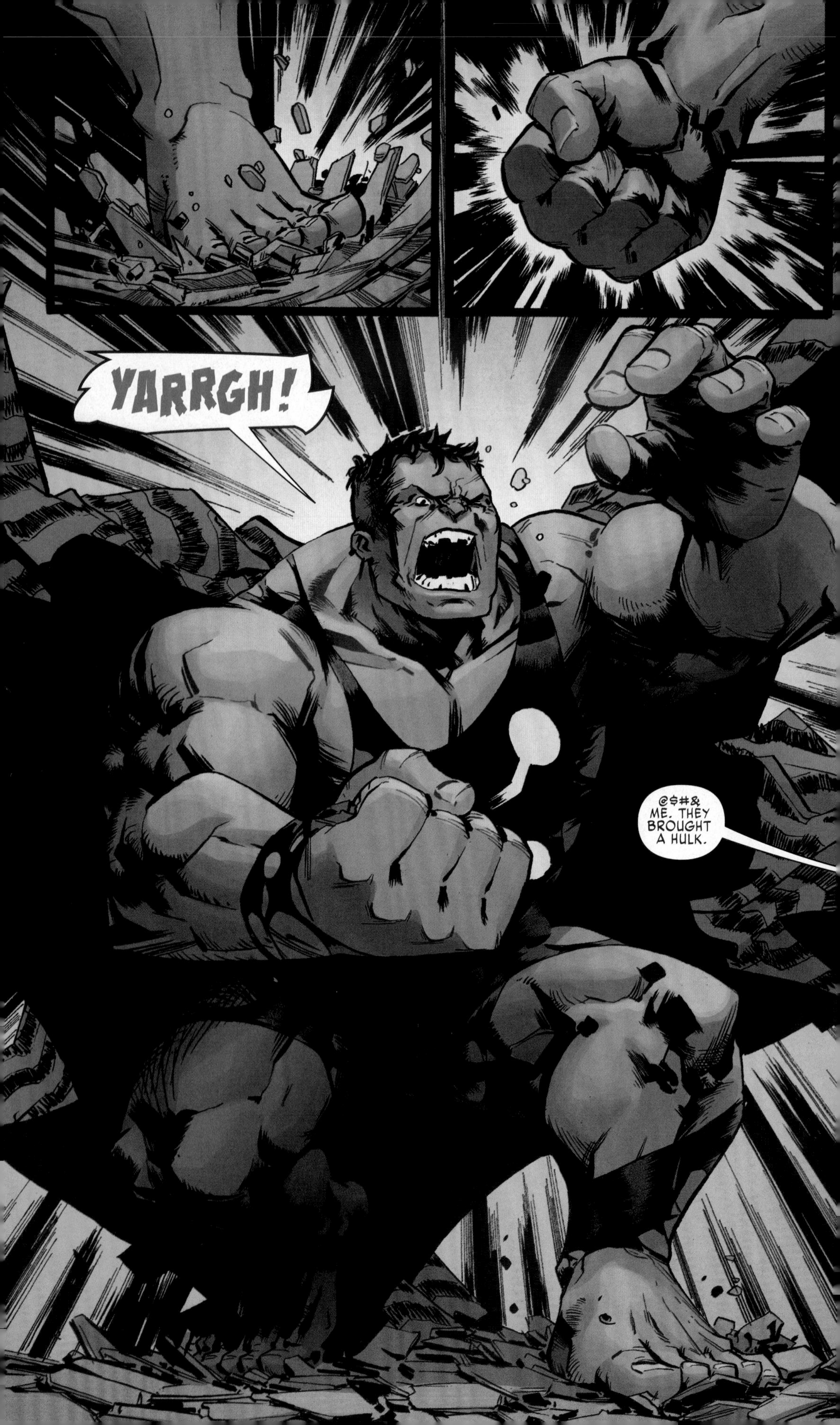
YARRGH!
@$#& ME. THEY BROUGHT A HULK.

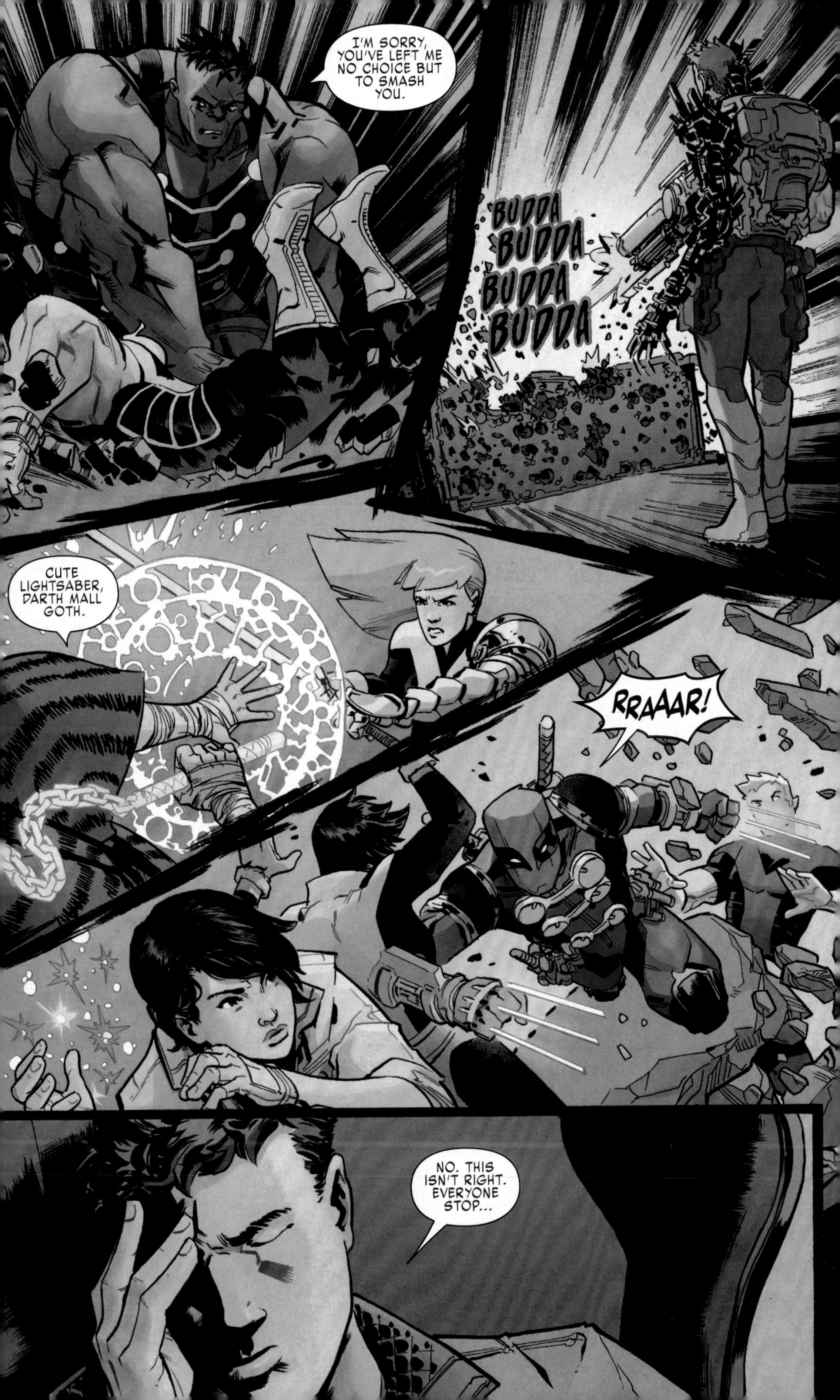
I'M SORRY, YOU'VE LEFT ME NO CHOICE BUT TO SMASH YOU.
BUDDA BUDDA BUDDA BUDDA
CUTE LIGHTSABER, DARTH MALL GOTH.
RRAAAR!
NO. THIS ISN'T RIGHT. EVERYONE STOP...

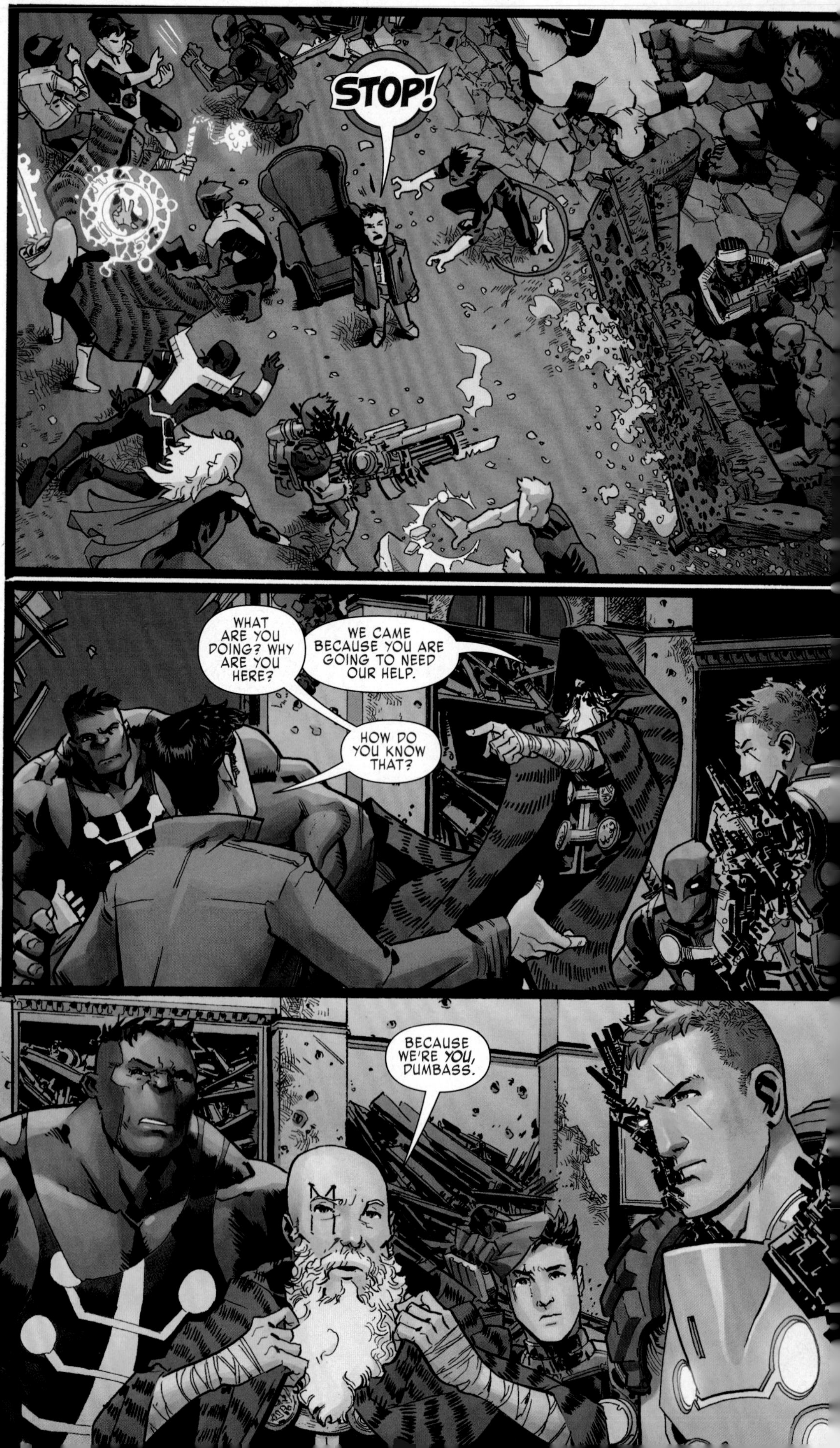
STOP!
WHAT ARE YOU DOING? WHY ARE YOU HERE?
WE CAME BECAUSE YOU ARE GOING TO NEED OUR HELP.
HOW DO YOU KNOW THAT?
BECAUSE WE'RE YOU, DUMBASS.

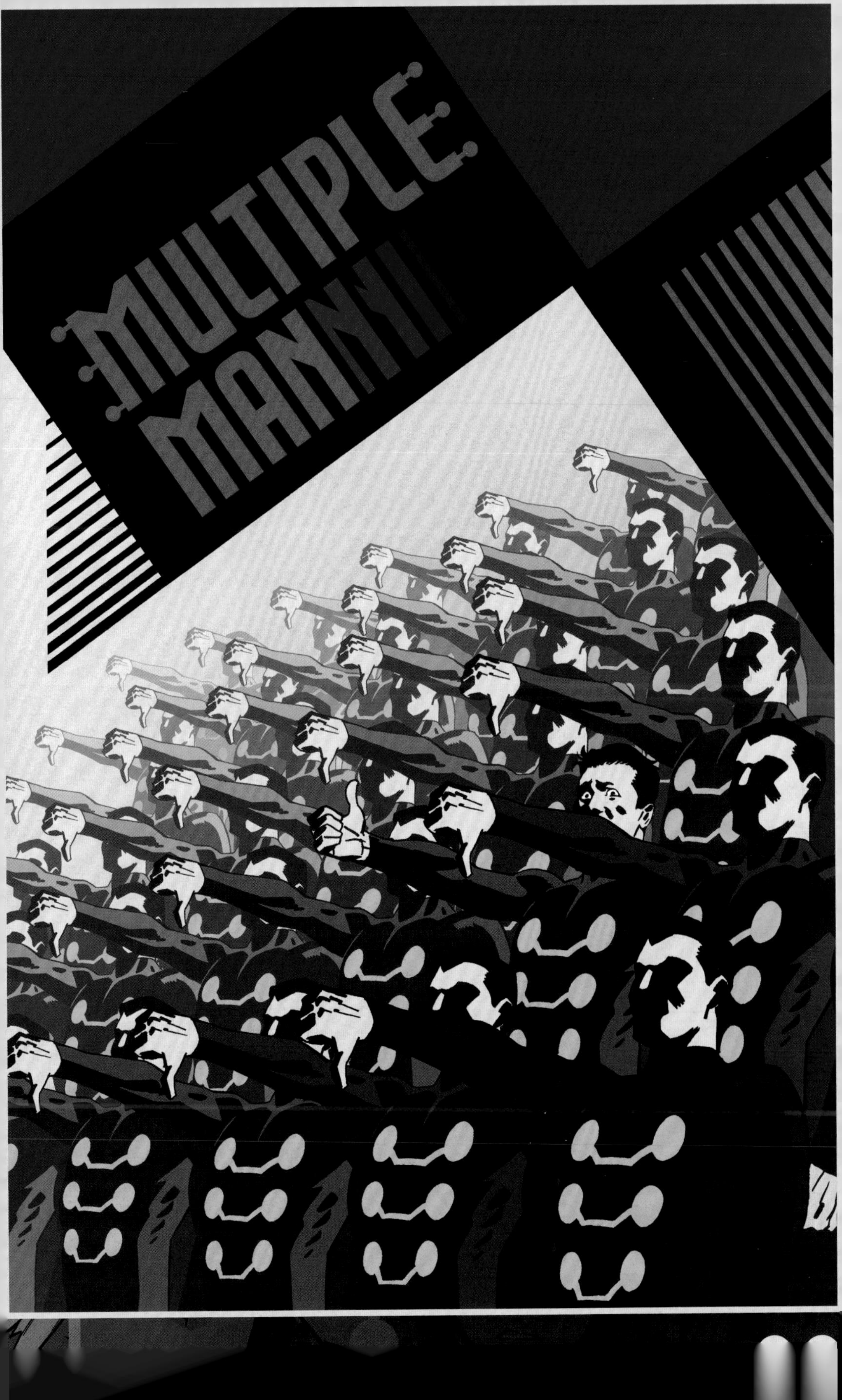
MULTIPLE MAN

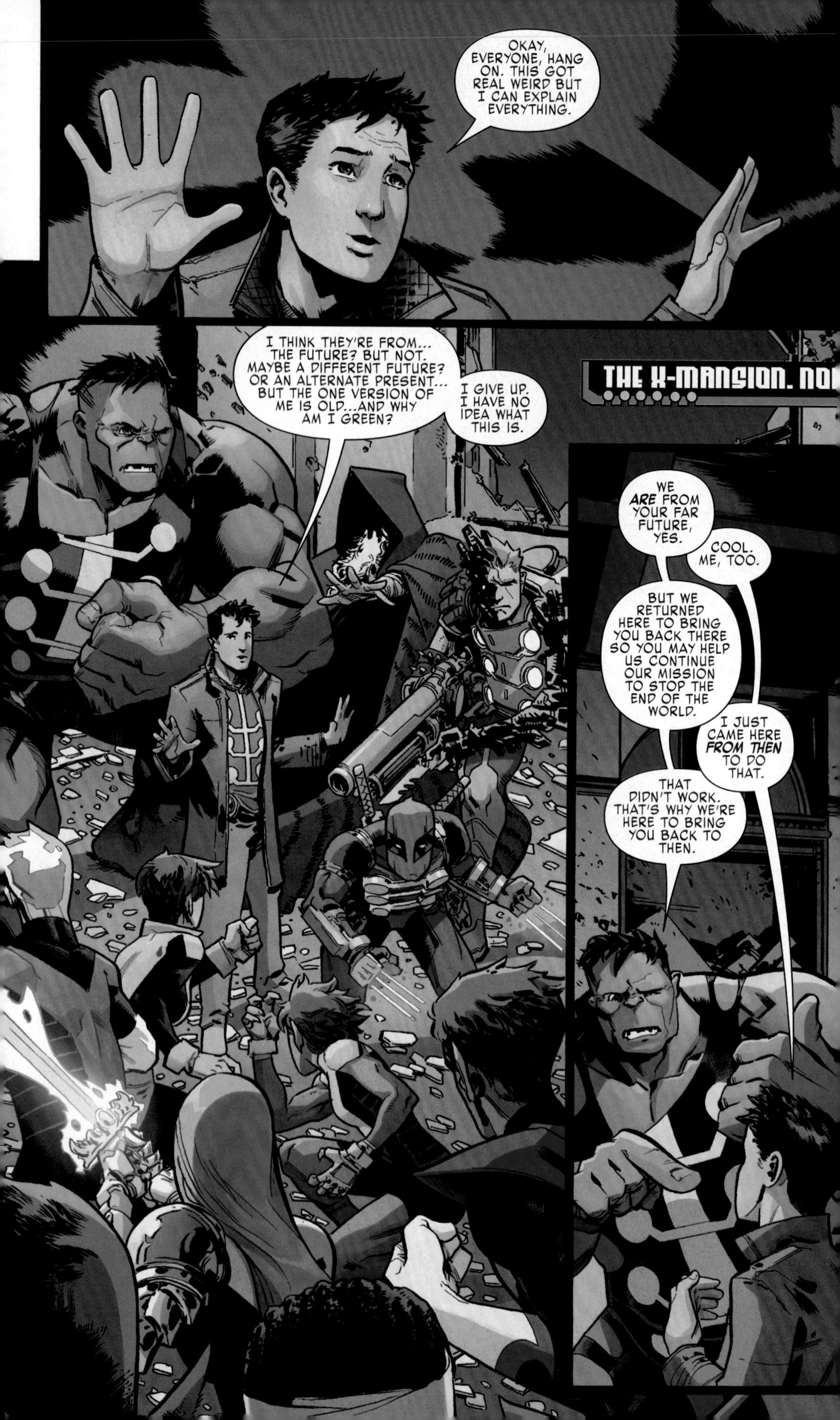
OKAY, EVERYONE, HANG ON. THIS GOT REAL WEIRD BUT I CAN EXPLAIN EVERYTHING.
I THINK THEY'RE FROM... THE FUTURE? BUT NOT. MAYBE A DIFFERENT FUTURE? OR AN ALTERNATE PRESENT... BUT THE ONE VERSION OF ME IS OLD...AND WHY AM I GREEN?
I GIVE UP. I HAVE NO IDEA WHAT THIS IS.
WE ARE FROM YOUR FAR FUTURE, YES.
COOL. ME, TOO.
BUT WE RETURNED HERE TO BRING YOU BACK THERE SO YOU MAY HELP US CONTINUE OUR MISSION TO STOP THE END OF THE WORLD.
I JUST CAME HERE FROM THEN TO DO THAT.
THAT DIDN'T WORK. THAT'S WHY WE'RE HERE TO BRING YOU BACK TO THEN.

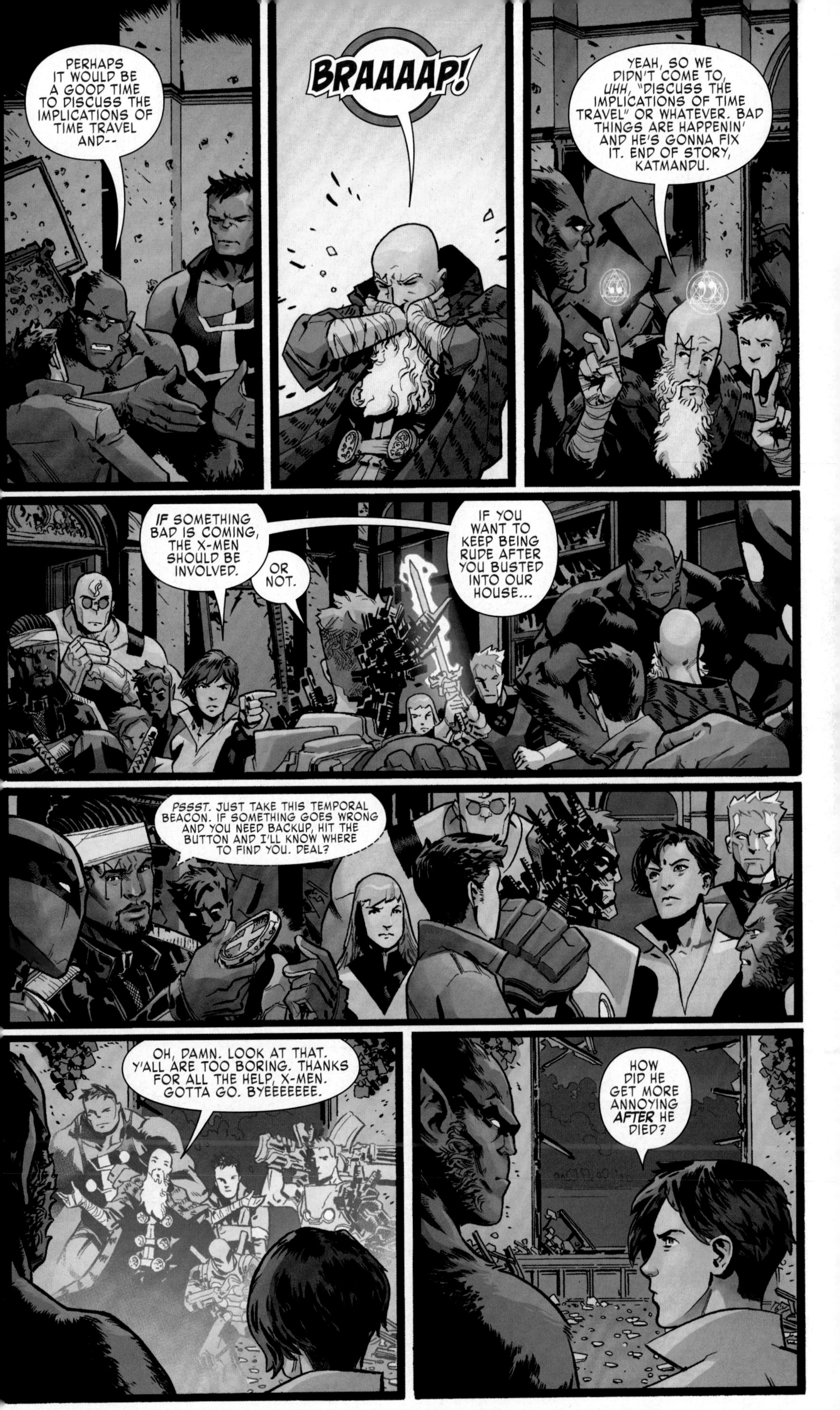

PERHAPS IT WOULD BE A GOOD TIME TO DISCUSS THE IMPLICATIONS OF TIME TRAVEL AND--
BRAAAAP!
YEAH, SO WE DIDN'T COME TO, UHH, "DISCUSS THE IMPLICATIONS OF TIME TRAVEL" OR WHATEVER. BAD THINGS ARE HAPPENIN' AND HE'S GONNA FIX IT. END OF STORY, KATMANDU.
IF SOMETHING BAD IS COMING, THE X-MEN SHOULD BE INVOLVED.
OR NOT.
IF YOU WANT TO KEEP BEING RUDE AFTER YOU BUSTED INTO OUR HOUSE...
PSSST. JUST TAKE THIS TEMPORAL BEACON. IF SOMETHING GOES WRONG AND YOU NEED BACKUP, HIT THE BUTTON AND I'LL KNOW WHERE TO FIND YOU. DEAL?
OH, DAMN. LOOK AT THAT. Y'ALL ARE TOO BORING. THANKS FOR ALL THE HELP, X-MEN. GOTTA GO. BYEEEEEEE.
HOW DID HE GET MORE ANNOYING AFTER HE DIED?

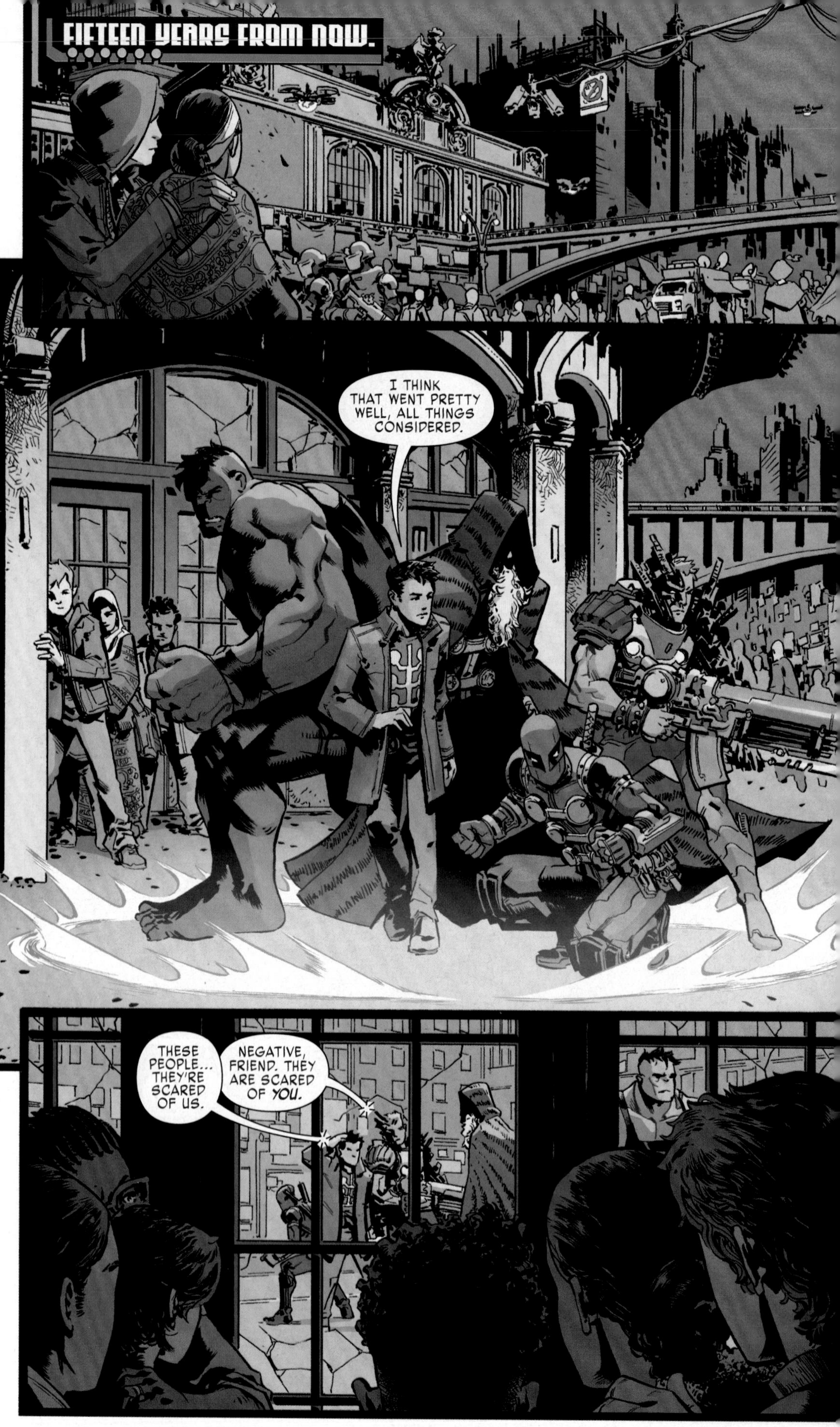
FIFTEEN YEARS FROM NOW.
I THINK THAT WENT PRETTY WELL, ALL THINGS CONSIDERED.
THESE PEOPLE... THEY'RE SCARED OF US.
NEGATIVE, FRIEND. THEY ARE SCARED OF *YOU*.

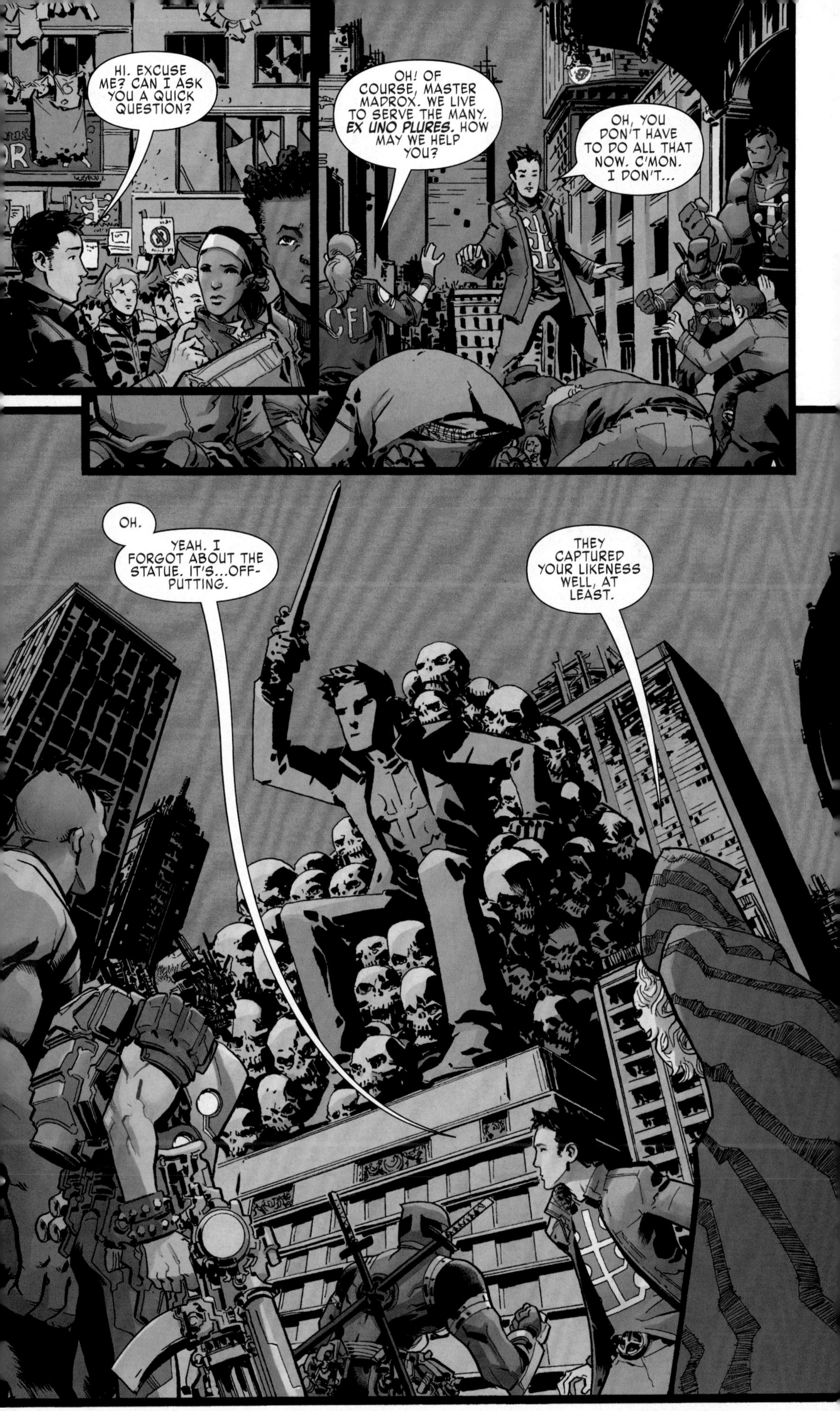
HI. EXCUSE ME? CAN I ASK YOU A QUICK QUESTION?
OH! OF COURSE, MASTER MADROX. WE LIVE TO SERVE THE MANY. *EX UNO PLURES.* HOW MAY WE HELP YOU?
OH, YOU DON'T HAVE TO DO ALL THAT NOW. C'MON. I DON'T...
OH.
YEAH. I FORGOT ABOUT THE STATUE. IT'S...OFF-PUTTING.
THEY CAPTURED YOUR LIKENESS WELL, AT LEAST.

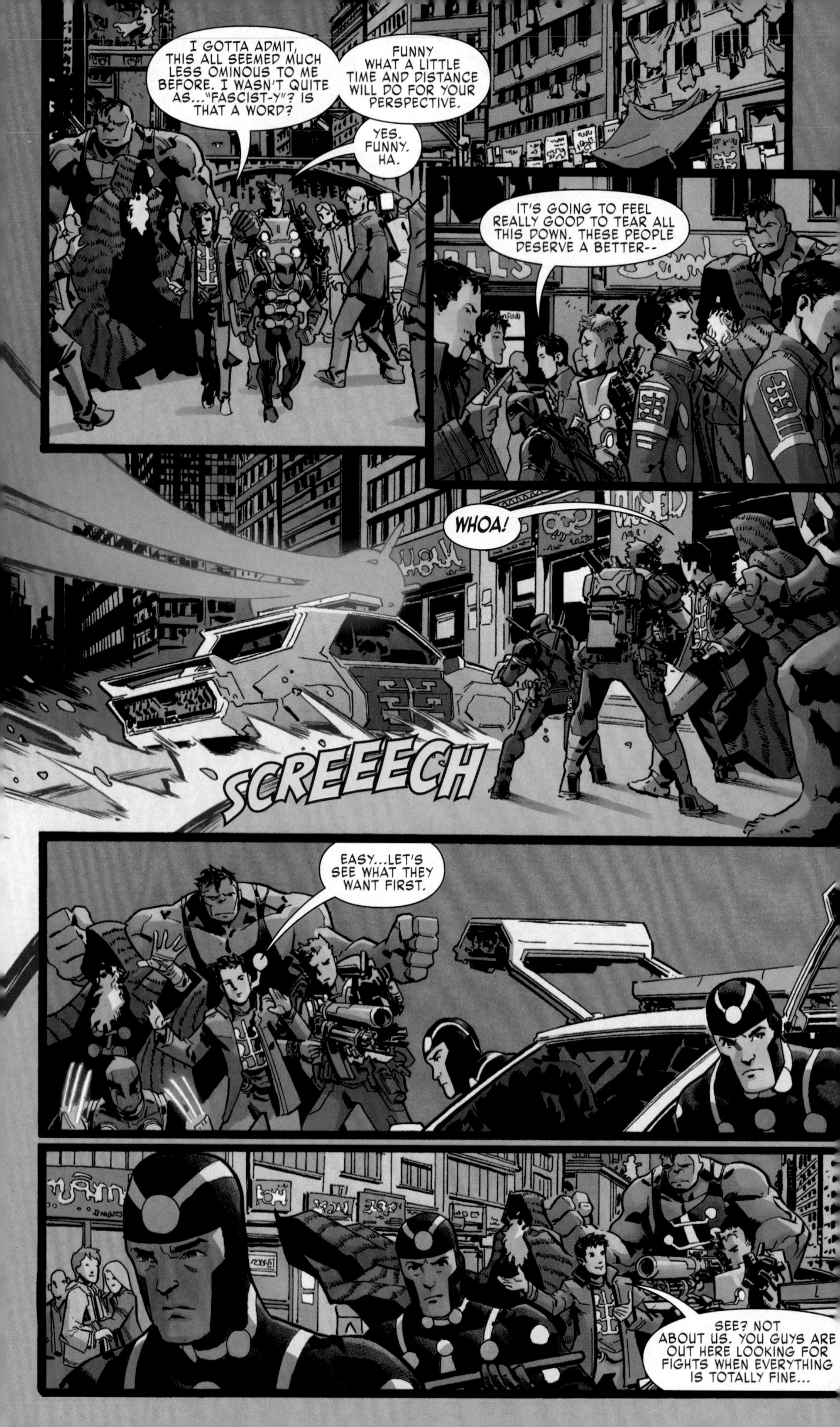
I GOTTA ADMIT, THIS ALL SEEMED MUCH LESS OMINOUS TO ME BEFORE. I WASN'T QUITE AS..."FASCIST-Y"? IS THAT A WORD?
FUNNY WHAT A LITTLE TIME AND DISTANCE WILL DO FOR YOUR PERSPECTIVE.
YES. FUNNY. HA.
IT'S GOING TO FEEL REALLY GOOD TO TEAR ALL THIS DOWN. THESE PEOPLE DESERVE A BETTER--
WHOA!
SCREEECH
EASY...LET'S SEE WHAT THEY WANT FIRST.
SEE? NOT ABOUT US. YOU GUYS ARE OUT HERE LOOKING FOR FIGHTS WHEN EVERYTHING IS TOTALLY FINE...

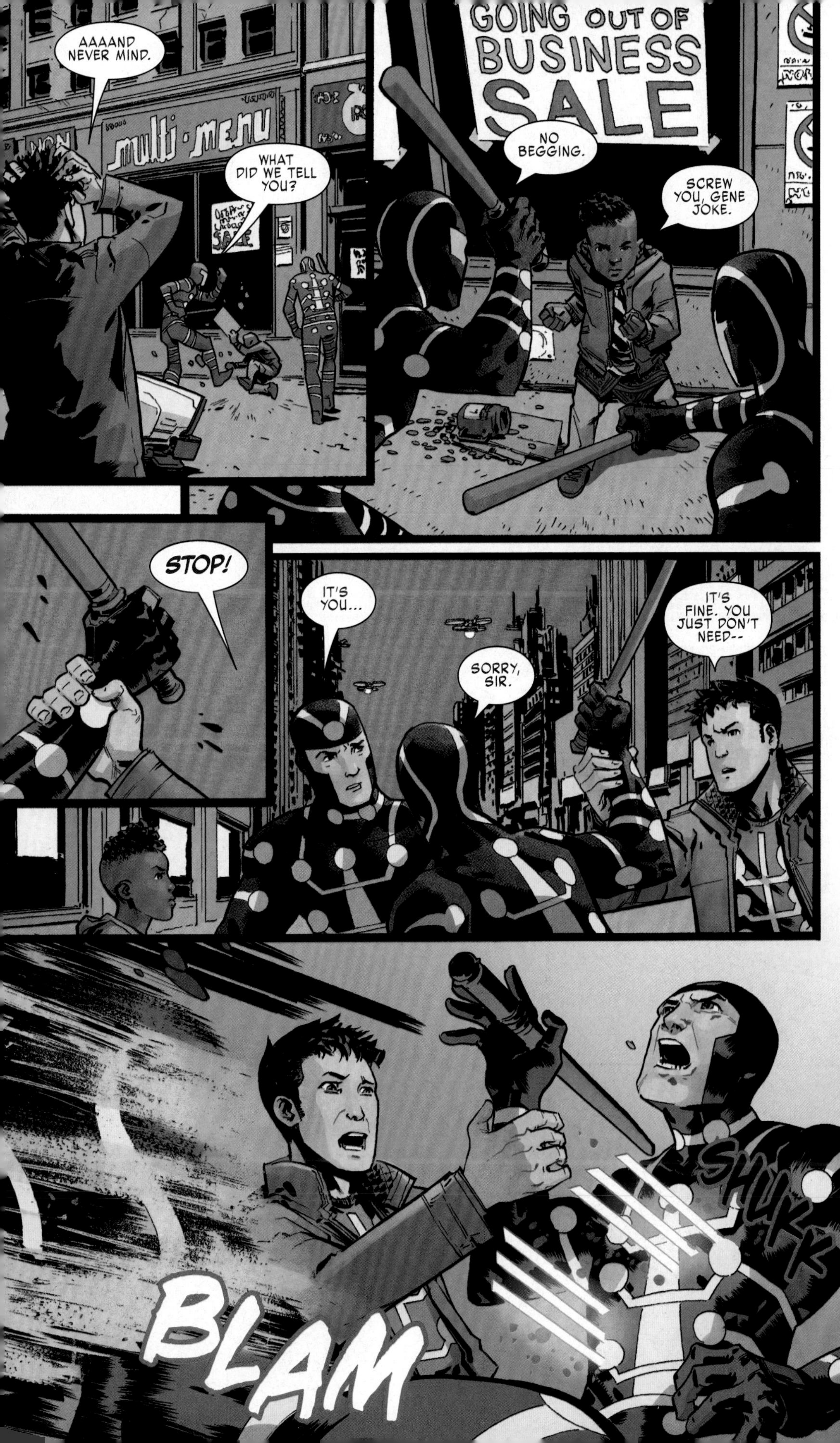
AAAAND NEVER MIND.
multi-menu
WHAT DID WE TELL YOU?
GOING OUT OF BUSINESS SALE
NO BEGGING.
SCREW YOU, GENE JOKE.
STOP!
IT'S YOU...
SORRY, SIR.
IT'S FINE. YOU JUST DON'T NEED--
SHUKK
BLAM

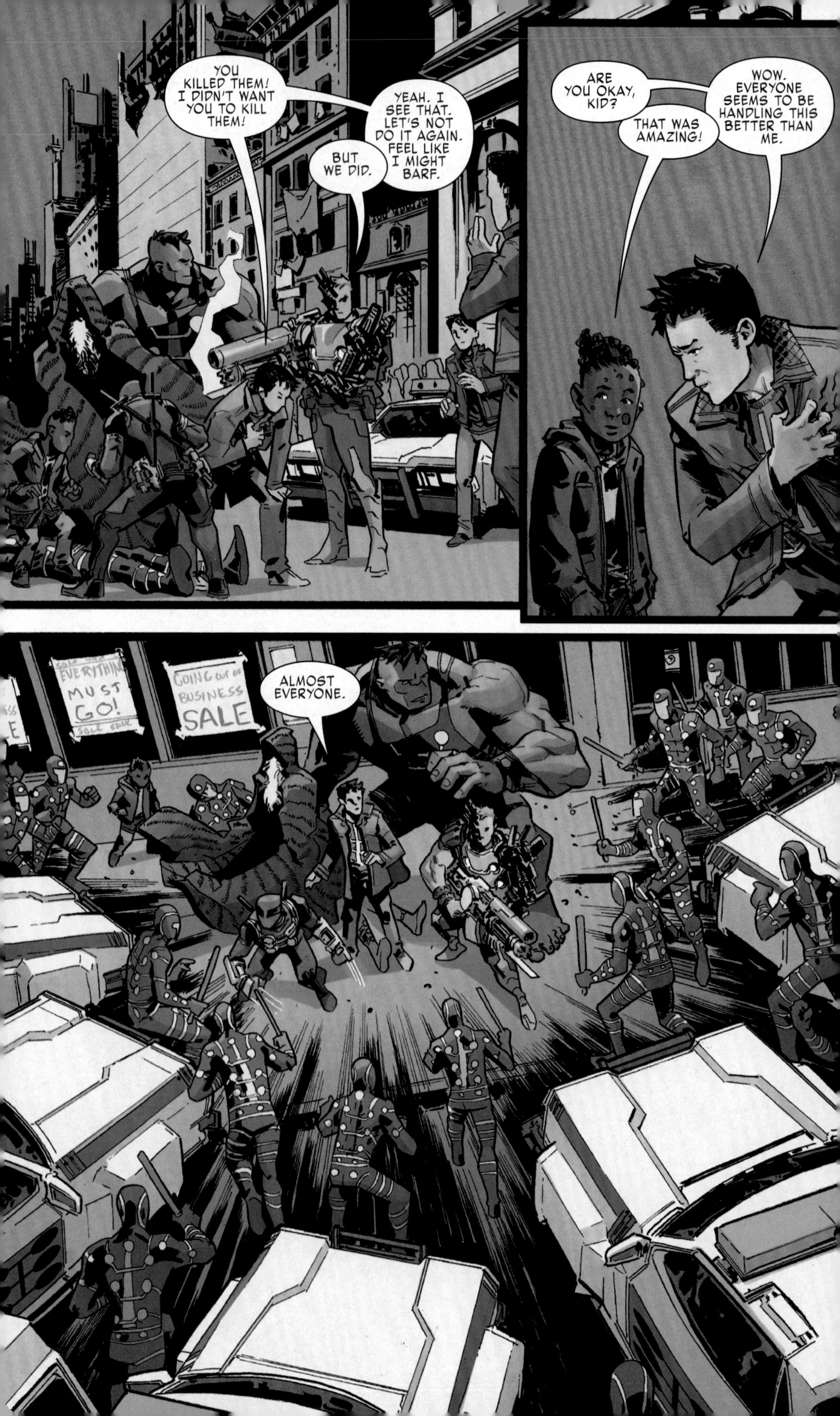
YOU KILLED THEM! I DIDN'T WANT YOU TO KILL THEM!
YEAH. I SEE THAT. LET'S NOT DO IT AGAIN. FEEL LIKE I MIGHT BARF.
BUT WE DID.
ARE YOU OKAY, KID?
WOW. EVERYONE SEEMS TO BE HANDLING THIS BETTER THAN ME.
THAT WAS AMAZING!
EVERYTHING MUST GO!
GOING OUT OF BUSINESS SALE
ALMOST EVERYONE.

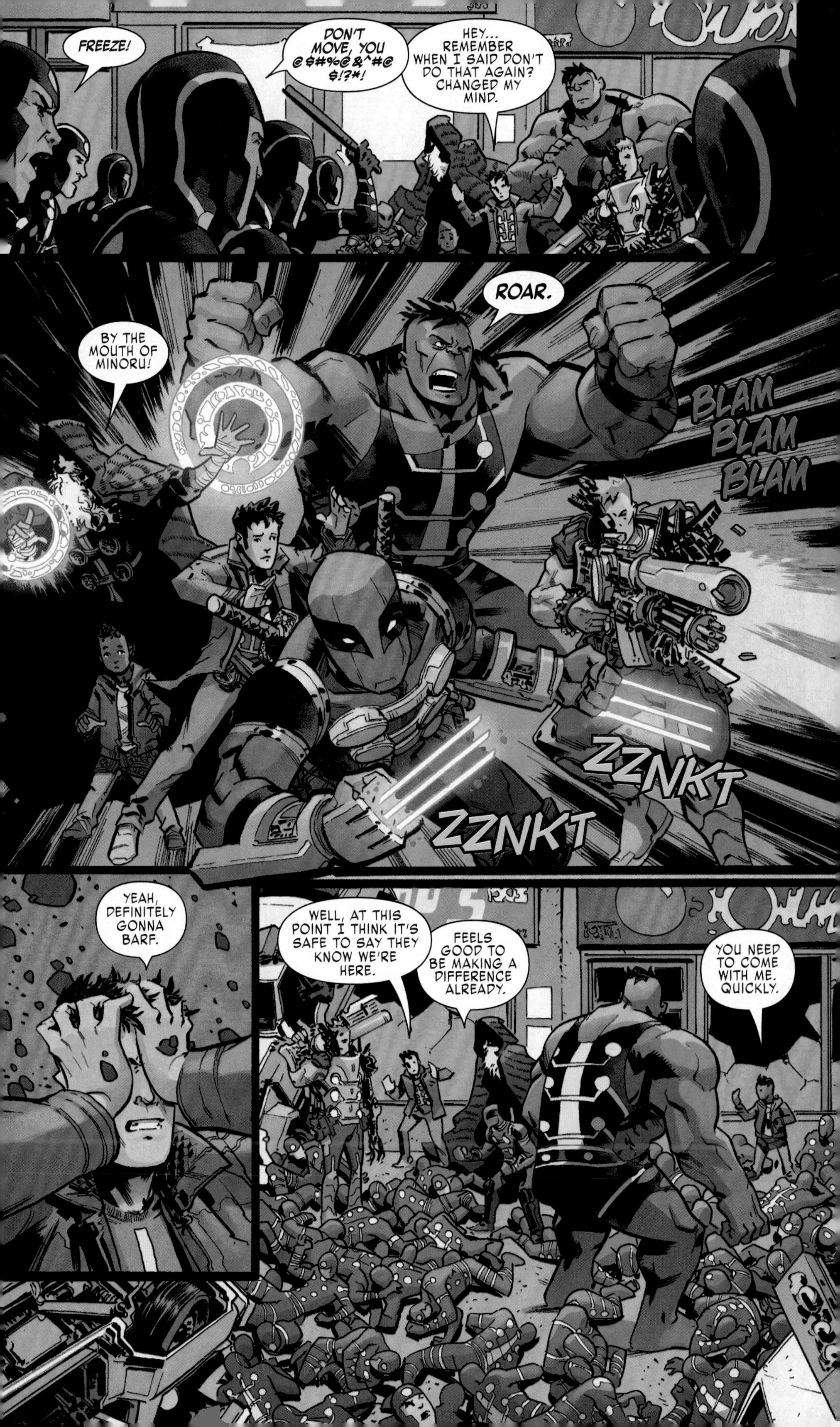
FREEZE!
DON'T MOVE, YOU @$#%@&^#@ $!?*!
HEY... REMEMBER WHEN I SAID DON'T DO THAT AGAIN? CHANGED MY MIND.
BY THE MOUTH OF MINORU!
ROAR.
BLAM BLAM BLAM
ZZNKT
ZZNKT
YEAH, DEFINITELY GONNA BARF.
WELL, AT THIS POINT I THINK IT'S SAFE TO SAY THEY KNOW WE'RE HERE.
FEELS GOOD TO BE MAKING A DIFFERENCE ALREADY.
YOU NEED TO COME WITH ME. QUICKLY.

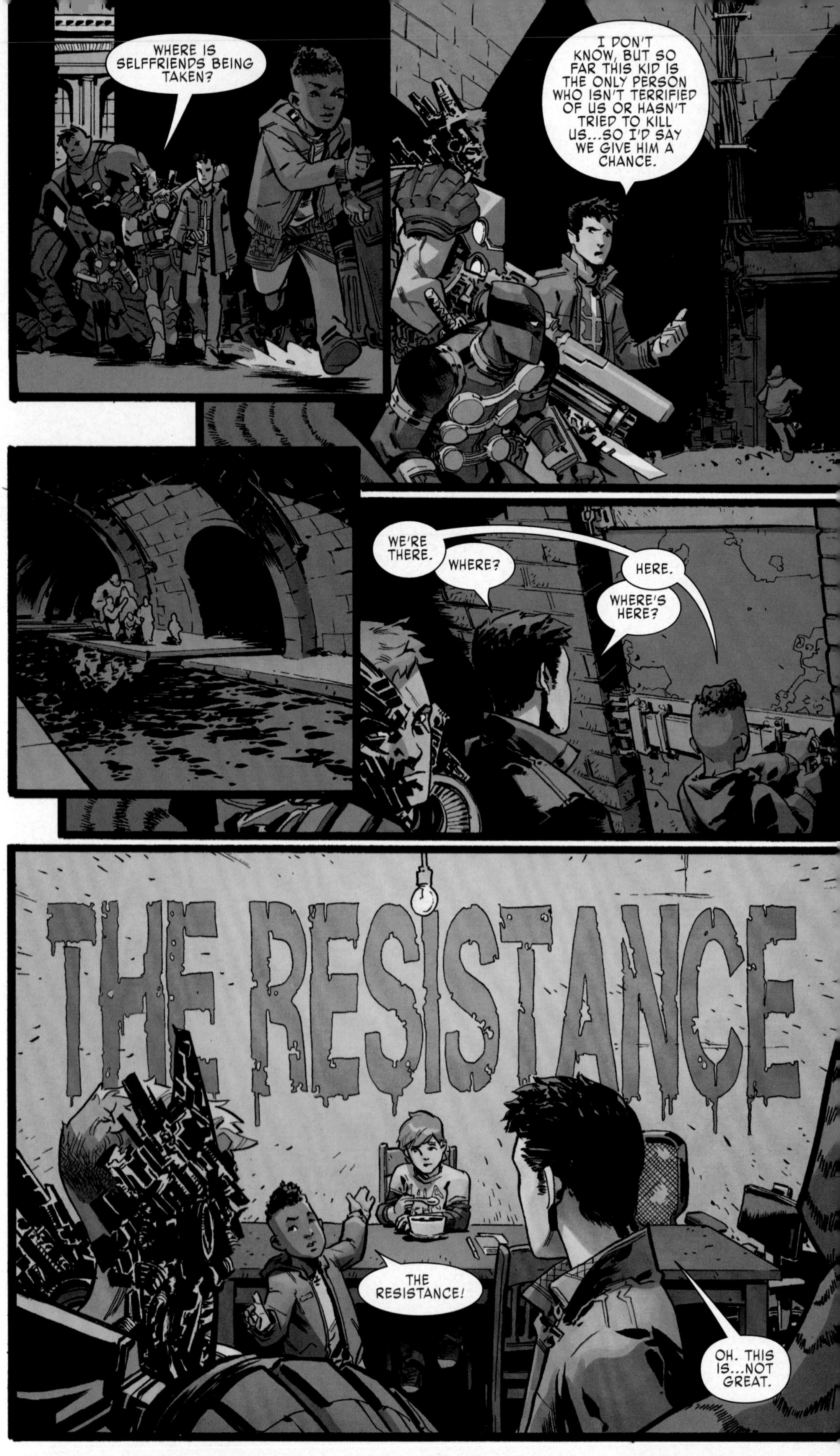
WHERE IS SELFFRIENDS BEING TAKEN?
I DON'T KNOW, BUT SO FAR THIS KID IS THE ONLY PERSON WHO ISN'T TERRIFIED OF US OR HASN'T TRIED TO KILL US...SO I'D SAY WE GIVE HIM A CHANCE.
WE'RE THERE.
WHERE?
HERE.
WHERE'S HERE?
THE RESISTANCE
THE RESISTANCE!
OH. THIS IS...NOT GREAT.

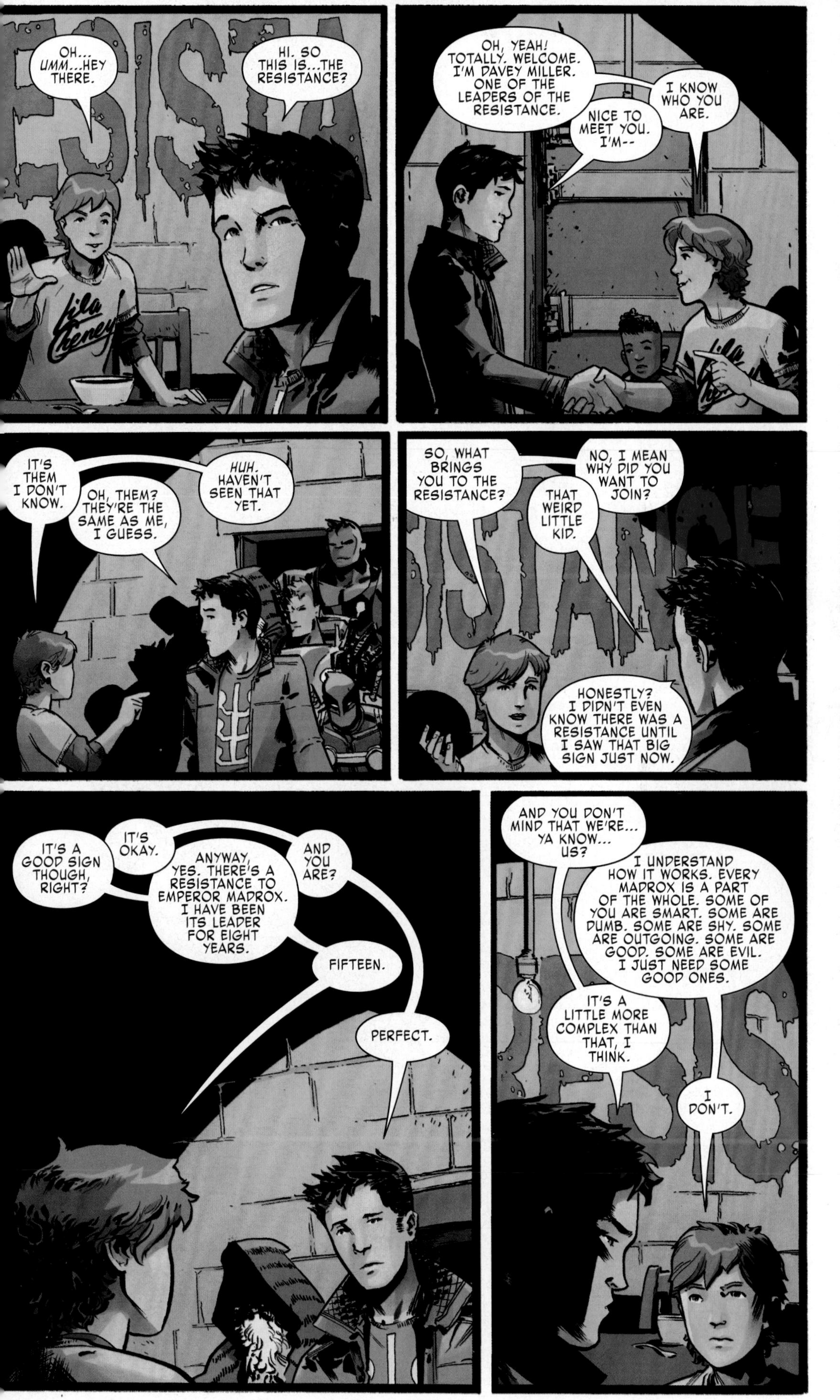

OH... UMM...HEY THERE.
HI. SO THIS IS...THE RESISTANCE?
Lila Cheney
OH, YEAH! TOTALLY. WELCOME. I'M DAVEY MILLER. ONE OF THE LEADERS OF THE RESISTANCE.
NICE TO MEET YOU. I'M--
I KNOW WHO YOU ARE.
IT'S THEM I DON'T KNOW.
HUH. HAVEN'T SEEN THAT YET.
OH, THEM? THEY'RE THE SAME AS ME, I GUESS.
SO, WHAT BRINGS YOU TO THE RESISTANCE?
NO, I MEAN WHY DID YOU WANT TO JOIN?
THAT WEIRD LITTLE KID.
HONESTLY? I DIDN'T EVEN KNOW THERE WAS A RESISTANCE UNTIL I SAW THAT BIG SIGN JUST NOW.
IT'S A GOOD SIGN THOUGH, RIGHT?
IT'S OKAY.
ANYWAY, YES. THERE'S A RESISTANCE TO EMPEROR MADROX. I HAVE BEEN ITS LEADER FOR EIGHT YEARS.
AND YOU ARE?
FIFTEEN.
PERFECT.
AND YOU DON'T MIND THAT WE'RE... YA KNOW... US?
I UNDERSTAND HOW IT WORKS. EVERY MADROX IS A PART OF THE WHOLE. SOME OF YOU ARE SMART. SOME ARE DUMB. SOME ARE SHY. SOME ARE OUTGOING. SOME ARE GOOD. SOME ARE EVIL. I JUST NEED SOME GOOD ONES.
IT'S A LITTLE MORE COMPLEX THAN THAT, I THINK.
I DON'T.

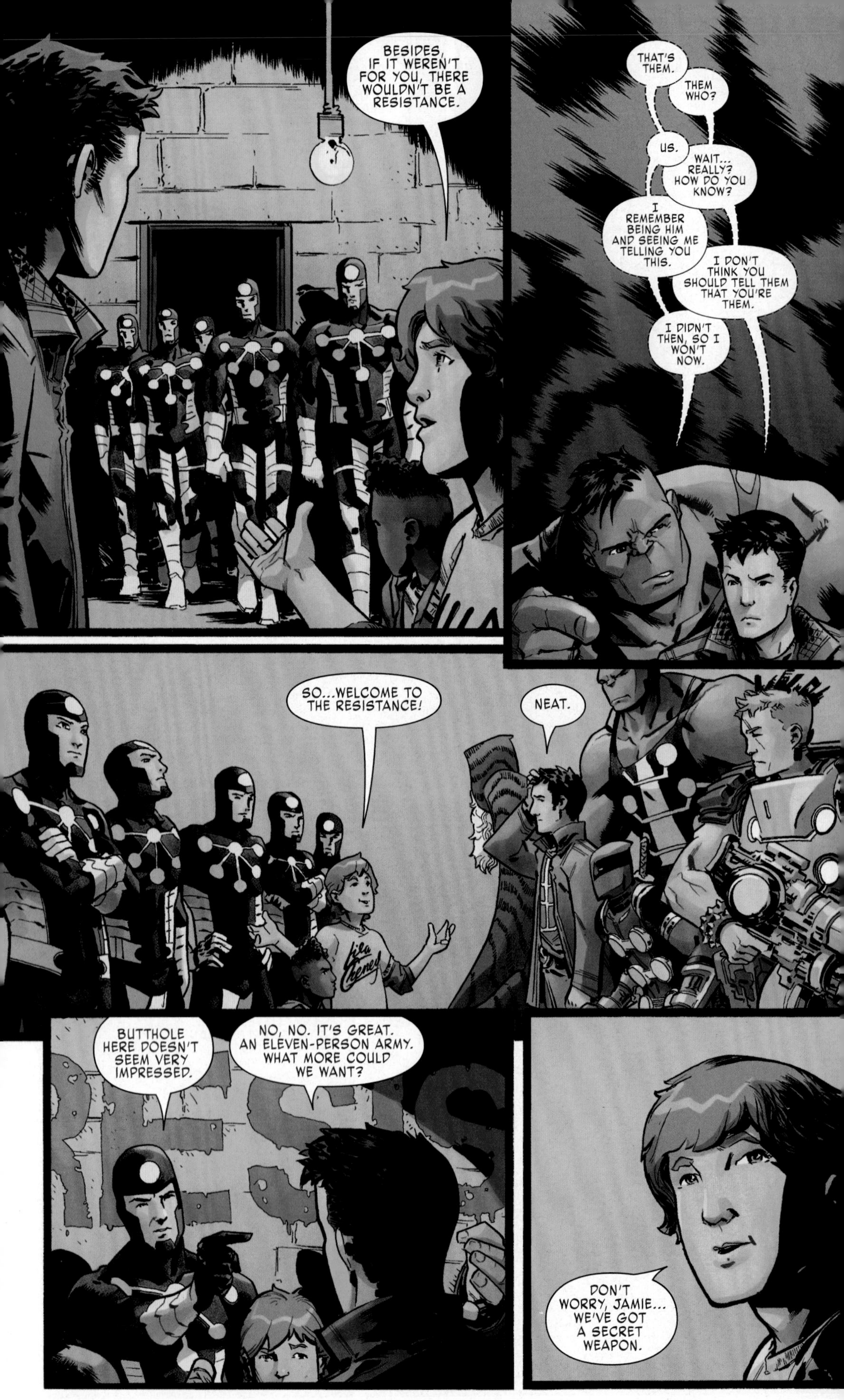
BESIDES, IF IT WEREN'T FOR YOU, THERE WOULDN'T BE A RESISTANCE.
THAT'S THEM.
THEM WHO?
US.
WAIT... REALLY? HOW DO YOU KNOW?
I REMEMBER BEING HIM AND SEEING ME TELLING YOU THIS.
I DON'T THINK YOU SHOULD TELL THEM THAT YOU'RE THEM.
I DIDN'T THEN, SO I WON'T NOW.
SO...WELCOME TO THE RESISTANCE!
NEAT.
BUTTHOLE HERE DOESN'T SEEM VERY IMPRESSED.
NO, NO. IT'S GREAT. AN ELEVEN-PERSON ARMY. WHAT MORE COULD WE WANT?
DON'T WORRY, JAMIE... WE'VE GOT A SECRET WEAPON.

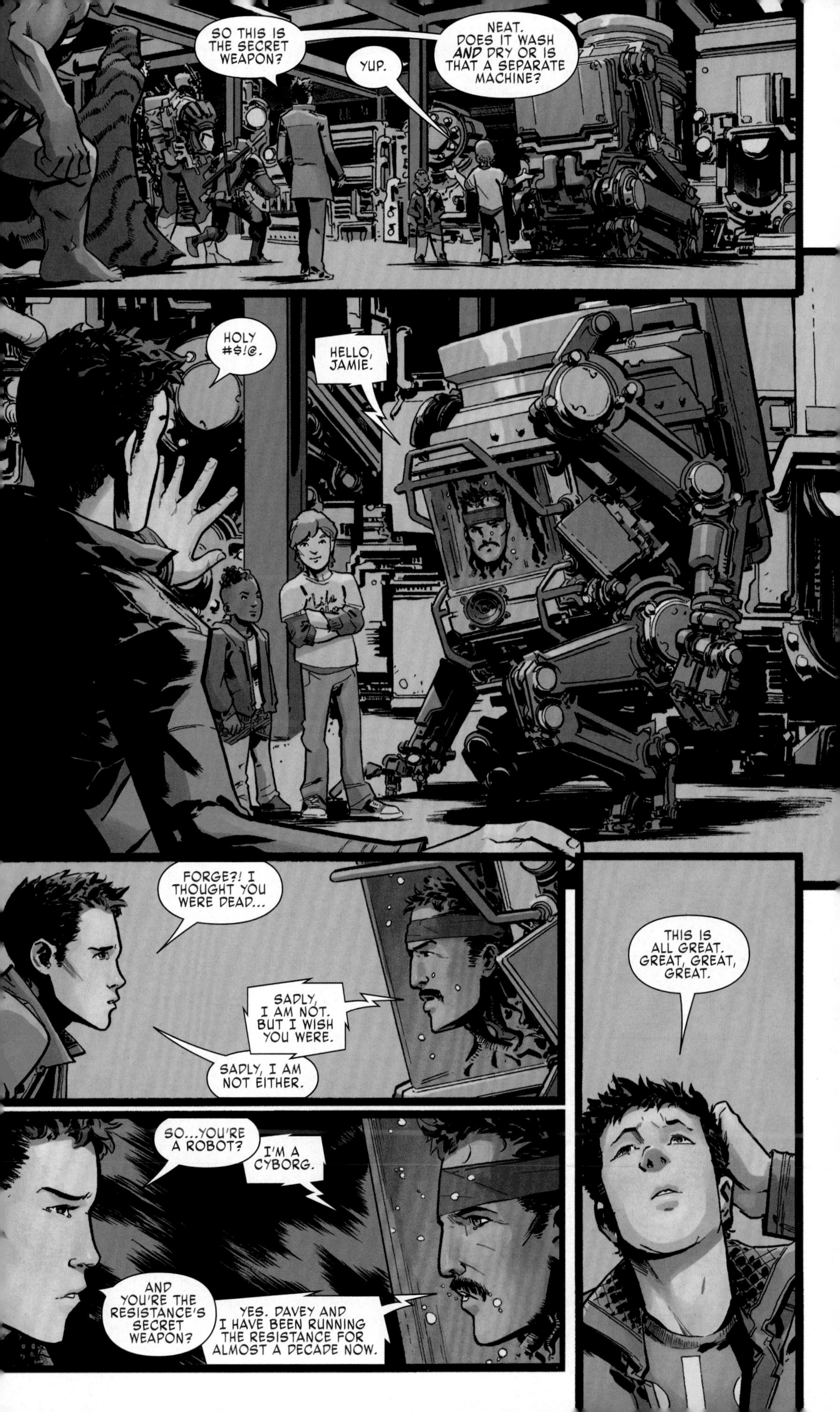
SO THIS IS THE SECRET WEAPON?
YUP.
NEAT. DOES IT WASH AND DRY OR IS THAT A SEPARATE MACHINE?
HOLY #$!@.
HELLO, JAMIE.
FORGE?! I THOUGHT YOU WERE DEAD...
SADLY, I AM NOT. BUT I WISH YOU WERE.
SADLY, I AM NOT EITHER.
THIS IS ALL GREAT. GREAT, GREAT, GREAT.
SO...YOU'RE A ROBOT?
I'M A CYBORG.
AND YOU'RE THE RESISTANCE'S SECRET WEAPON?
YES. DAVEY AND I HAVE BEEN RUNNING THE RESISTANCE FOR ALMOST A DECADE NOW.

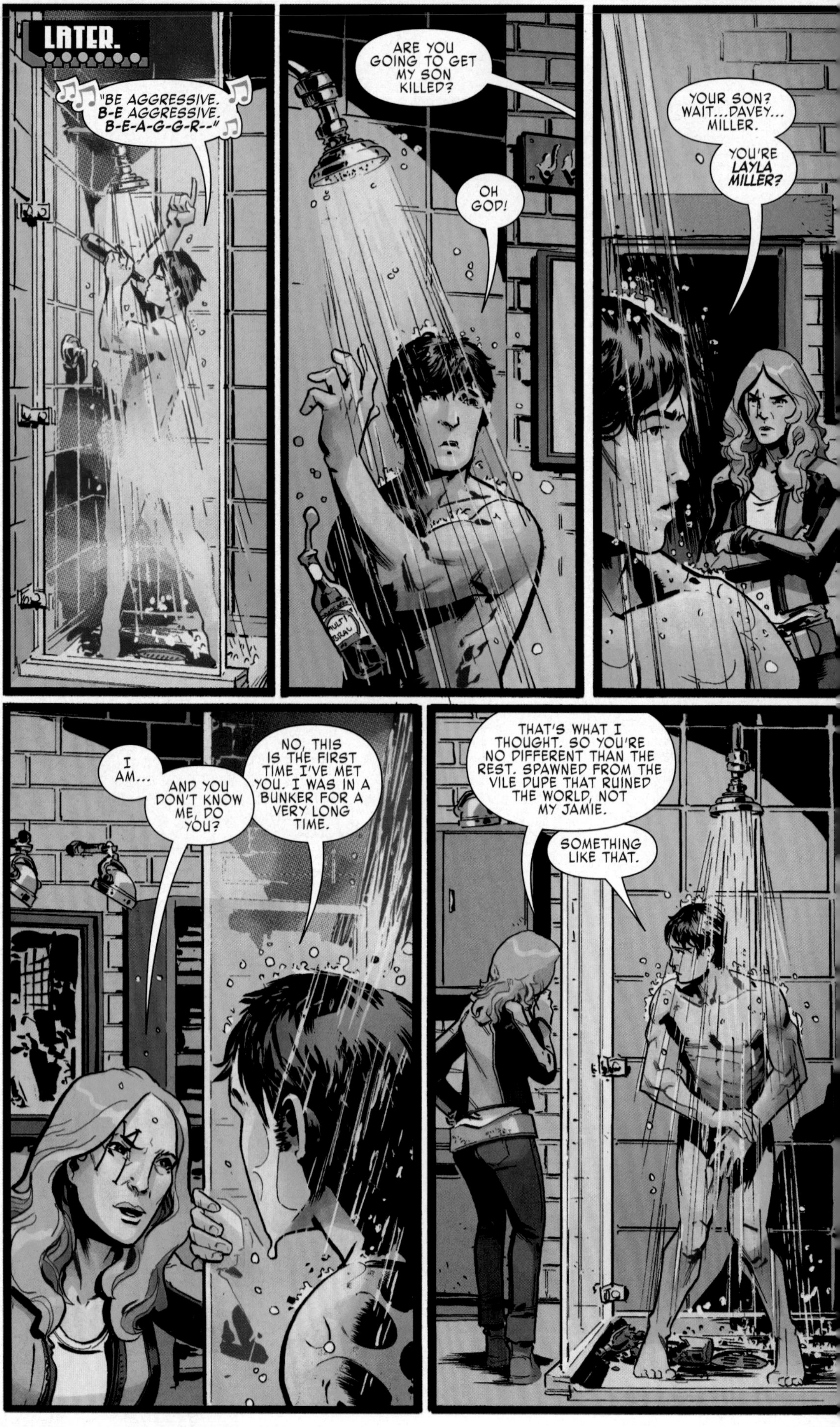
LATER.
"BE AGGRESSIVE. B-E AGGRESSIVE. B-E-A-G-G-R--"
ARE YOU GOING TO GET MY SON KILLED?
OH GOD!
YOUR SON? WAIT...DAVEY... MILLER.
YOU'RE LAYLA MILLER?
I AM...
AND YOU DON'T KNOW ME, DO YOU?
NO, THIS IS THE FIRST TIME I'VE MET YOU. I WAS IN A BUNKER FOR A VERY LONG TIME.
THAT'S WHAT I THOUGHT. SO YOU'RE NO DIFFERENT THAN THE REST. SPAWNED FROM THE VILE DUPE THAT RUINED THE WORLD, NOT MY JAMIE.
SOMETHING LIKE THAT.

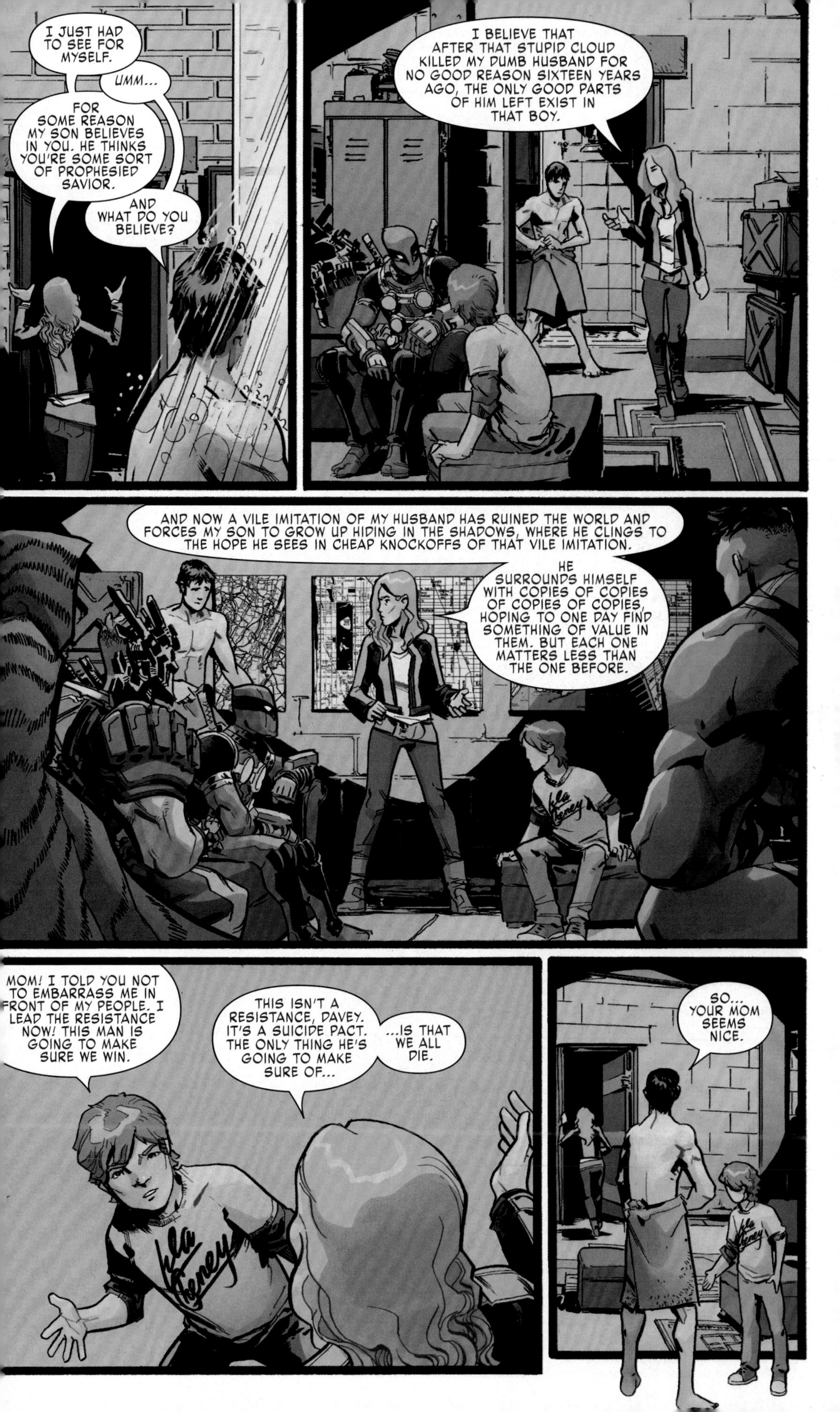
I JUST HAD TO SEE FOR MYSELF.
UMM...
FOR SOME REASON MY SON BELIEVES IN YOU. HE THINKS YOU'RE SOME SORT OF PROPHESIED SAVIOR.
AND WHAT DO YOU BELIEVE?
I BELIEVE THAT AFTER THAT STUPID CLOUD KILLED MY DUMB HUSBAND FOR NO GOOD REASON SIXTEEN YEARS AGO, THE ONLY GOOD PARTS OF HIM LEFT EXIST IN THAT BOY.
AND NOW A VILE IMITATION OF MY HUSBAND HAS RUINED THE WORLD AND FORCES MY SON TO GROW UP HIDING IN THE SHADOWS, WHERE HE CLINGS TO THE HOPE HE SEES IN CHEAP KNOCKOFFS OF THAT VILE IMITATION.
HE SURROUNDS HIMSELF WITH COPIES OF COPIES OF COPIES OF COPIES, HOPING TO ONE DAY FIND SOMETHING OF VALUE IN THEM. BUT EACH ONE MATTERS LESS THAN THE ONE BEFORE.
MOM! I TOLD YOU NOT TO EMBARRASS ME IN FRONT OF MY PEOPLE. I LEAD THE RESISTANCE NOW! THIS MAN IS GOING TO MAKE SURE WE WIN.
THIS ISN'T A RESISTANCE, DAVEY. IT'S A SUICIDE PACT. THE ONLY THING HE'S GOING TO MAKE SURE OF...
...IS THAT WE ALL DIE.
SO... YOUR MOM SEEMS NICE.

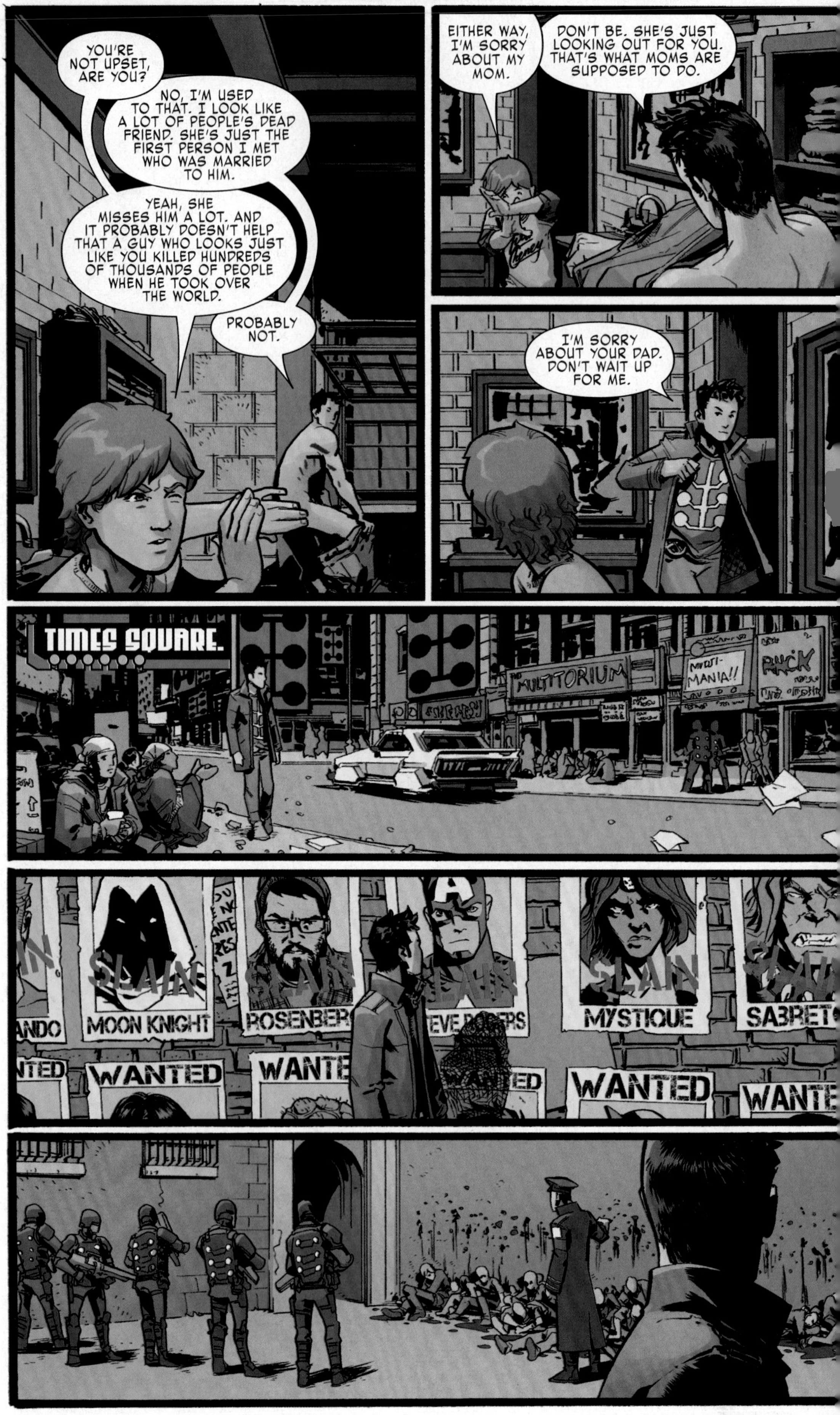
YOU'RE NOT UPSET, ARE YOU?
NO, I'M USED TO THAT. I LOOK LIKE A LOT OF PEOPLE'S DEAD FRIEND. SHE'S JUST THE FIRST PERSON I MET WHO WAS MARRIED TO HIM.
YEAH, SHE MISSES HIM A LOT. AND IT PROBABLY DOESN'T HELP THAT A GUY WHO LOOKS JUST LIKE YOU KILLED HUNDREDS OF THOUSANDS OF PEOPLE WHEN HE TOOK OVER THE WORLD.
PROBABLY NOT.
EITHER WAY, I'M SORRY ABOUT MY MOM.
DON'T BE. SHE'S JUST LOOKING OUT FOR YOU. THAT'S WHAT MOMS ARE SUPPOSED TO DO.
I'M SORRY ABOUT YOUR DAD. DON'T WAIT UP FOR ME.
TIMES SQUARE.
MULTITORIUM
MULTI-MANIA!!
SLAIN
MOON KNIGHT
ROSENBER
EVE ROGERS
MYSTIQUE
SABRET
ANDO
WANTED
WANTE

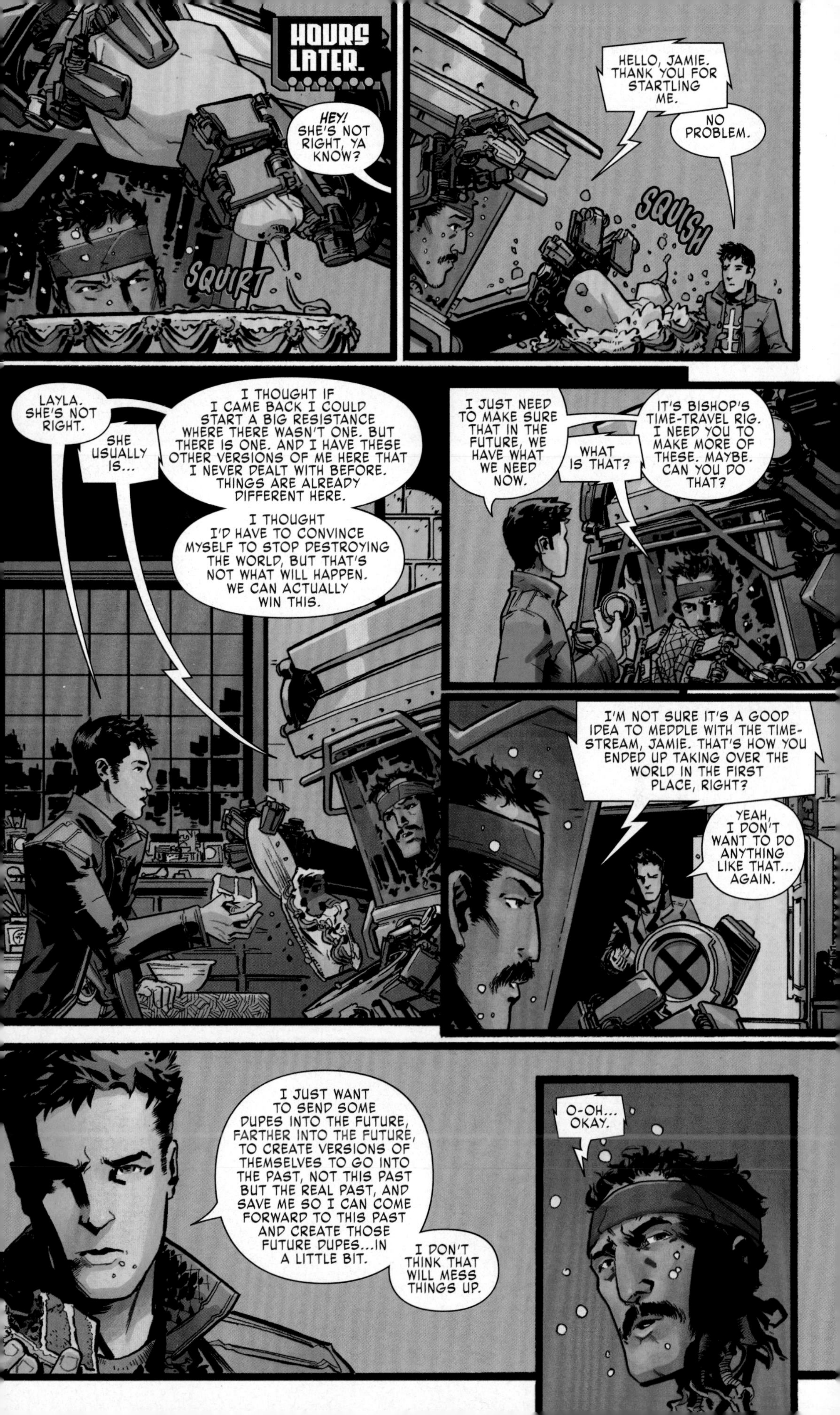
HOURS LATER.
HEY! SHE'S NOT RIGHT, YA KNOW?
SQUIRT
HELLO, JAMIE. THANK YOU FOR STARTLING ME.
NO PROBLEM.
SQUISH
LAYLA. SHE'S NOT RIGHT.
SHE USUALLY IS...
I THOUGHT IF I CAME BACK I COULD START A BIG RESISTANCE WHERE THERE WASN'T ONE. BUT THERE IS ONE. AND I HAVE THESE OTHER VERSIONS OF ME HERE THAT I NEVER DEALT WITH BEFORE. THINGS ARE ALREADY DIFFERENT HERE.
I THOUGHT I'D HAVE TO CONVINCE MYSELF TO STOP DESTROYING THE WORLD, BUT THAT'S NOT WHAT WILL HAPPEN. WE CAN ACTUALLY WIN THIS.
I JUST NEED TO MAKE SURE THAT IN THE FUTURE, WE HAVE WHAT WE NEED NOW.
WHAT IS THAT?
IT'S BISHOP'S TIME-TRAVEL RIG. I NEED YOU TO MAKE MORE OF THESE. MAYBE. CAN YOU DO THAT?
I'M NOT SURE IT'S A GOOD IDEA TO MEDDLE WITH THE TIME-STREAM, JAMIE. THAT'S HOW YOU ENDED UP TAKING OVER THE WORLD IN THE FIRST PLACE, RIGHT?
YEAH, I DON'T WANT TO DO ANYTHING LIKE THAT... AGAIN.
I JUST WANT TO SEND SOME DUPES INTO THE FUTURE, FARTHER INTO THE FUTURE, TO CREATE VERSIONS OF THEMSELVES TO GO INTO THE PAST, NOT THIS PAST BUT THE REAL PAST, AND SAVE ME SO I CAN COME FORWARD TO THIS PAST AND CREATE THOSE FUTURE DUPES...IN A LITTLE BIT.
I DON'T THINK THAT WILL MESS THINGS UP.
O-OH... OKAY.

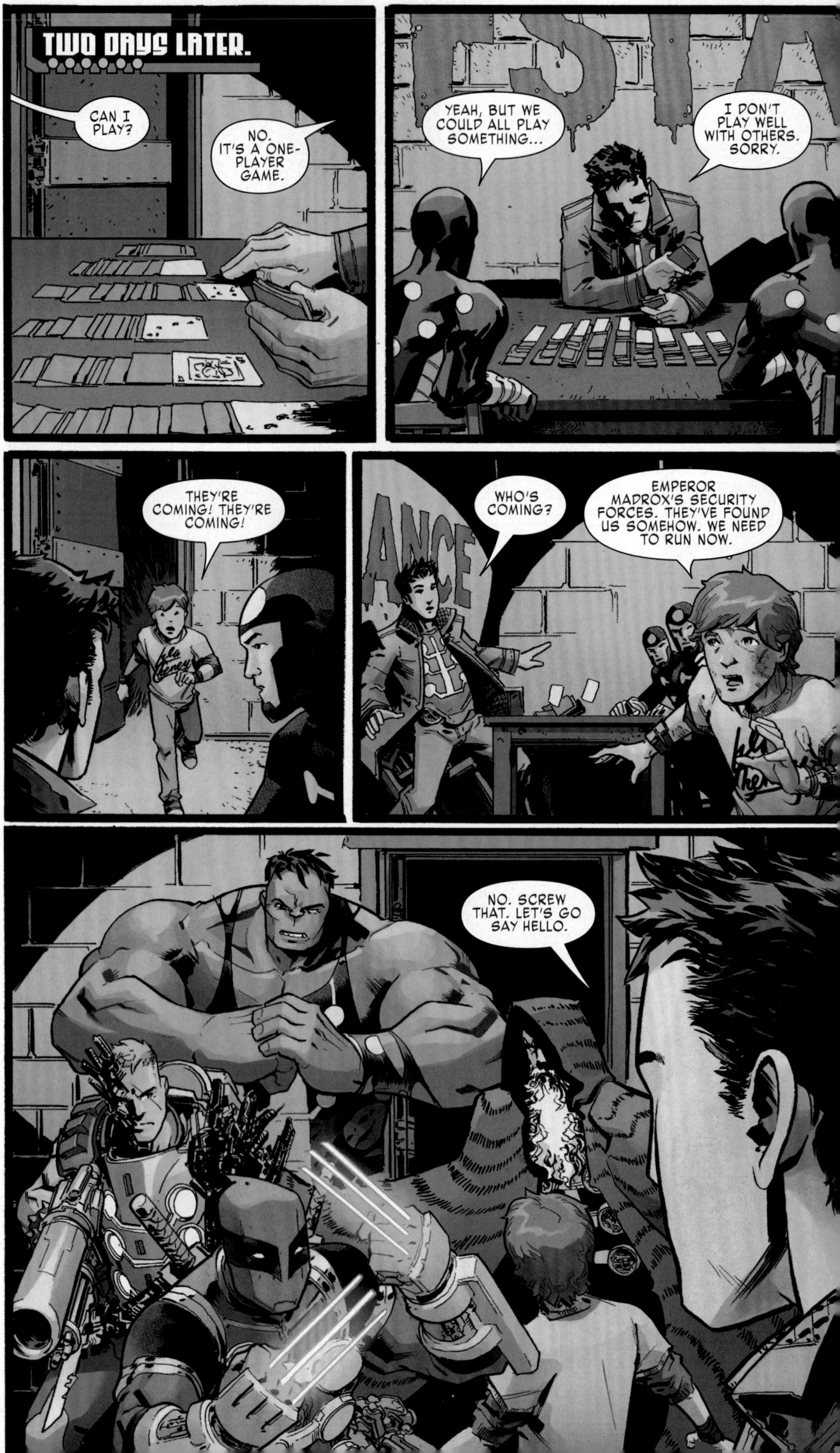
TWO DAYS LATER.
CAN I PLAY?
NO. IT'S A ONE-PLAYER GAME.
YEAH, BUT WE COULD ALL PLAY SOMETHING...
I DON'T PLAY WELL WITH OTHERS. SORRY.
THEY'RE COMING! THEY'RE COMING!
WHO'S COMING?
EMPEROR MADROX'S SECURITY FORCES. THEY'VE FOUND US SOMEHOW. WE NEED TO RUN NOW.
NO. SCREW THAT. LET'S GO SAY HELLO.

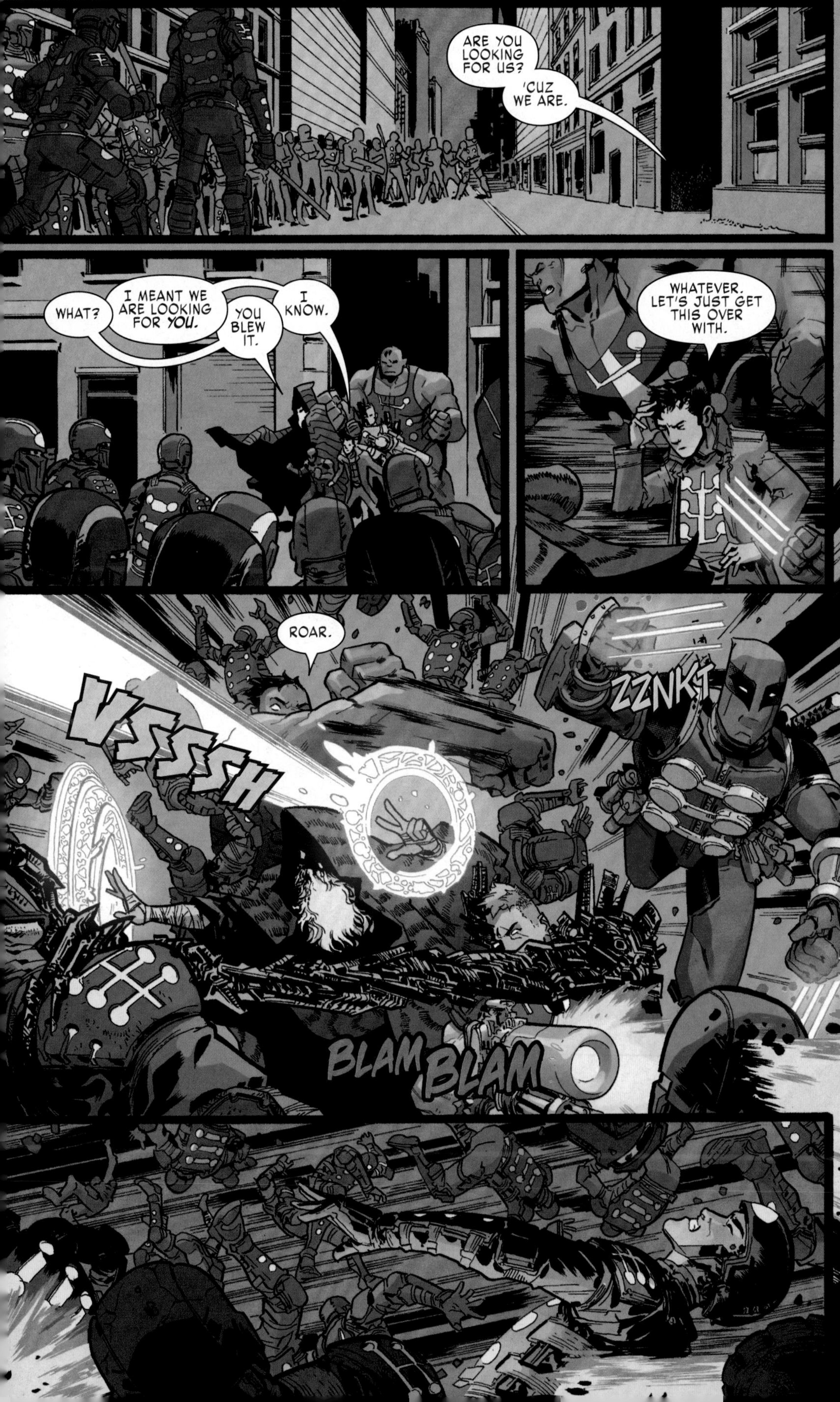

ARE YOU LOOKING FOR US?
'CUZ WE ARE.
WHAT?
I MEANT WE ARE LOOKING FOR *YOU.*
YOU BLEW IT.
I KNOW.
WHATEVER. LET'S JUST GET THIS OVER WITH.
ROAR.
VSSSH
ZZNKT
BLAM BLAM

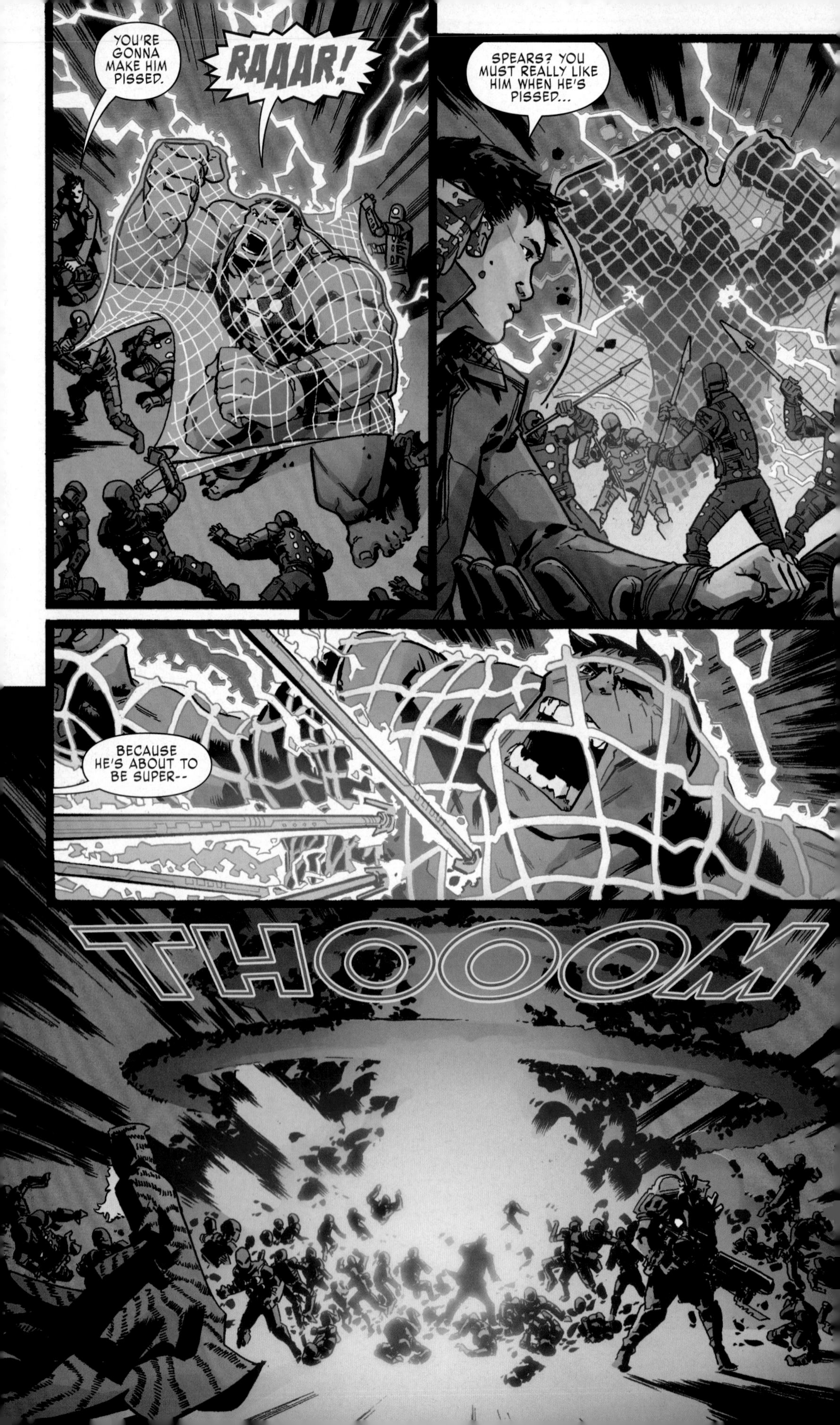
YOU'RE GONNA MAKE HIM PISSED.
RAAAR!
SPEARS? YOU MUST REALLY LIKE HIM WHEN HE'S PISSED...
BECAUSE HE'S ABOUT TO BE SUPER--
THOOOM

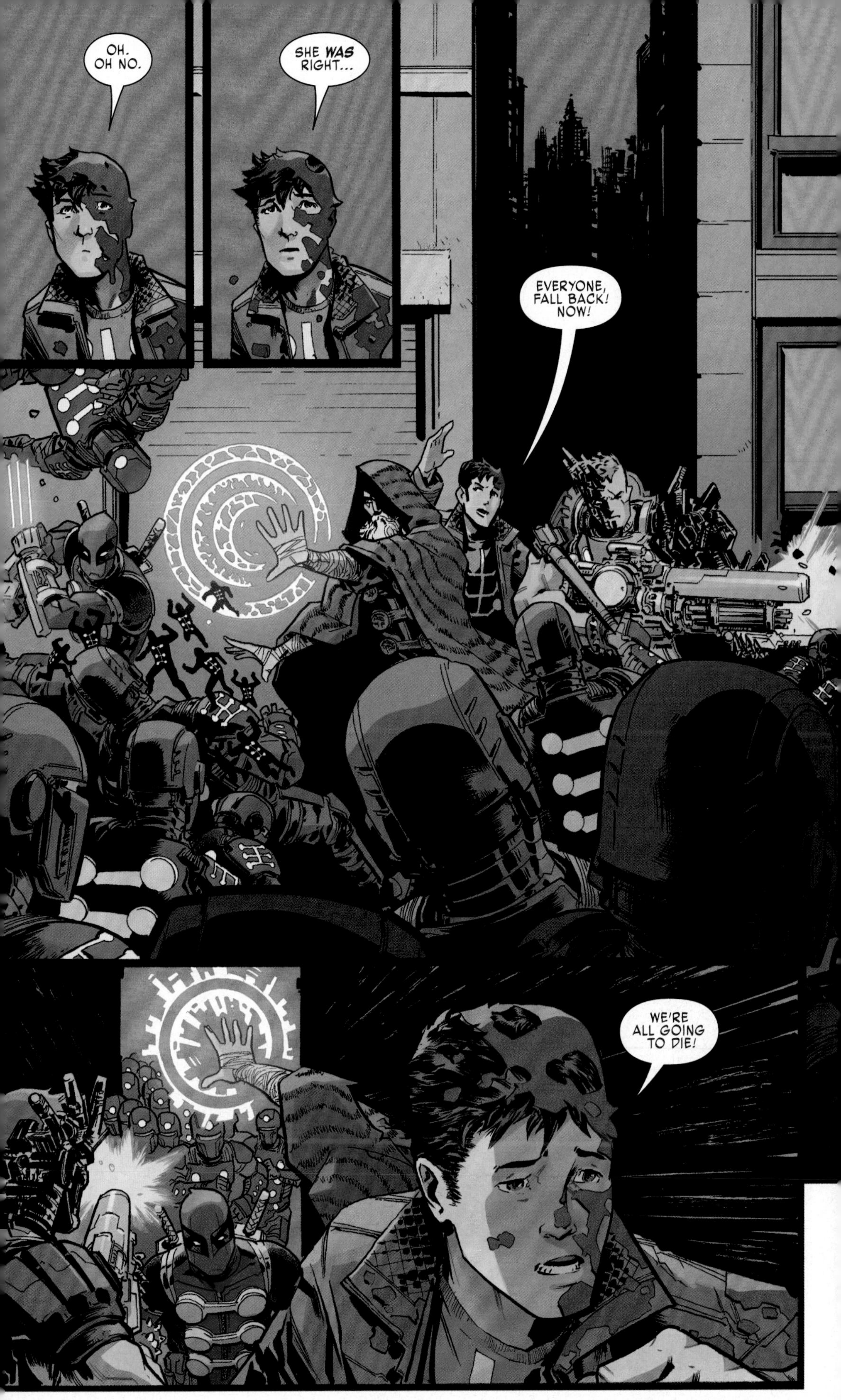
OH.
OH NO.
SHE *WAS* RIGHT...
EVERYONE, FALL BACK! NOW!
WE'RE ALL GOING TO DIE!

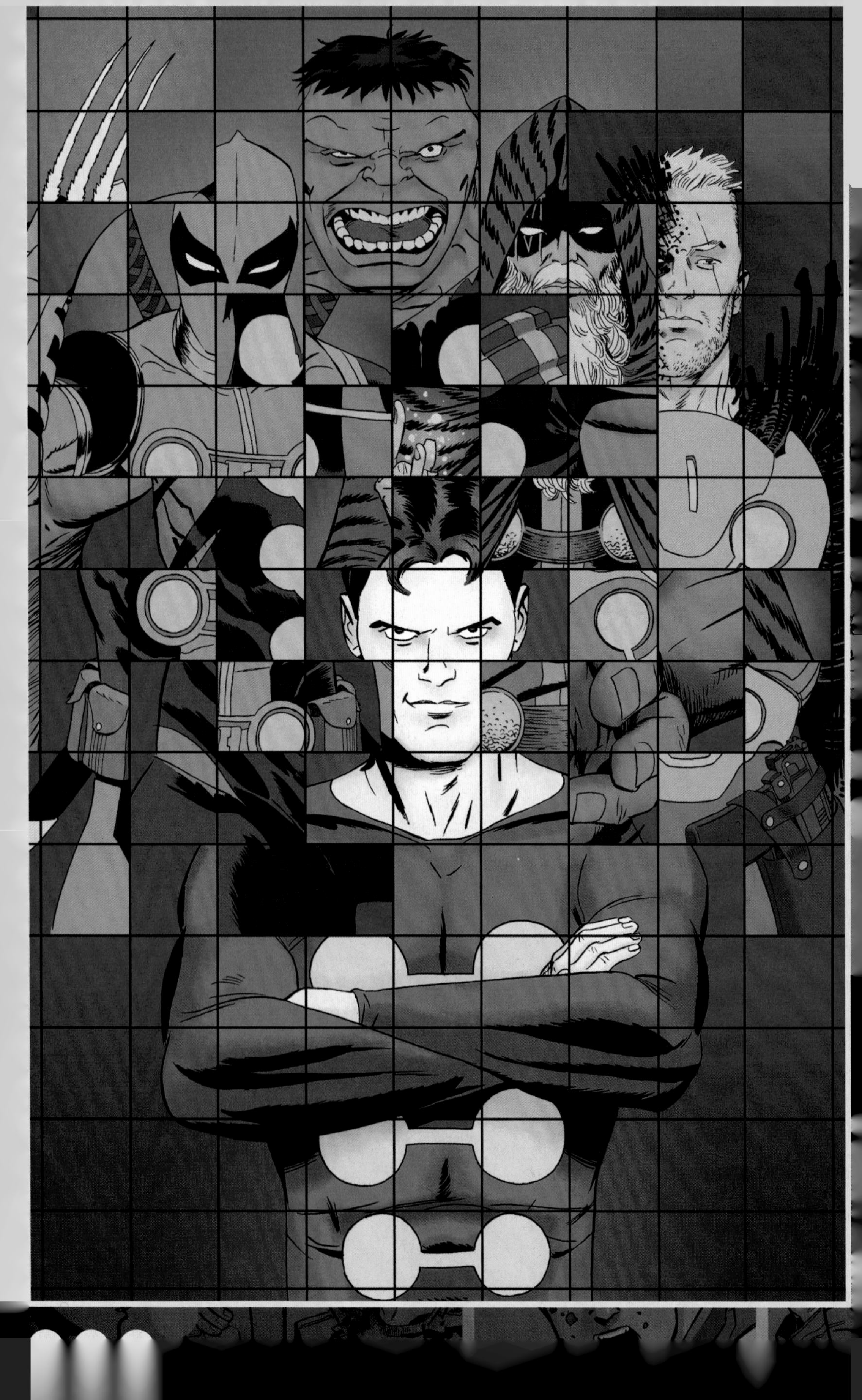

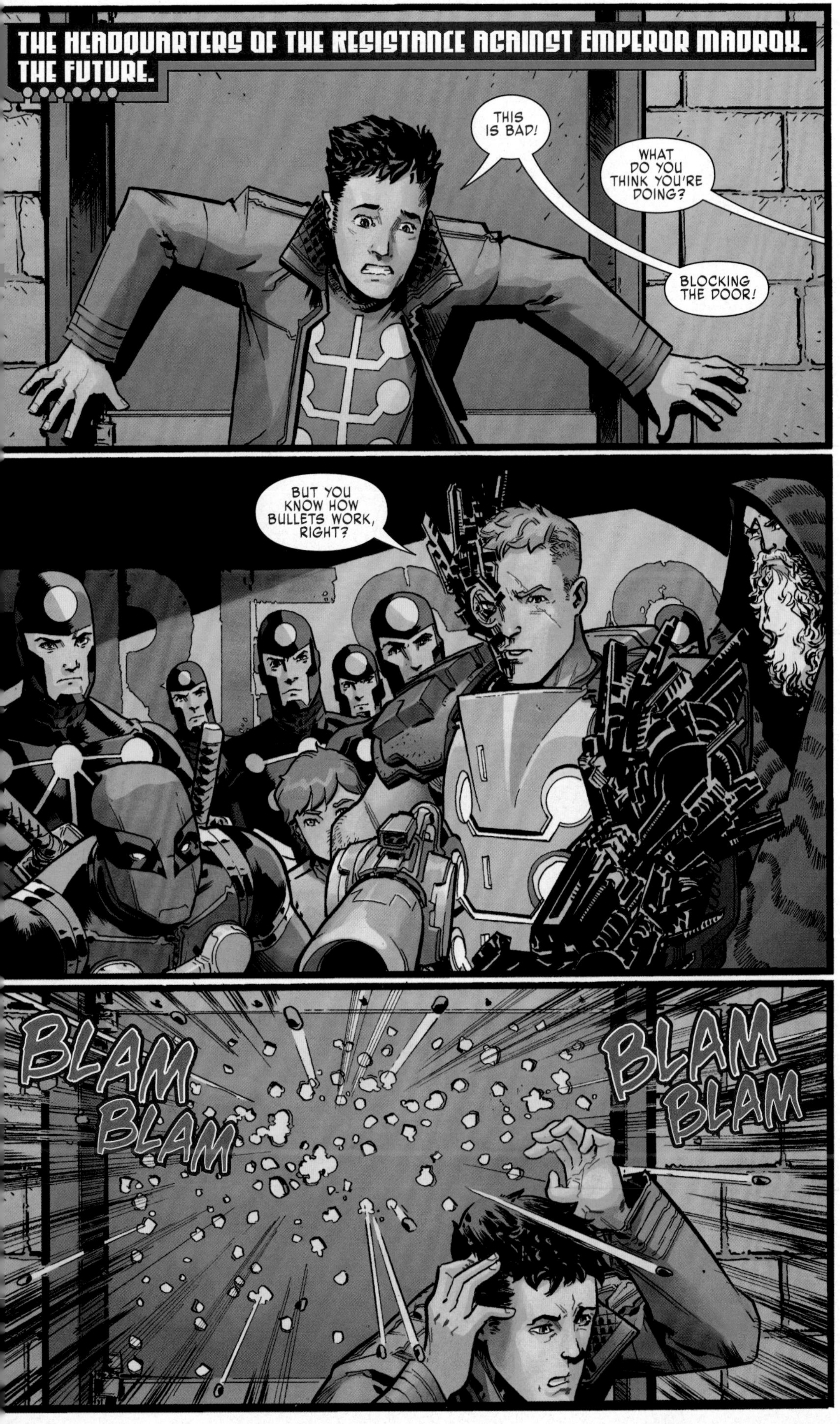
THE HEADQUARTERS OF THE RESISTANCE AGAINST EMPEROR MADROX. THE FUTURE.
THIS IS BAD!
WHAT DO YOU THINK YOU'RE DOING?
BLOCKING THE DOOR!
BUT YOU KNOW HOW BULLETS WORK, RIGHT?
BLAM BLAM
BLAM BLAM

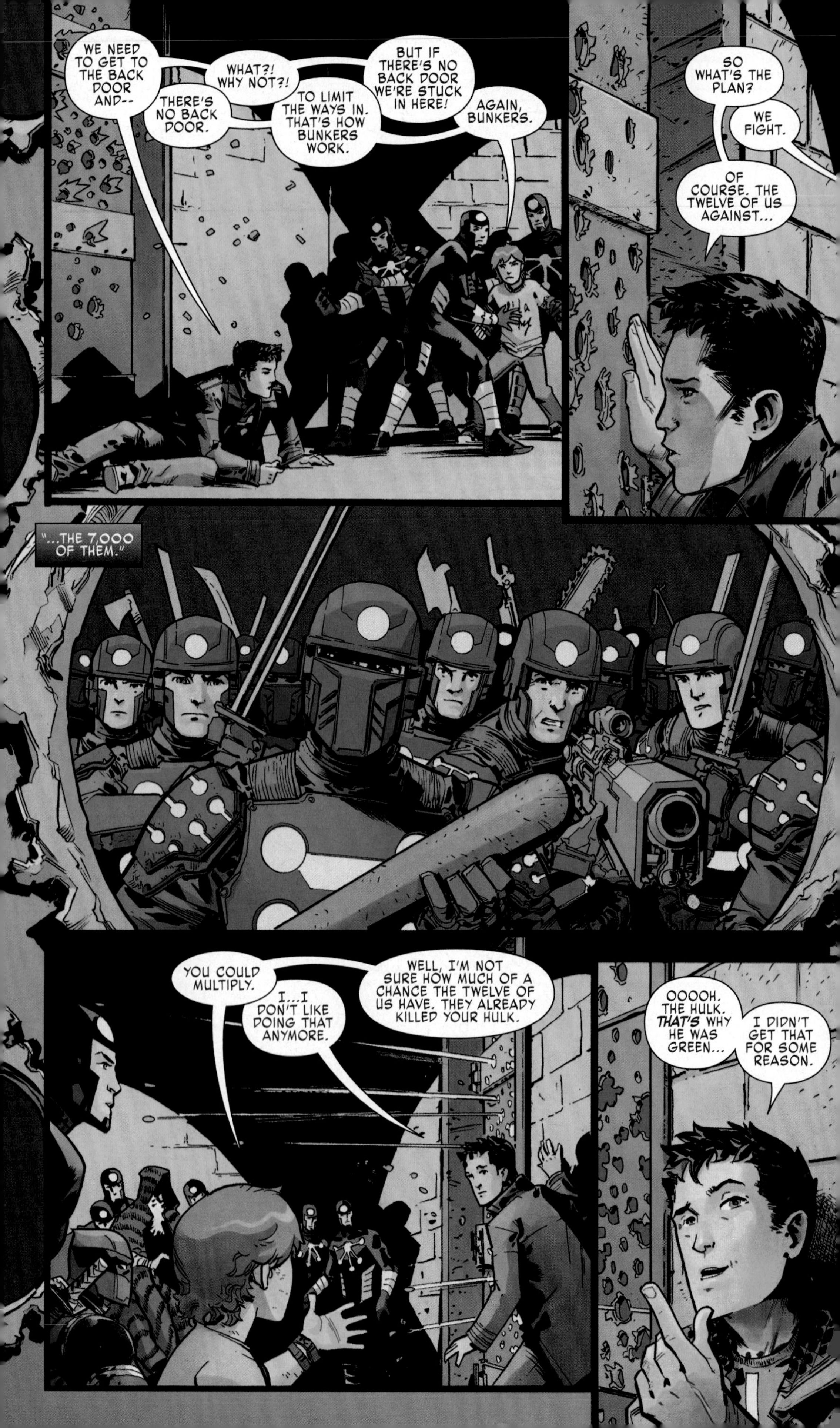
WE NEED TO GET TO THE BACK DOOR AND--
THERE'S NO BACK DOOR.
WHAT?! WHY NOT?!
TO LIMIT THE WAYS IN. THAT'S HOW BUNKERS WORK.
BUT IF THERE'S NO BACK DOOR WE'RE STUCK IN HERE!
AGAIN, BUNKERS.
SO WHAT'S THE PLAN?
WE FIGHT.
OF COURSE. THE TWELVE OF US AGAINST...
"...THE 7,000 OF THEM."
YOU COULD MULTIPLY.
I...I DON'T LIKE DOING THAT ANYMORE.
WELL, I'M NOT SURE HOW MUCH OF A CHANCE THE TWELVE OF US HAVE. THEY ALREADY KILLED YOUR HULK.
OOOOH. THE HULK. THAT'S WHY HE WAS GREEN...
I DIDN'T GET THAT FOR SOME REASON.

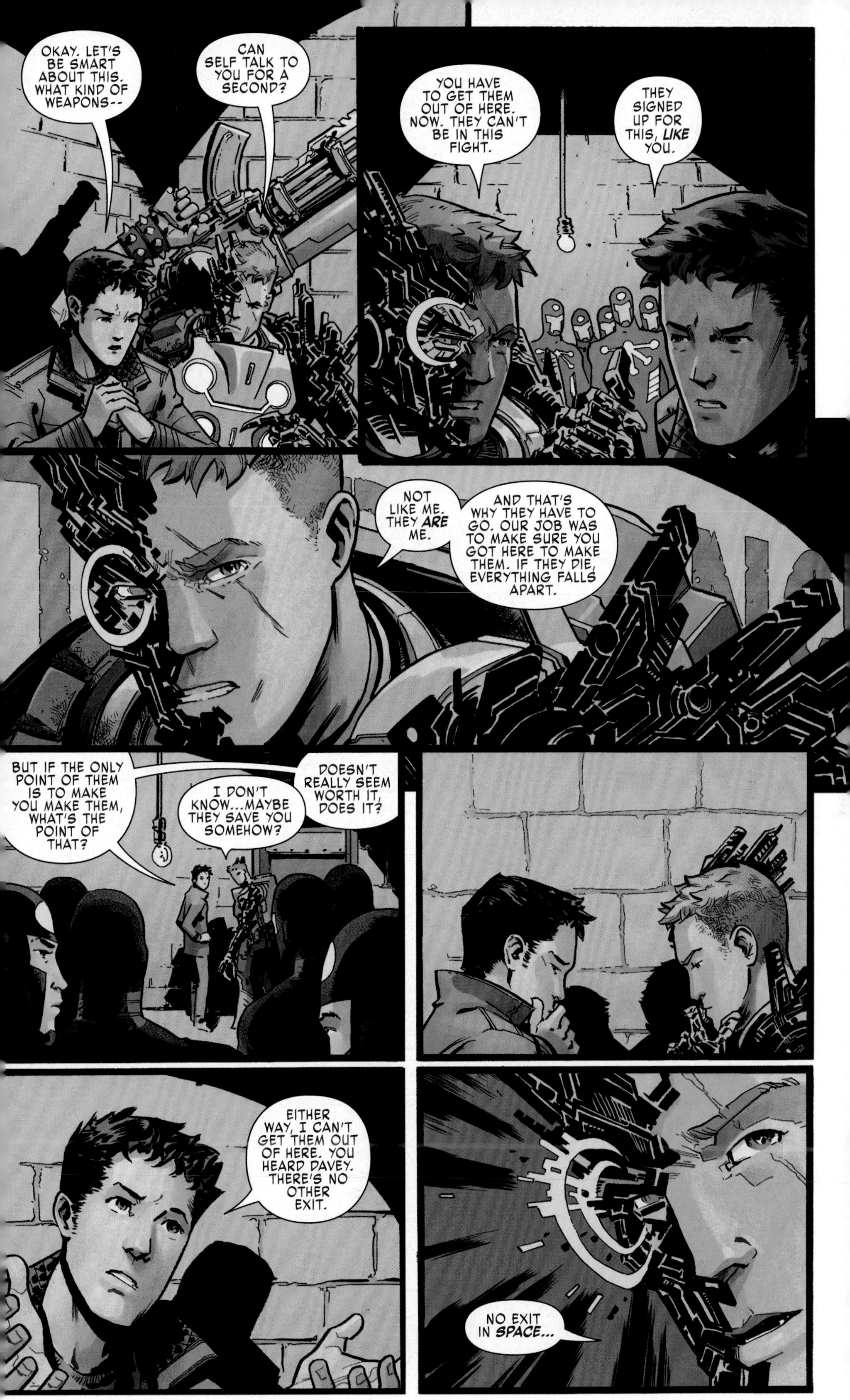
OKAY. LET'S BE SMART ABOUT THIS. WHAT KIND OF WEAPONS--
CAN SELF TALK TO YOU FOR A SECOND?
YOU HAVE TO GET THEM OUT OF HERE. NOW. THEY CAN'T BE IN THIS FIGHT.
THEY SIGNED UP FOR THIS, *LIKE* YOU.
NOT LIKE ME. THEY *ARE* ME.
AND THAT'S WHY THEY HAVE TO GO. OUR JOB WAS TO MAKE SURE YOU GOT HERE TO MAKE THEM. IF THEY DIE, EVERYTHING FALLS APART.
BUT IF THE ONLY POINT OF THEM IS TO MAKE YOU MAKE THEM, WHAT'S THE POINT OF THAT?
I DON'T KNOW...MAYBE THEY SAVE YOU SOMEHOW?
DOESN'T REALLY SEEM WORTH IT, DOES IT?
EITHER WAY, I CAN'T GET THEM OUT OF HERE. YOU HEARD DAVEY. THERE'S NO OTHER EXIT.
NO EXIT IN *SPACE...*

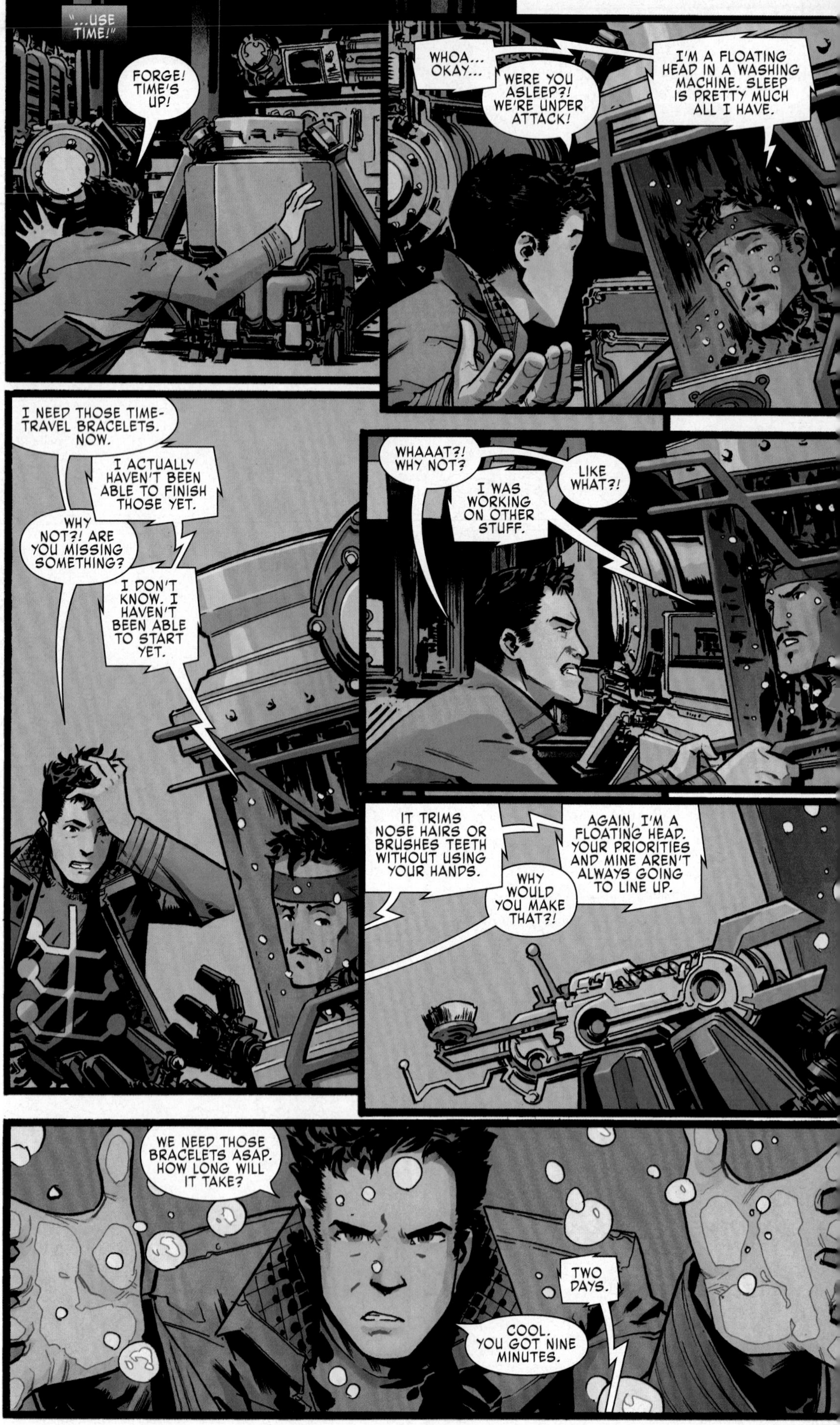
"...USE TIME!"
FORGE! TIME'S UP!
WHOA... OKAY...
I'M A FLOATING HEAD IN A WASHING MACHINE. SLEEP IS PRETTY MUCH ALL I HAVE.
WERE YOU ASLEEP?! WE'RE UNDER ATTACK!
I NEED THOSE TIME-TRAVEL BRACELETS. NOW.
I ACTUALLY HAVEN'T BEEN ABLE TO FINISH THOSE YET.
WHY NOT?! ARE YOU MISSING SOMETHING?
I DON'T KNOW. I HAVEN'T BEEN ABLE TO START YET.
WHAAAT?! WHY NOT?
I WAS WORKING ON OTHER STUFF.
LIKE WHAT?!
IT TRIMS NOSE HAIRS OR BRUSHES TEETH WITHOUT USING YOUR HANDS.
WHY WOULD YOU MAKE THAT?!
AGAIN, I'M A FLOATING HEAD. YOUR PRIORITIES AND MINE AREN'T ALWAYS GOING TO LINE UP.
WE NEED THOSE BRACELETS ASAP. HOW LONG WILL IT TAKE?
TWO DAYS.
COOL. YOU GOT NINE MINUTES.

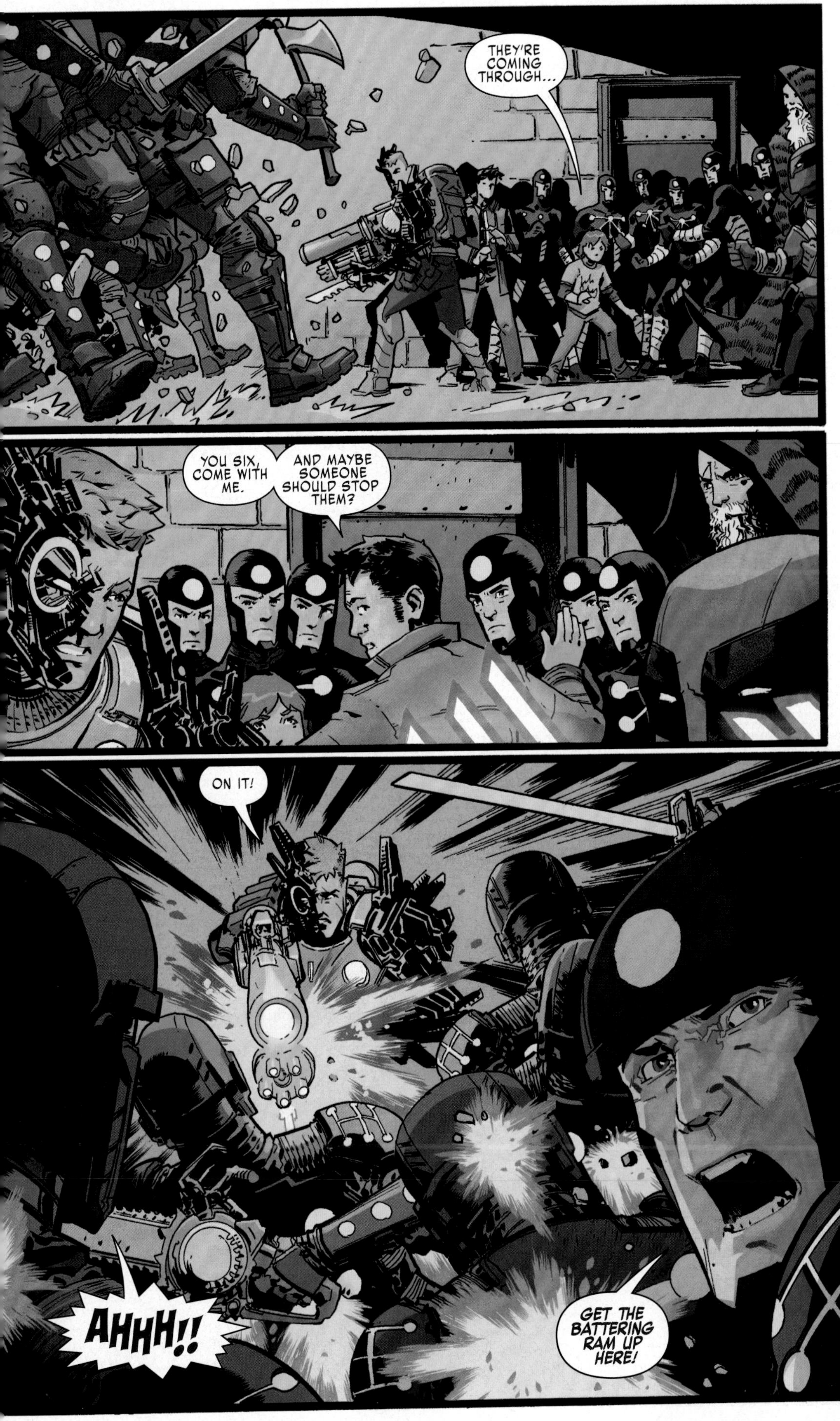
THEY'RE COMING THROUGH...
YOU SIX, COME WITH ME.
AND MAYBE SOMEONE SHOULD STOP THEM?
ON IT!
AHHH!!
GET THE BATTERING RAM UP HERE!

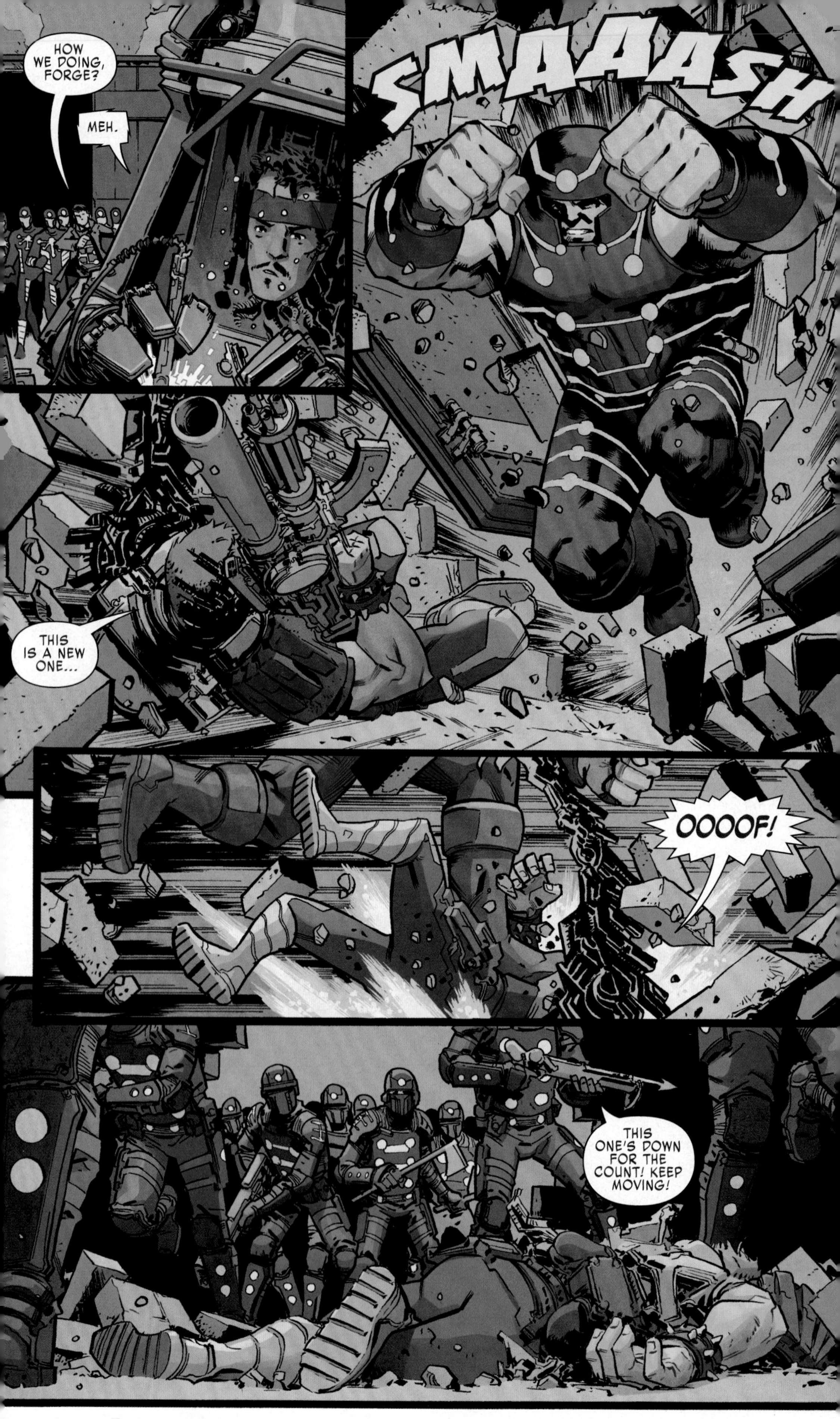
HOW WE DOING, FORGE?
MEH.
SMAAASH
THIS IS A NEW ONE...
OOOOF!
THIS ONE'S DOWN FOR THE COUNT! KEEP MOVING!

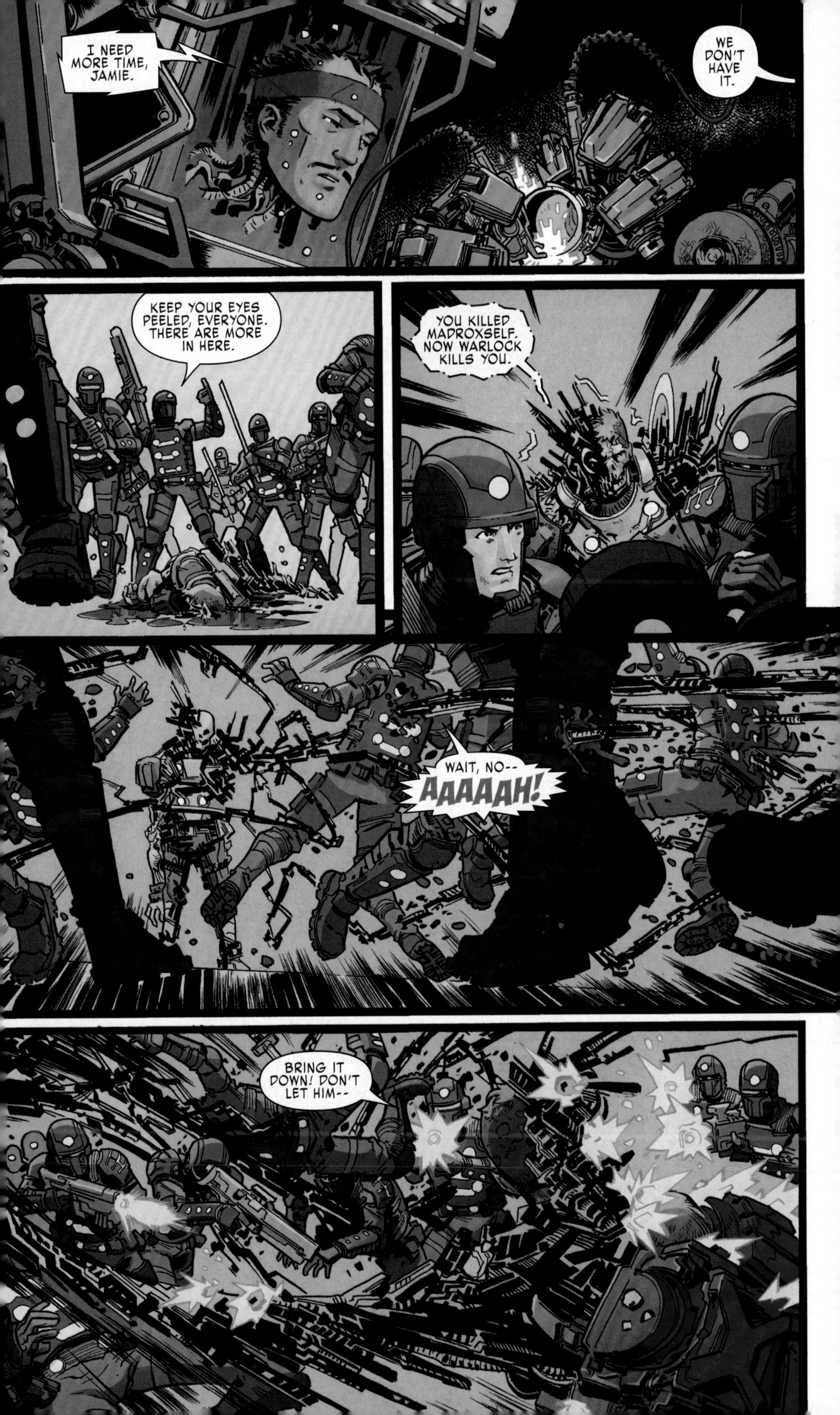
I NEED MORE TIME, JAMIE.
WE DON'T HAVE IT.
KEEP YOUR EYES PEELED, EVERYONE. THERE ARE MORE IN HERE.
YOU KILLED MADROXSELF. NOW WARLOCK KILLS YOU.
WAIT, NO--
AAAAAH!
BRING IT DOWN! DON'T LET HIM--

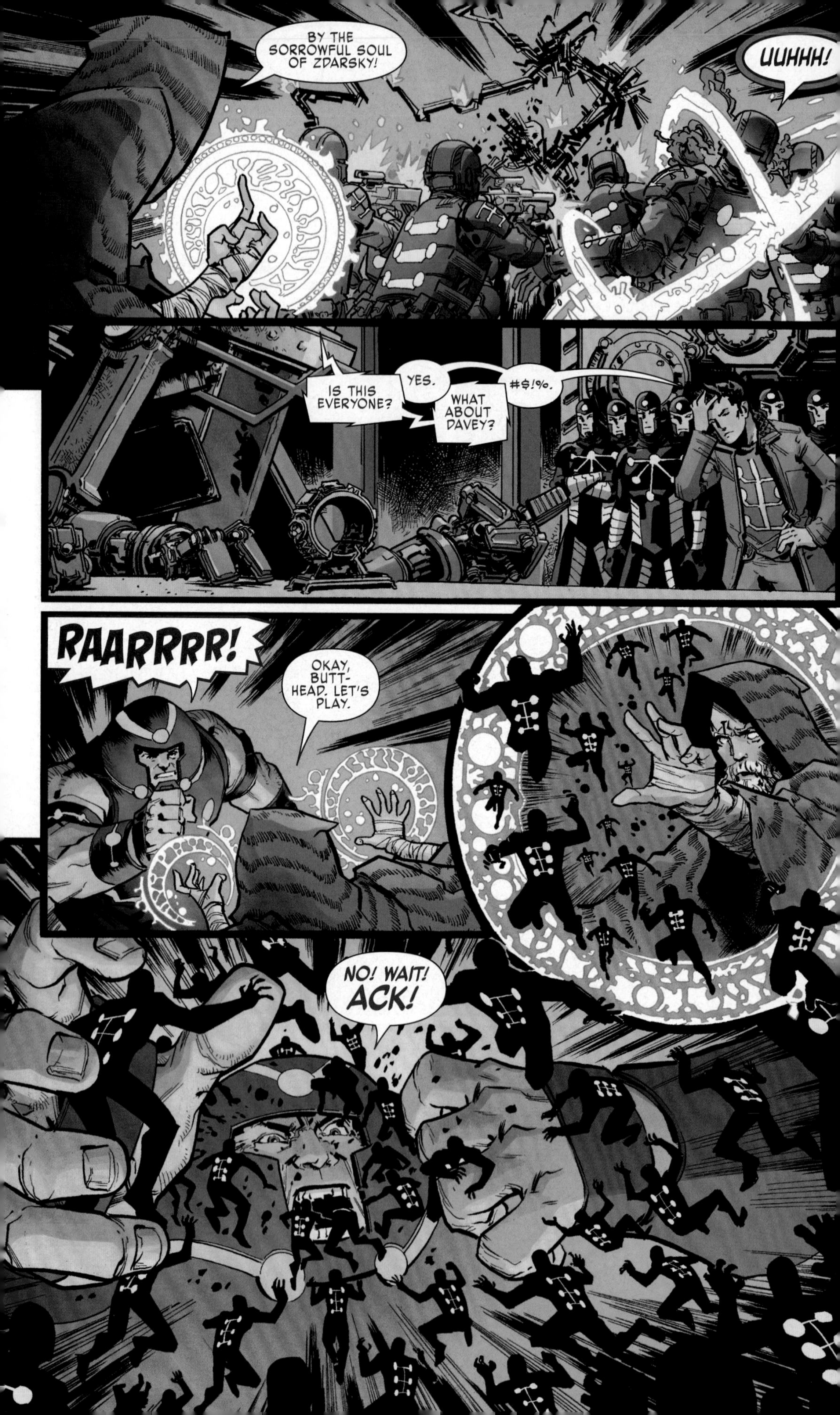

BY THE SORROWFUL SOUL OF ZDARSKY!
UUHHH!
IS THIS EVERYONE?
YES.
WHAT ABOUT DAVEY?
#$!%.
RAARRRR!
OKAY, BUTT-HEAD. LET'S PLAY.
NO! WAIT! ACK!

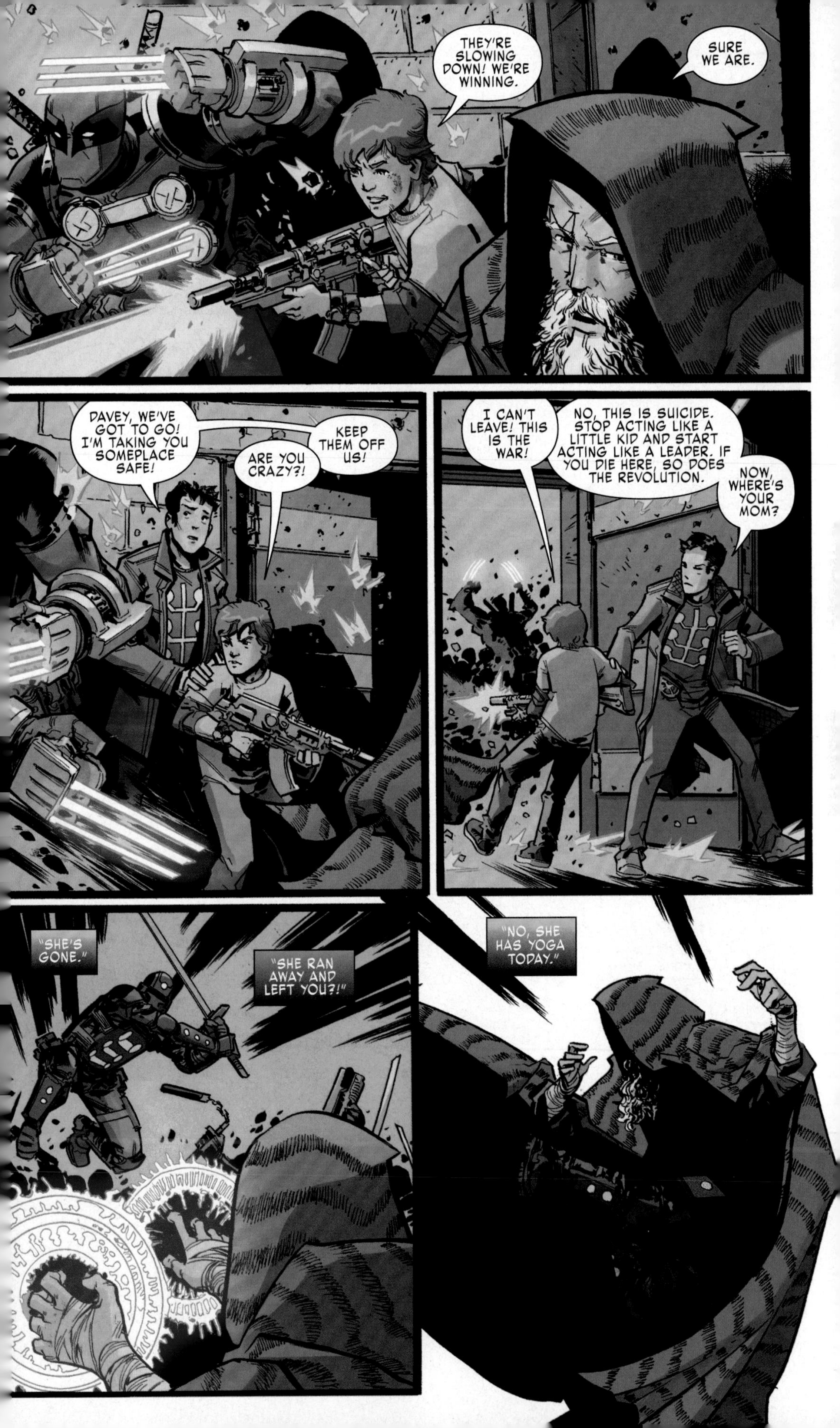
THEY'RE SLOWING DOWN! WE'RE WINNING.
SURE WE ARE.
DAVEY, WE'VE GOT TO GO! I'M TAKING YOU SOMEPLACE SAFE!
ARE YOU CRAZY?!
KEEP THEM OFF US!
I CAN'T LEAVE! THIS IS THE WAR!
NO, THIS IS SUICIDE. STOP ACTING LIKE A LITTLE KID AND START ACTING LIKE A LEADER. IF YOU DIE HERE, SO DOES THE REVOLUTION.
NOW, WHERE'S YOUR MOM?
"SHE'S GONE."
"SHE RAN AWAY AND LEFT YOU?!"
"NO, SHE HAS YOGA TODAY."

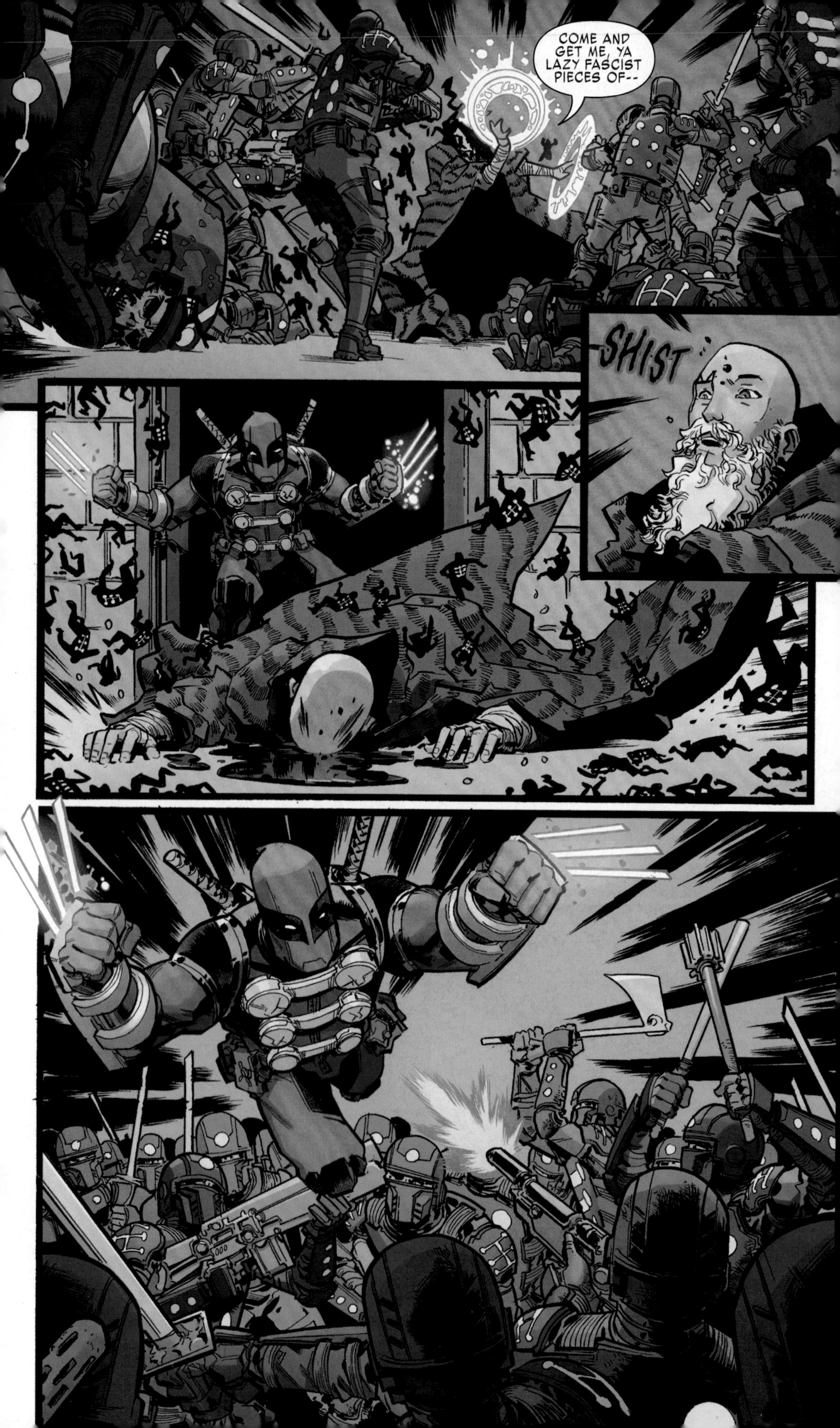
COME AND GET ME, YA LAZY FASCIST PIECES OF--
SHIST

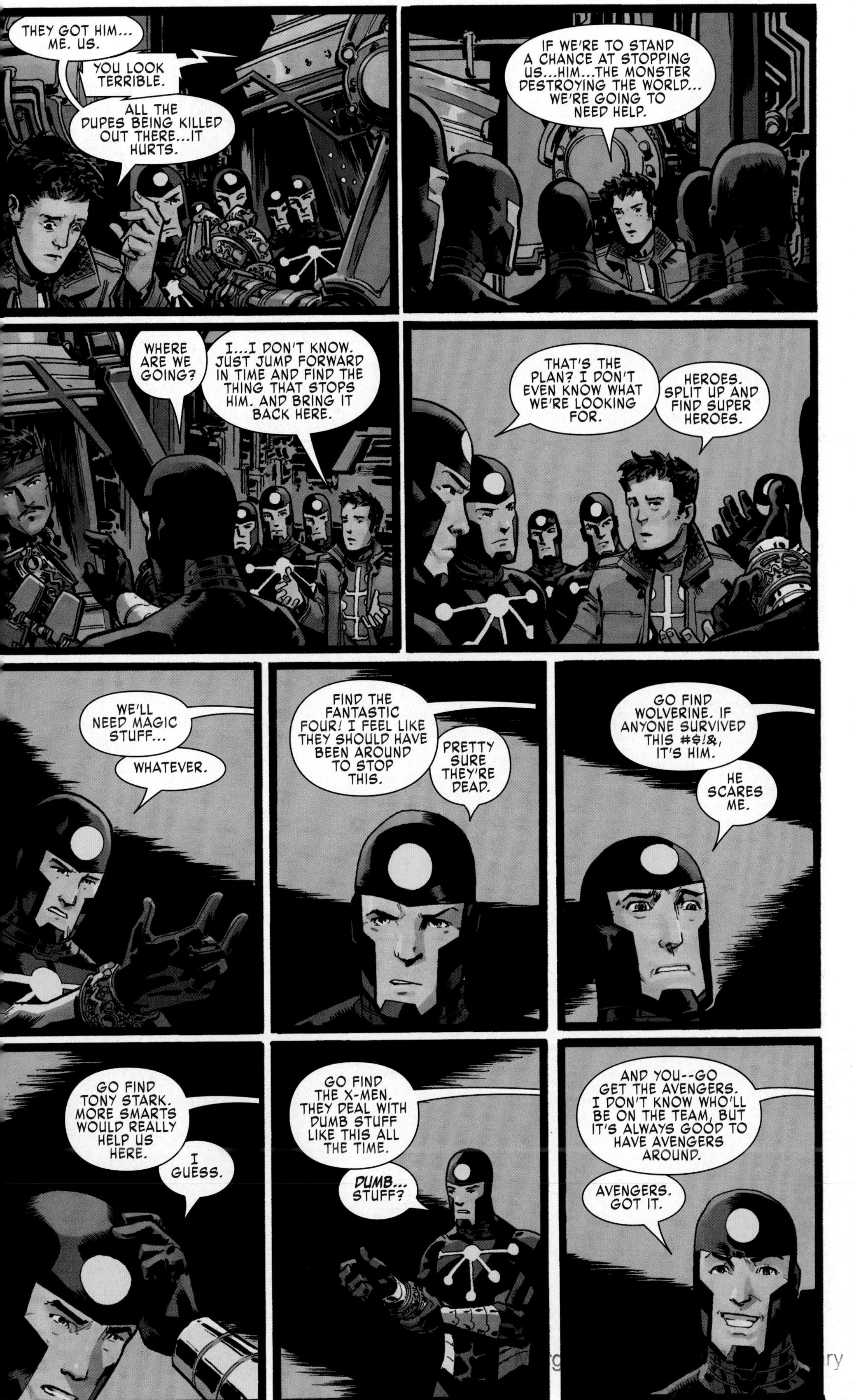
THEY GOT HIM... ME. US.
YOU LOOK TERRIBLE.
ALL THE DUPES BEING KILLED OUT THERE...IT HURTS.
IF WE'RE TO STAND A CHANCE AT STOPPING US...HIM...THE MONSTER DESTROYING THE WORLD... WE'RE GOING TO NEED HELP.
WHERE ARE WE GOING?
I...I DON'T KNOW. JUST JUMP FORWARD IN TIME AND FIND THE THING THAT STOPS HIM. AND BRING IT BACK HERE.
THAT'S THE PLAN? I DON'T EVEN KNOW WHAT WE'RE LOOKING FOR.
HEROES. SPLIT UP AND FIND SUPER HEROES.
WE'LL NEED MAGIC STUFF...
WHATEVER.
FIND THE FANTASTIC FOUR! I FEEL LIKE THEY SHOULD HAVE BEEN AROUND TO STOP THIS.
PRETTY SURE THEY'RE DEAD.
GO FIND WOLVERINE. IF ANYONE SURVIVED THIS #$!&, IT'S HIM.
HE SCARES ME.
GO FIND TONY STARK. MORE SMARTS WOULD REALLY HELP US HERE.
I GUESS.
GO FIND THE X-MEN. THEY DEAL WITH DUMB STUFF LIKE THIS ALL THE TIME.
DUMB... STUFF?
AND YOU--GO GET THE AVENGERS. I DON'T KNOW WHO'LL BE ON THE TEAM, BUT IT'S ALWAYS GOOD TO HAVE AVENGERS AROUND.
AVENGERS. GOT IT.

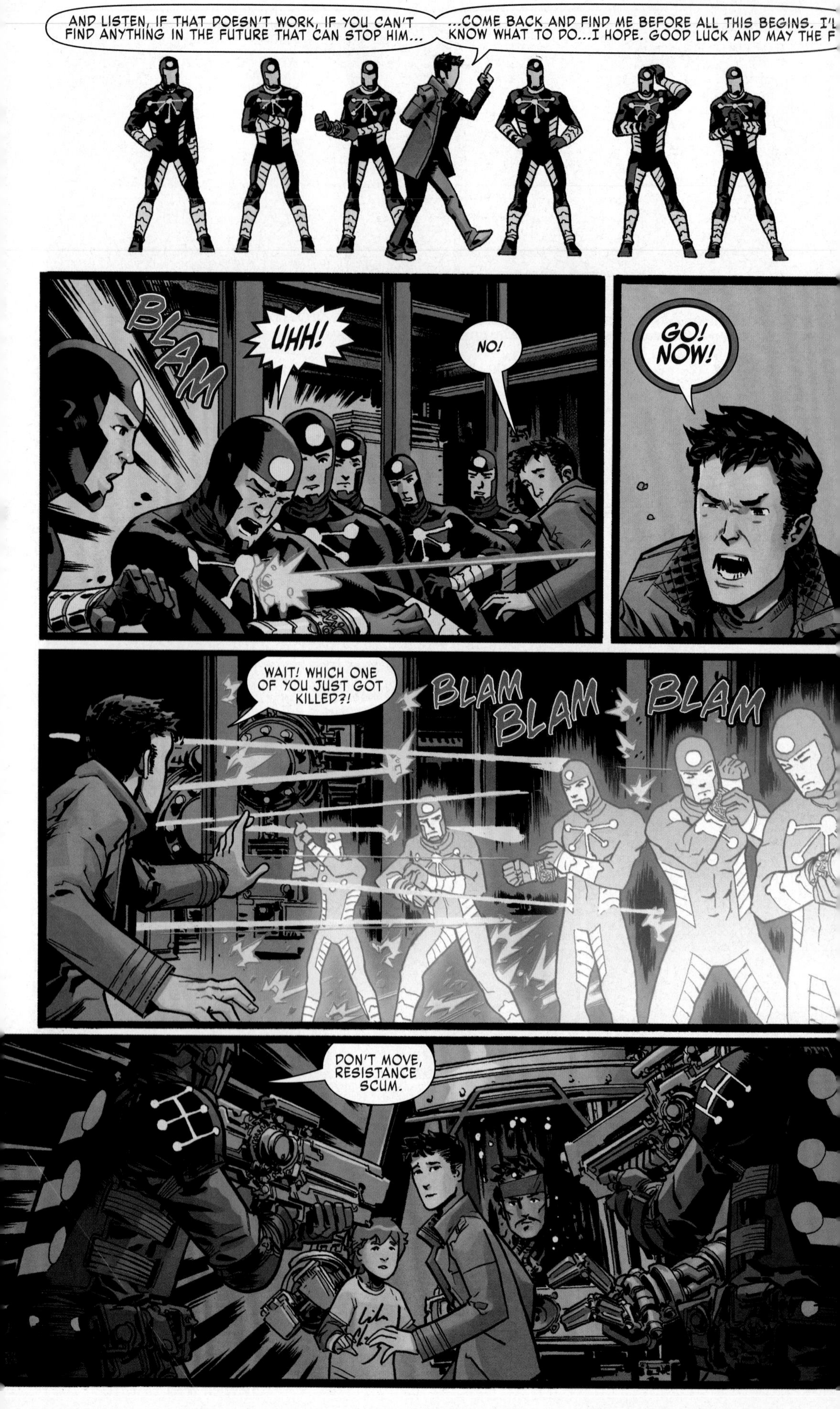

AND LISTEN, IF THAT DOESN'T WORK, IF YOU CAN'T FIND ANYTHING IN THE FUTURE THAT CAN STOP HIM...
...COME BACK AND FIND ME BEFORE ALL THIS BEGINS. I'L KNOW WHAT TO DO...I HOPE. GOOD LUCK AND MAY THE F
BLAM
UHH!
NO!
GO! NOW!
WAIT! WHICH ONE OF YOU JUST GOT KILLED?!
BLAM
BLAM
BLAM
DON'T MOVE, RESISTANCE SCUM.

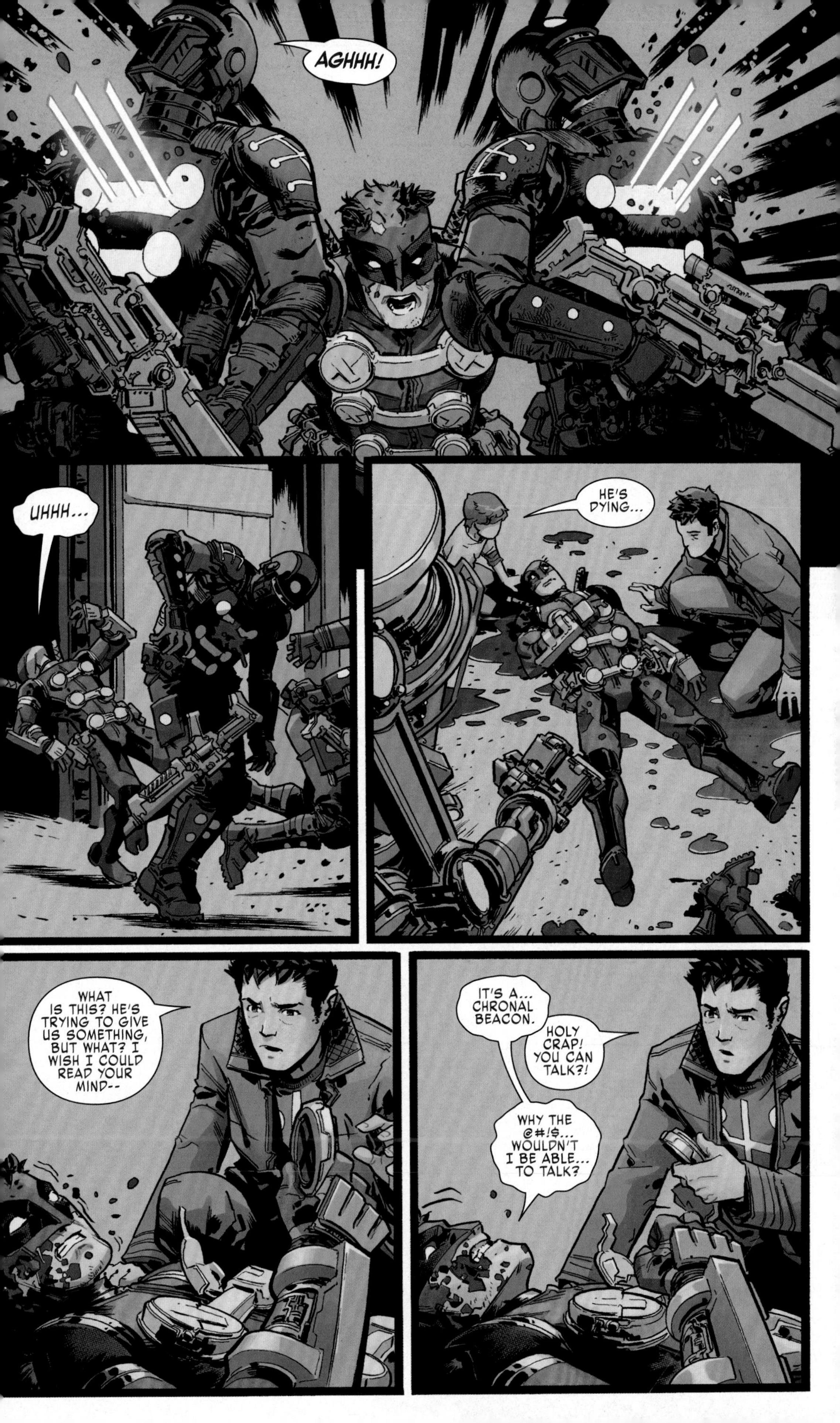
AGHHH!
UHHH...
HE'S DYING...
WHAT IS THIS? HE'S TRYING TO GIVE US SOMETHING, BUT WHAT? I WISH I COULD READ YOUR MIND--
IT'S A... CHRONAL BEACON.
HOLY CRAP! YOU CAN TALK?!
WHY THE @#!$... WOULDN'T I BE ABLE... TO TALK?

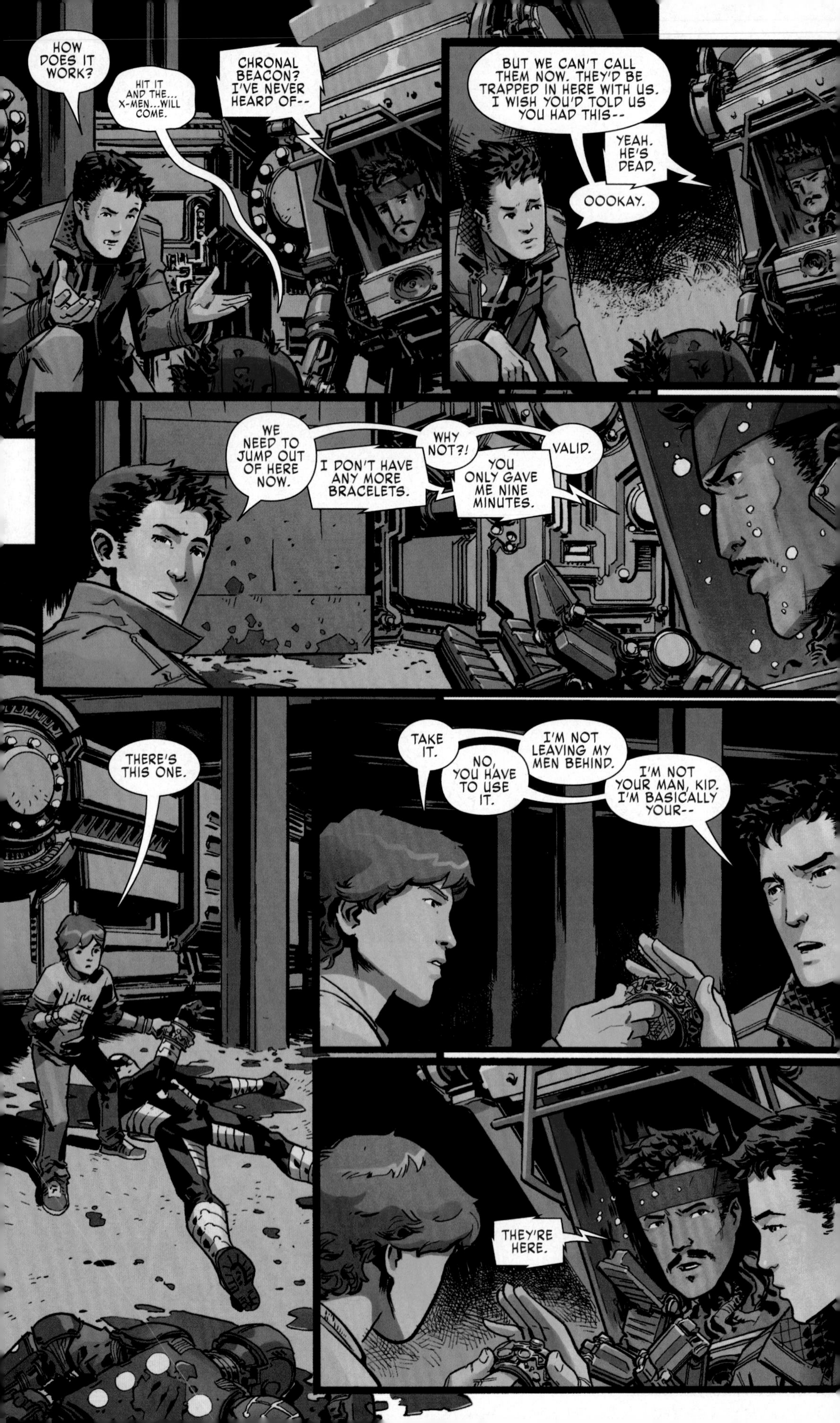
HOW DOES IT WORK?
HIT IT AND THE... X-MEN...WILL COME.
CHRONAL BEACON? I'VE NEVER HEARD OF--
BUT WE CAN'T CALL THEM NOW. THEY'D BE TRAPPED IN HERE WITH US. I WISH YOU'D TOLD US YOU HAD THIS--
YEAH. HE'S DEAD.
OOOKAY.
WE NEED TO JUMP OUT OF HERE NOW.
I DON'T HAVE ANY MORE BRACELETS.
WHY NOT?!
YOU ONLY GAVE ME NINE MINUTES.
VALID.
THERE'S THIS ONE.
TAKE IT.
NO, YOU HAVE TO USE IT.
I'M NOT LEAVING MY MEN BEHIND.
I'M NOT YOUR MAN, KID. I'M BASICALLY YOUR--
THEY'RE HERE.

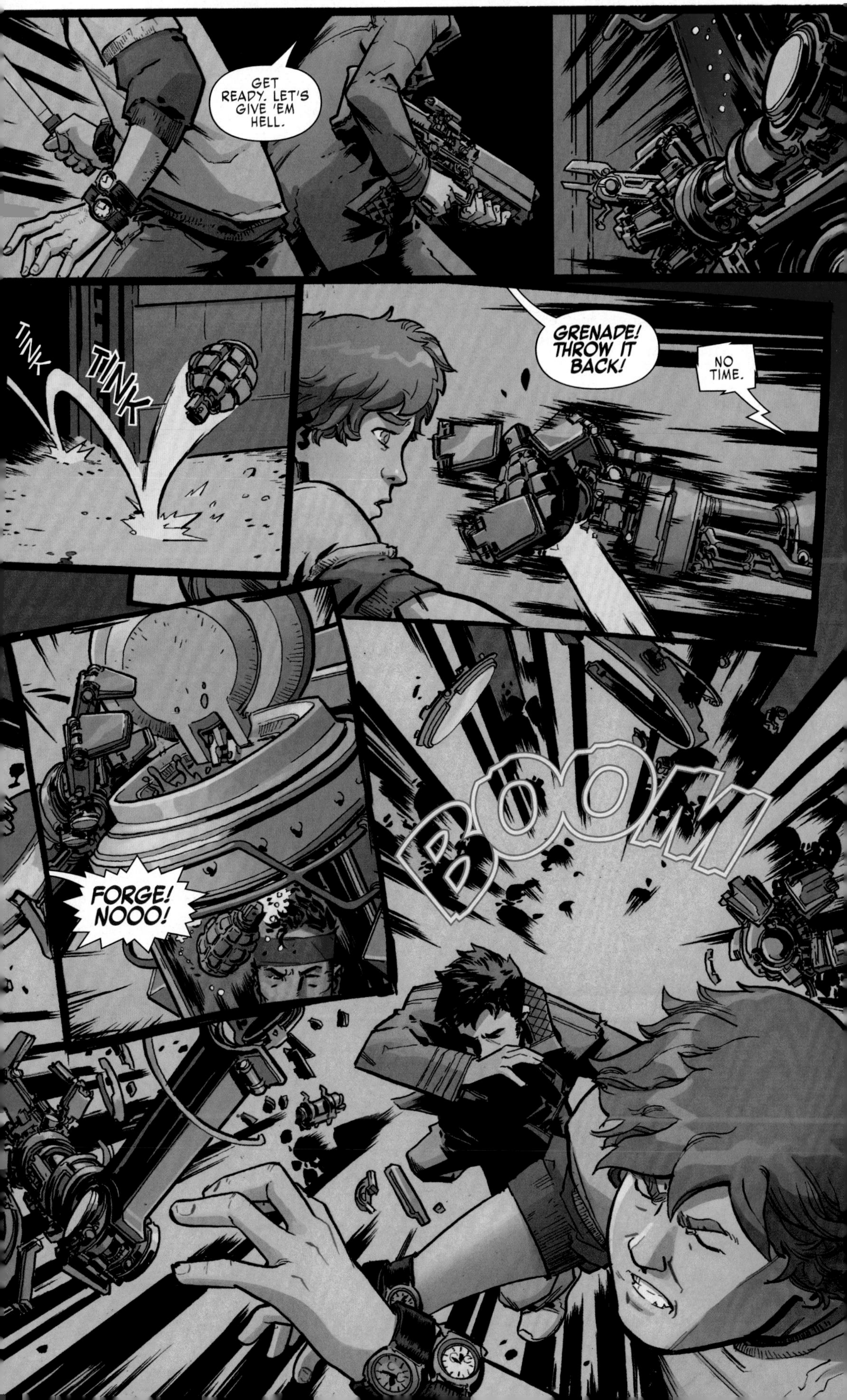
GET READY. LET'S GIVE 'EM HELL.
TINK
TINK
GRENADE! THROW IT BACK!
NO TIME.
FORGE! NOOO!
BOOM

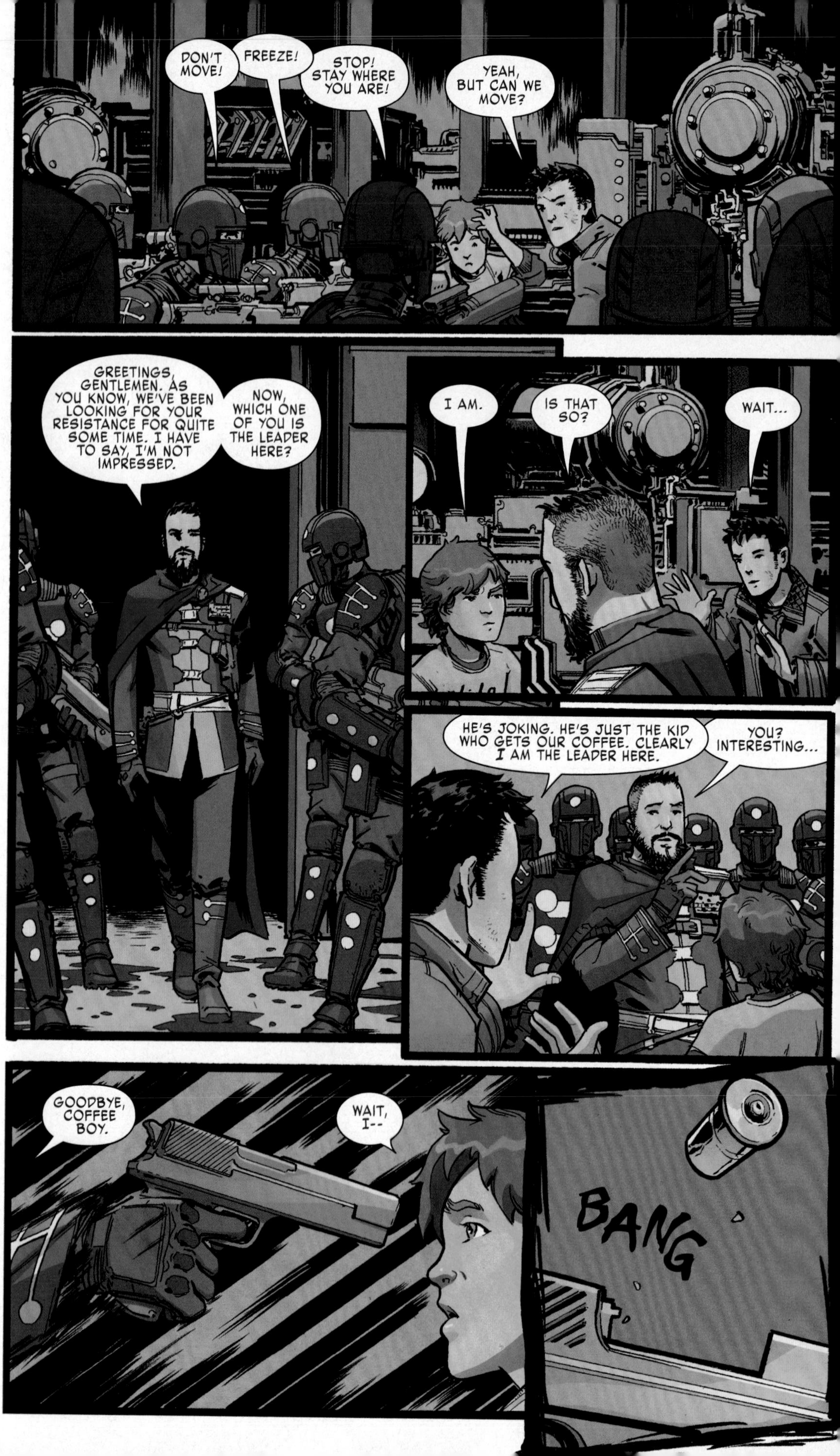
DON'T MOVE!
FREEZE!
STOP! STAY WHERE YOU ARE!
YEAH, BUT CAN WE MOVE?
GREETINGS, GENTLEMEN. AS YOU KNOW, WE'VE BEEN LOOKING FOR YOUR RESISTANCE FOR QUITE SOME TIME. I HAVE TO SAY, I'M NOT IMPRESSED.
NOW, WHICH ONE OF YOU IS THE LEADER HERE?
I AM.
IS THAT SO?
WAIT...
HE'S JOKING. HE'S JUST THE KID WHO GETS OUR COFFEE. CLEARLY I AM THE LEADER HERE.
YOU? INTERESTING...
GOODBYE, COFFEE BOY.
WAIT, I--
BANG

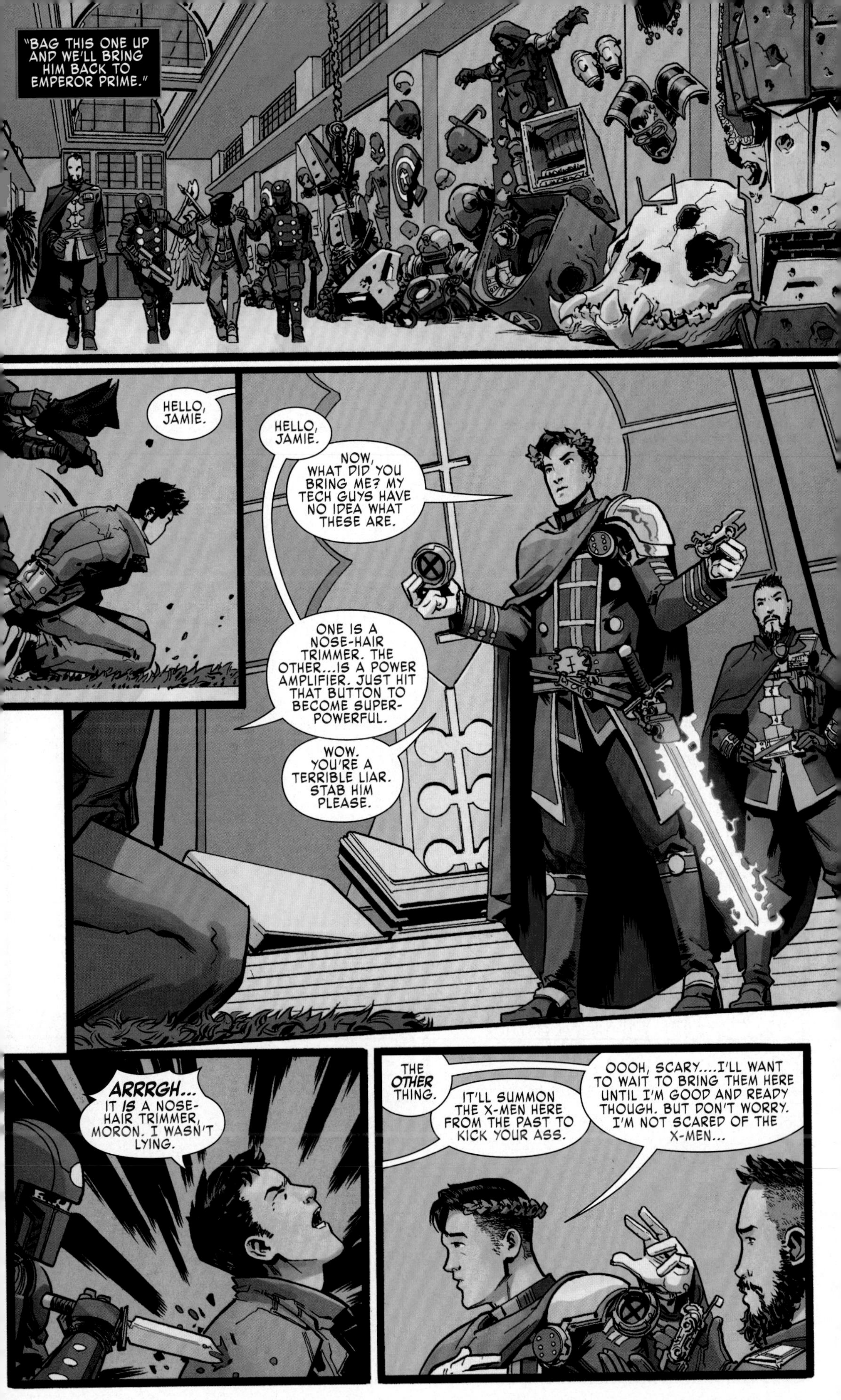
"BAG THIS ONE UP AND WE'LL BRING HIM BACK TO EMPEROR PRIME."
HELLO, JAMIE.
HELLO, JAMIE.
NOW, WHAT DID YOU BRING ME? MY TECH GUYS HAVE NO IDEA WHAT THESE ARE.
ONE IS A NOSE-HAIR TRIMMER. THE OTHER...IS A POWER AMPLIFIER. JUST HIT THAT BUTTON TO BECOME SUPER-POWERFUL.
WOW. YOU'RE A TERRIBLE LIAR. STAB HIM PLEASE.
ARRRGH... IT IS A NOSE-HAIR TRIMMER, MORON. I WASN'T LYING.
THE OTHER THING.
IT'LL SUMMON THE X-MEN HERE FROM THE PAST TO KICK YOUR ASS.
OOOH, SCARY....I'LL WANT TO WAIT TO BRING THEM HERE UNTIL I'M GOOD AND READY THOUGH. BUT DON'T WORRY. I'M NOT SCARED OF THE X-MEN...

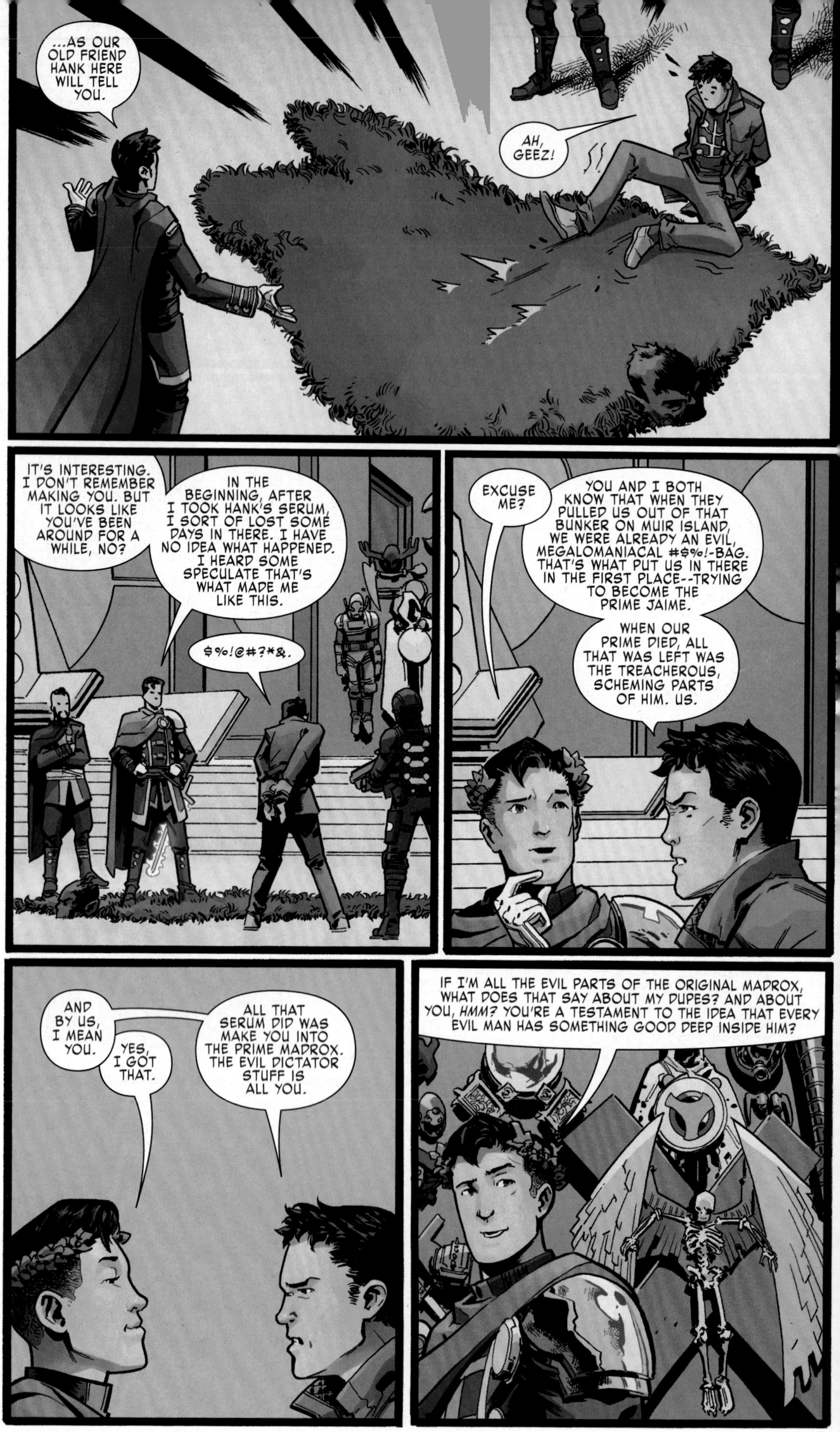
...AS OUR OLD FRIEND HANK HERE WILL TELL YOU.
AH, GEEZ!
IT'S INTERESTING. I DON'T REMEMBER MAKING YOU. BUT IT LOOKS LIKE YOU'VE BEEN AROUND FOR A WHILE, NO?
IN THE BEGINNING, AFTER I TOOK HANK'S SERUM, I SORT OF LOST SOME DAYS IN THERE. I HAVE NO IDEA WHAT HAPPENED. I HEARD SOME SPECULATE THAT'S WHAT MADE ME LIKE THIS.
$%!@#?*&.
EXCUSE ME?
YOU AND I BOTH KNOW THAT WHEN THEY PULLED US OUT OF THAT BUNKER ON MUIR ISLAND, WE WERE ALREADY AN EVIL, MEGALOMANIACAL #$%!-BAG. THAT'S WHAT PUT US IN THERE IN THE FIRST PLACE--TRYING TO BECOME THE PRIME JAIME.
WHEN OUR PRIME DIED, ALL THAT WAS LEFT WAS THE TREACHEROUS, SCHEMING PARTS OF HIM. US.
AND BY US, I MEAN YOU.
YES, I GOT THAT.
ALL THAT SERUM DID WAS MAKE YOU INTO THE PRIME MADROX. THE EVIL DICTATOR STUFF IS ALL YOU.
IF I'M ALL THE EVIL PARTS OF THE ORIGINAL MADROX, WHAT DOES THAT SAY ABOUT MY DUPES? AND ABOUT YOU, *HMM*? YOU'RE A TESTAMENT TO THE IDEA THAT EVERY EVIL MAN HAS SOMETHING GOOD DEEP INSIDE HIM?

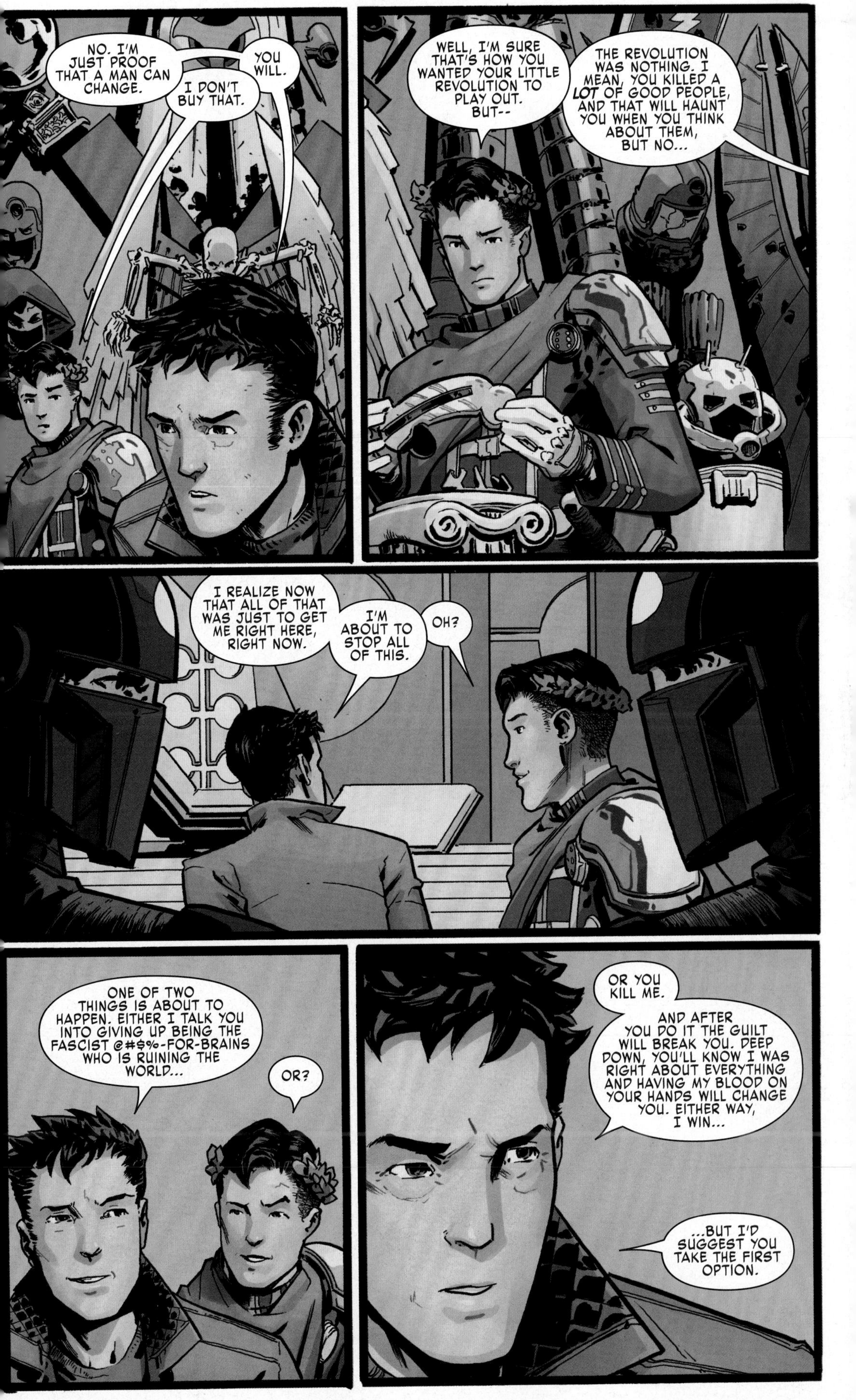
NO. I'M JUST PROOF THAT A MAN CAN CHANGE.
I DON'T BUY THAT.
YOU WILL.
WELL, I'M SURE THAT'S HOW YOU WANTED YOUR LITTLE REVOLUTION TO PLAY OUT. BUT--
THE REVOLUTION WAS NOTHING. I MEAN, YOU KILLED A *LOT* OF GOOD PEOPLE, AND THAT WILL HAUNT YOU WHEN YOU THINK ABOUT THEM, BUT NO...
I REALIZE NOW THAT ALL OF THAT WAS JUST TO GET ME RIGHT HERE, RIGHT NOW.
I'M ABOUT TO STOP ALL OF THIS.
OH?
ONE OF TWO THINGS IS ABOUT TO HAPPEN. EITHER I TALK YOU INTO GIVING UP BEING THE FASCIST @#$%-FOR-BRAINS WHO IS RUINING THE WORLD...
OR?
OR YOU KILL ME.
AND AFTER YOU DO IT THE GUILT WILL BREAK YOU. DEEP DOWN, YOU'LL KNOW I WAS RIGHT ABOUT EVERYTHING AND HAVING MY BLOOD ON YOUR HANDS WILL CHANGE YOU. EITHER WAY, I WIN...
...BUT I'D SUGGEST YOU TAKE THE FIRST OPTION.

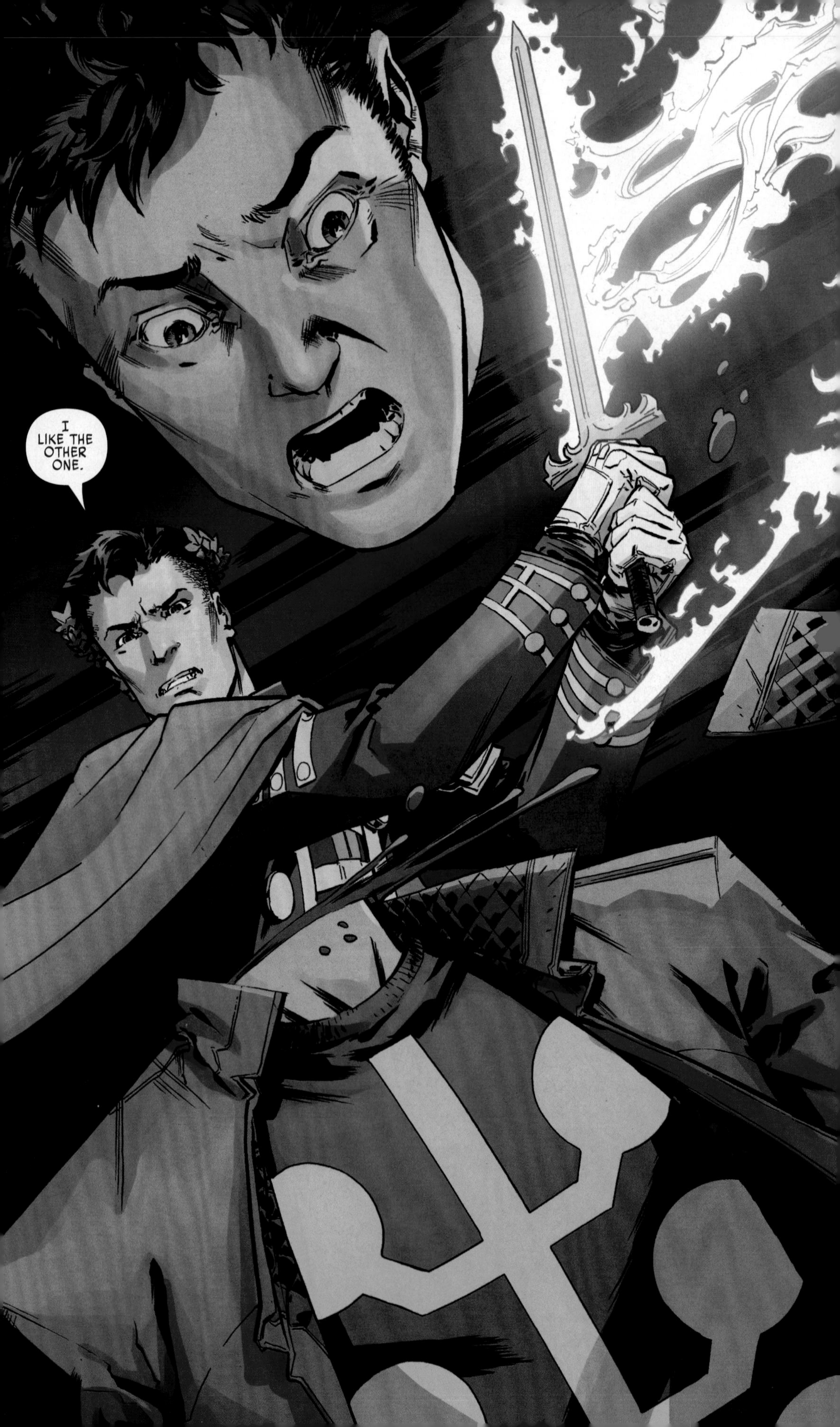
I LIKE THE OTHER ONE.

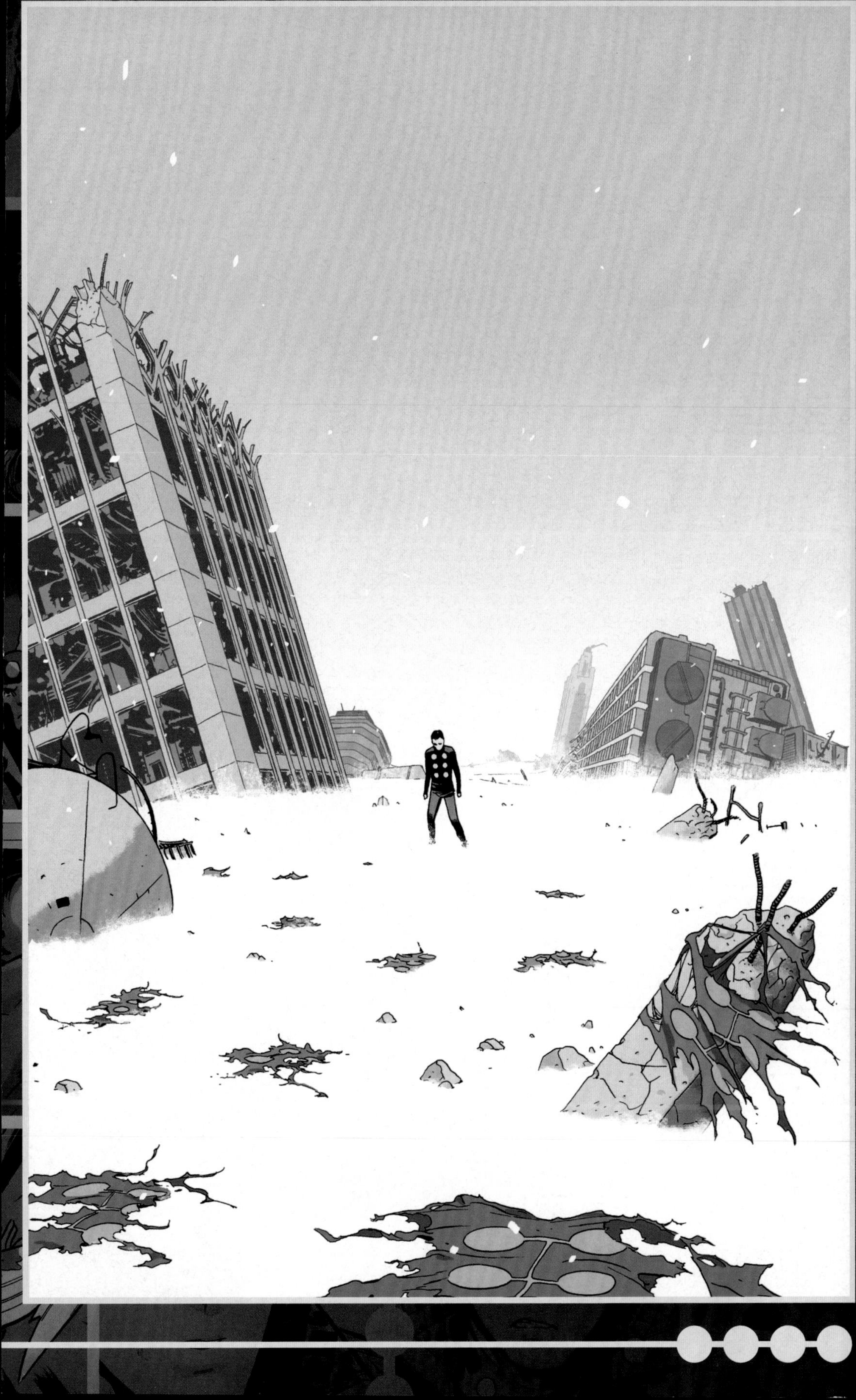

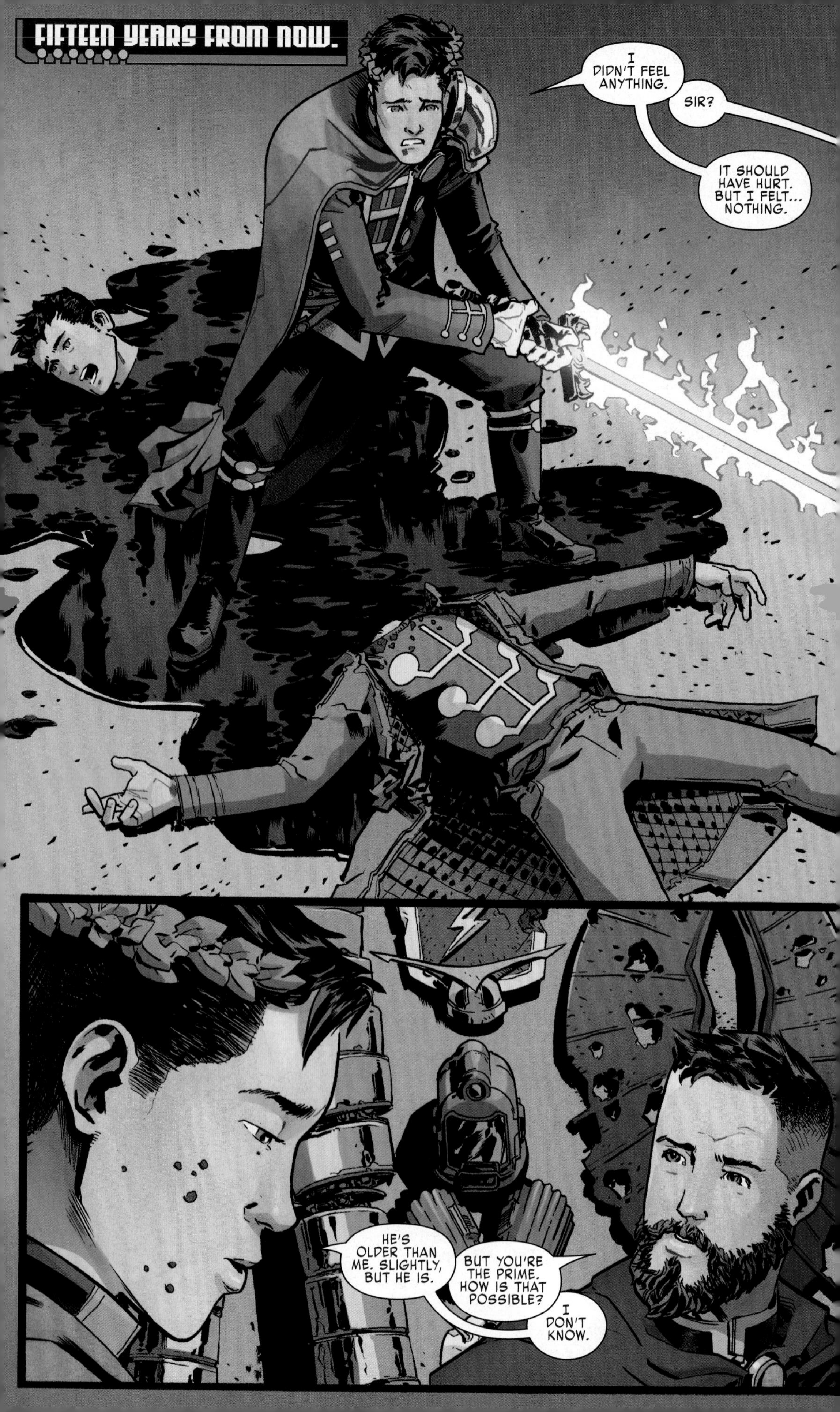
FIFTEEN YEARS FROM NOW.
I DIDN'T FEEL ANYTHING.
SIR?
IT SHOULD HAVE HURT. BUT I FELT... NOTHING.
HE'S OLDER THAN ME. SLIGHTLY, BUT HE IS.
BUT YOU'RE THE PRIME. HOW IS THAT POSSIBLE?
I DON'T KNOW.

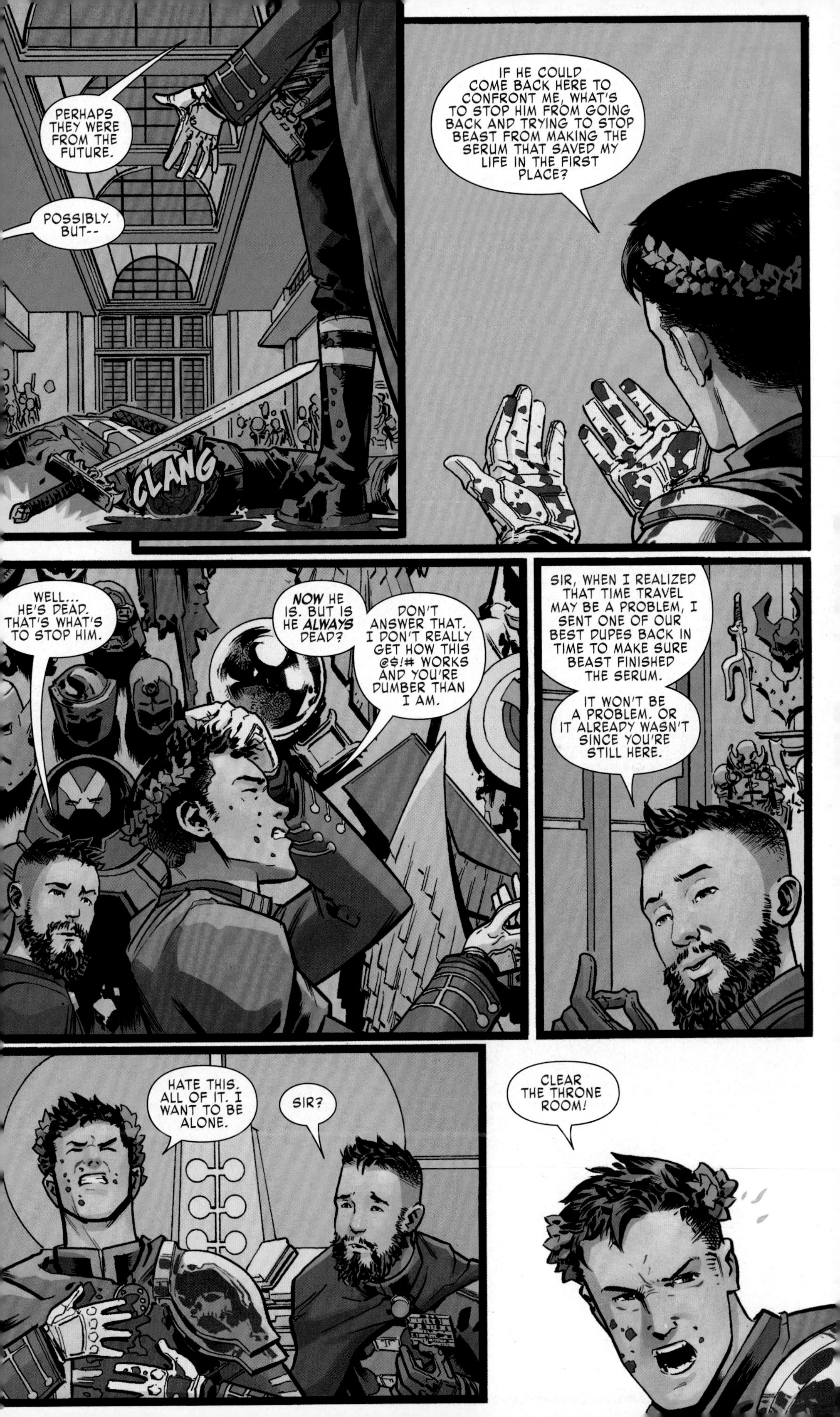
PERHAPS THEY WERE FROM THE FUTURE.
POSSIBLY. BUT--
CLANG
IF HE COULD COME BACK HERE TO CONFRONT ME, WHAT'S TO STOP HIM FROM GOING BACK AND TRYING TO STOP BEAST FROM MAKING THE SERUM THAT SAVED MY LIFE IN THE FIRST PLACE?
WELL... HE'S DEAD. THAT'S WHAT'S TO STOP HIM.
NOW HE IS. BUT IS HE ALWAYS DEAD?
DON'T ANSWER THAT. I DON'T REALLY GET HOW THIS @$!# WORKS AND YOU'RE DUMBER THAN I AM.
SIR, WHEN I REALIZED THAT TIME TRAVEL MAY BE A PROBLEM, I SENT ONE OF OUR BEST DUPES BACK IN TIME TO MAKE SURE BEAST FINISHED THE SERUM.
IT WON'T BE A PROBLEM. OR IT ALREADY WASN'T SINCE YOU'RE STILL HERE.
HATE THIS. ALL OF IT. I WANT TO BE ALONE.
SIR?
CLEAR THE THRONE ROOM!

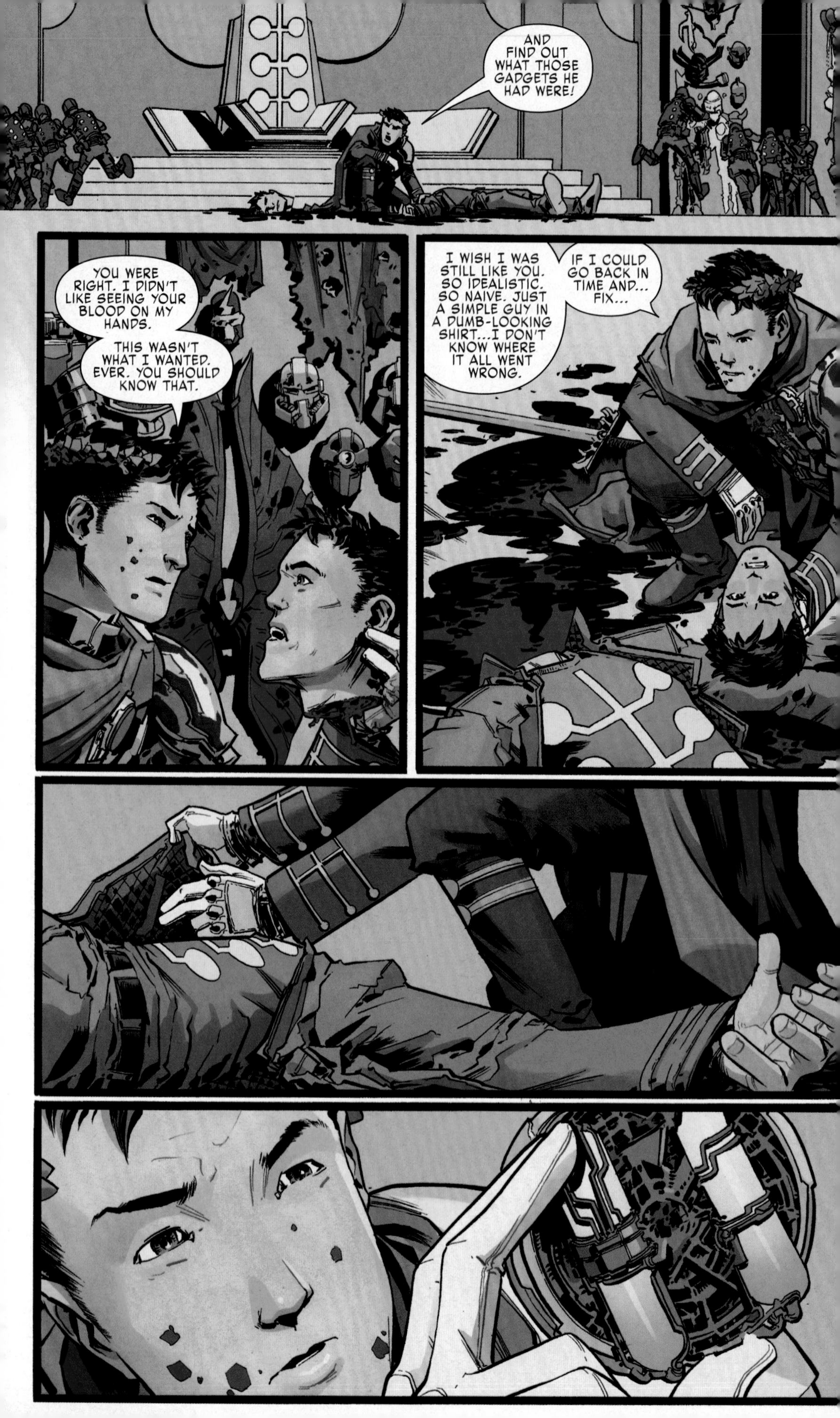
AND FIND OUT WHAT THOSE GADGETS HE HAD WERE!
YOU WERE RIGHT. I DIDN'T LIKE SEEING YOUR BLOOD ON MY HANDS.
THIS WASN'T WHAT I WANTED. EVER. YOU SHOULD KNOW THAT.
I WISH I WAS STILL LIKE YOU. SO IDEALISTIC. SO NAIVE. JUST A SIMPLE GUY IN A DUMB-LOOKING SHIRT...I DON'T KNOW WHERE IT ALL WENT WRONG.
IF I COULD GO BACK IN TIME AND... FIX...

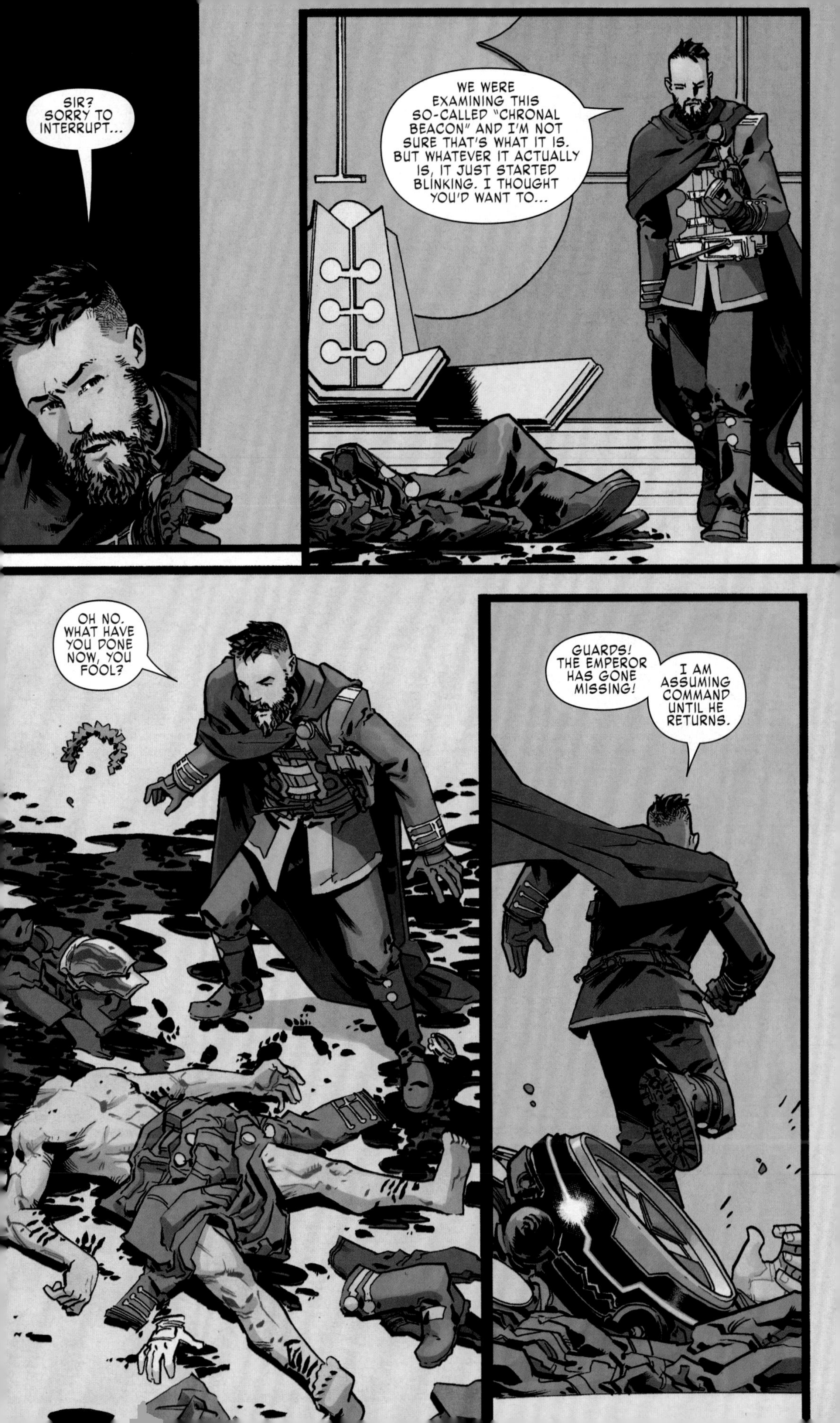

SIR? SORRY TO INTERRUPT...
WE WERE EXAMINING THIS SO-CALLED "CHRONAL BEACON" AND I'M NOT SURE THAT'S WHAT IT IS. BUT WHATEVER IT ACTUALLY IS, IT JUST STARTED BLINKING. I THOUGHT YOU'D WANT TO...
OH NO. WHAT HAVE YOU DONE NOW, YOU FOOL?
GUARDS! THE EMPEROR HAS GONE MISSING!
I AM ASSUMING COMMAND UNTIL HE RETURNS.

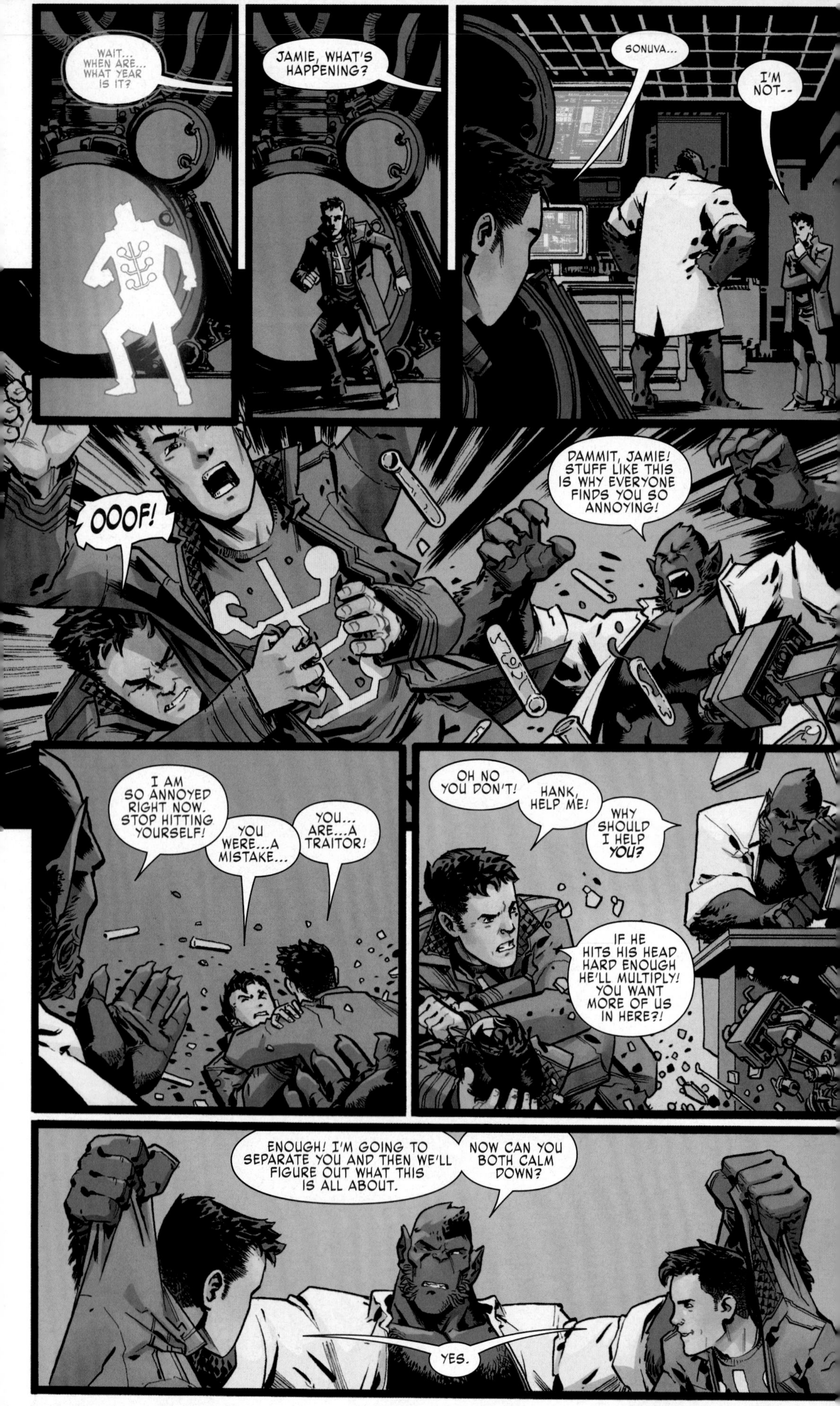

WAIT... WHEN ARE... WHAT YEAR IS IT?
JAMIE, WHAT'S HAPPENING?
SONUVA...
I'M NOT--
OOOF!
DAMMIT, JAMIE! STUFF LIKE THIS IS WHY EVERYONE FINDS YOU SO ANNOYING!
I AM SO ANNOYED RIGHT NOW. STOP HITTING YOURSELF!
YOU WERE...A MISTAKE...
YOU... ARE...A TRAITOR!
OH NO YOU DON'T!
HANK, HELP ME!
WHY SHOULD I HELP YOU?
IF HE HITS HIS HEAD HARD ENOUGH HE'LL MULTIPLY! YOU WANT MORE OF US IN HERE?!
ENOUGH! I'M GOING TO SEPARATE YOU AND THEN WE'LL FIGURE OUT WHAT THIS IS ALL ABOUT.
NOW CAN YOU BOTH CALM DOWN?
YES.

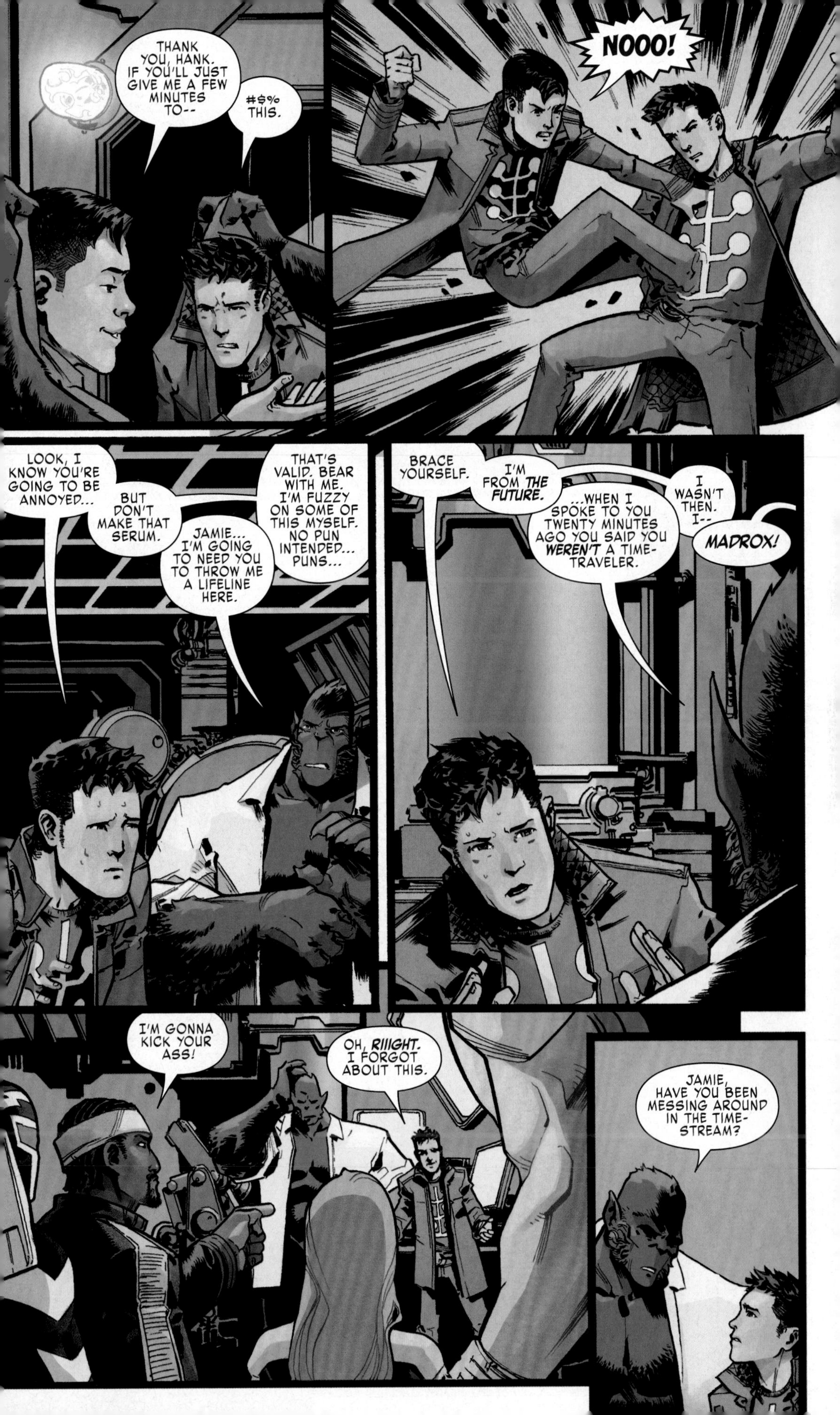
THANK YOU, HANK. IF YOU'LL JUST GIVE ME A FEW MINUTES TO--
#$% THIS.
NOOO!
LOOK, I KNOW YOU'RE GOING TO BE ANNOYED...
BUT DON'T MAKE THAT SERUM.
JAMIE... I'M GOING TO NEED YOU TO THROW ME A LIFELINE HERE.
THAT'S VALID. BEAR WITH ME. I'M FUZZY ON SOME OF THIS MYSELF. NO PUN INTENDED... PUNS...
BRACE YOURSELF.
I'M FROM THE FUTURE.
...WHEN I SPOKE TO YOU TWENTY MINUTES AGO YOU SAID YOU WEREN'T A TIME-TRAVELER.
I WASN'T THEN. I--
MADROX!
I'M GONNA KICK YOUR ASS!
OH, RIIIGHT. I FORGOT ABOUT THIS.
JAMIE, HAVE YOU BEEN MESSING AROUND IN THE TIME-STREAM?

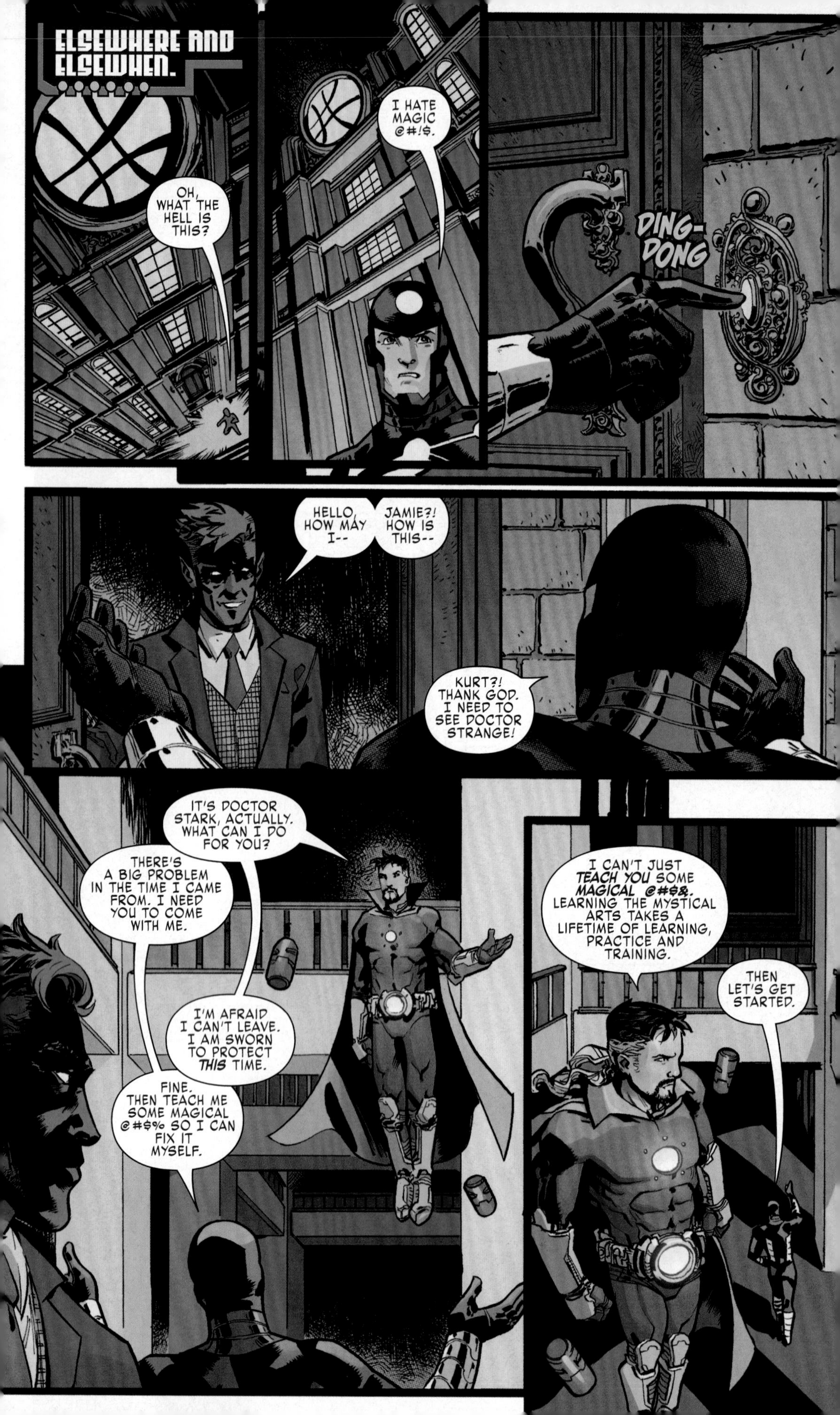

ELSEWHERE AND ELSEWHEN.
OH, WHAT THE HELL IS THIS?
I HATE MAGIC @#!$.
DING-DONG
HELLO, HOW MAY I--
JAMIE?! HOW IS THIS--
KURT?! THANK GOD. I NEED TO SEE DOCTOR STRANGE!
IT'S DOCTOR STARK, ACTUALLY. WHAT CAN I DO FOR YOU?
THERE'S A BIG PROBLEM IN THE TIME I CAME FROM. I NEED YOU TO COME WITH ME.
I'M AFRAID I CAN'T LEAVE. I AM SWORN TO PROTECT *THIS* TIME.
FINE. THEN TEACH ME SOME MAGICAL @#$% SO I CAN FIX IT MYSELF.
I CAN'T JUST *TEACH YOU* SOME *MAGICAL @#$&.* LEARNING THE MYSTICAL ARTS TAKES A LIFETIME OF LEARNING, PRACTICE AND TRAINING.
THEN LET'S GET STARTED.

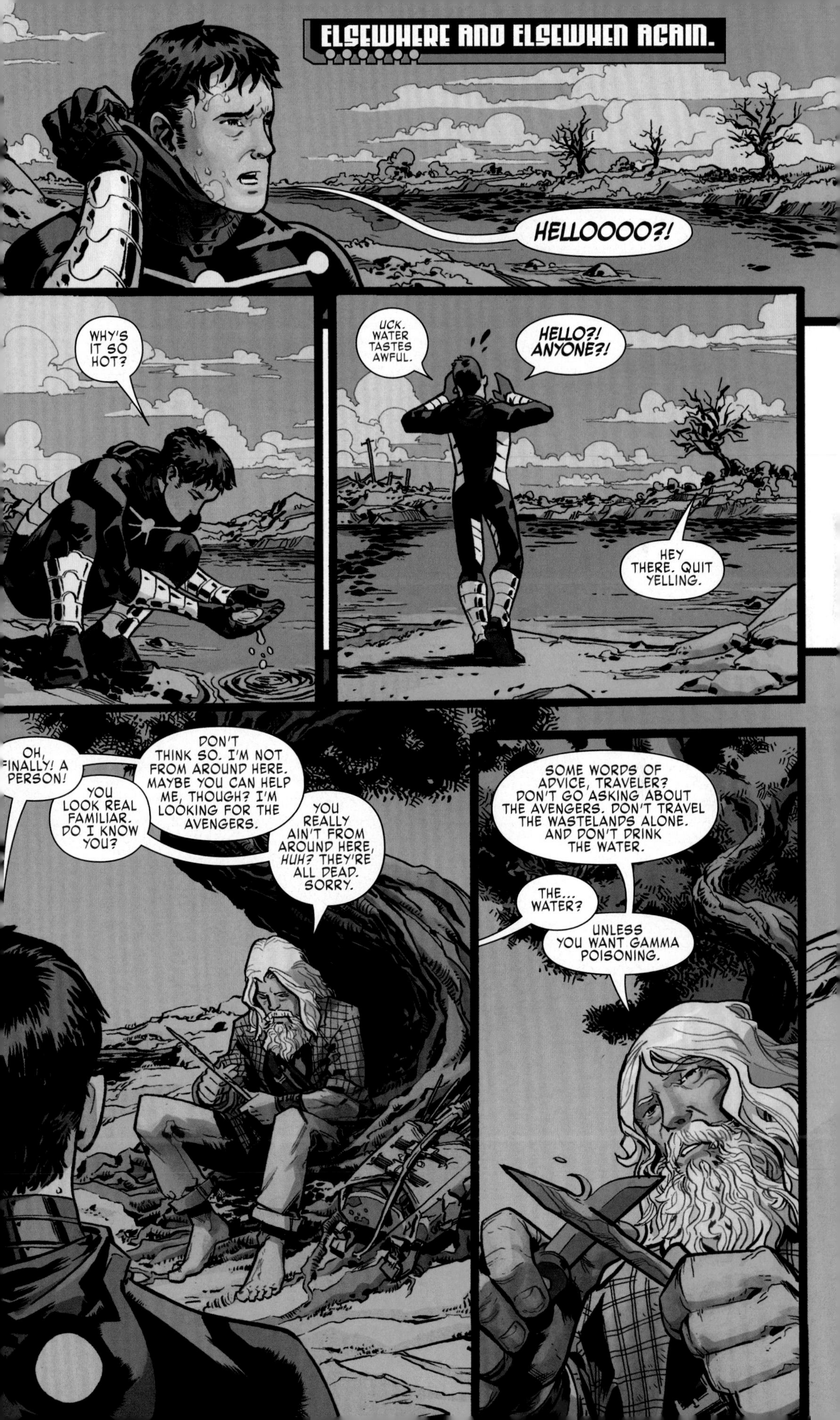
ELSEWHERE AND ELSEWHEN AGAIN.
HELLOOOO?!
WHY'S IT SO HOT?
UCK. WATER TASTES AWFUL.
HELLO?! ANYONE?!
HEY THERE. QUIT YELLING.
OH, FINALLY! A PERSON!
YOU LOOK REAL FAMILIAR. DO I KNOW YOU?
DON'T THINK SO. I'M NOT FROM AROUND HERE. MAYBE YOU CAN HELP ME, THOUGH? I'M LOOKING FOR THE AVENGERS.
YOU REALLY AIN'T FROM AROUND HERE, HUH? THEY'RE ALL DEAD. SORRY.
SOME WORDS OF ADVICE, TRAVELER? DON'T GO ASKING ABOUT THE AVENGERS. DON'T TRAVEL THE WASTELANDS ALONE. AND DON'T DRINK THE WATER.
THE... WATER?
UNLESS YOU WANT GAMMA POISONING.

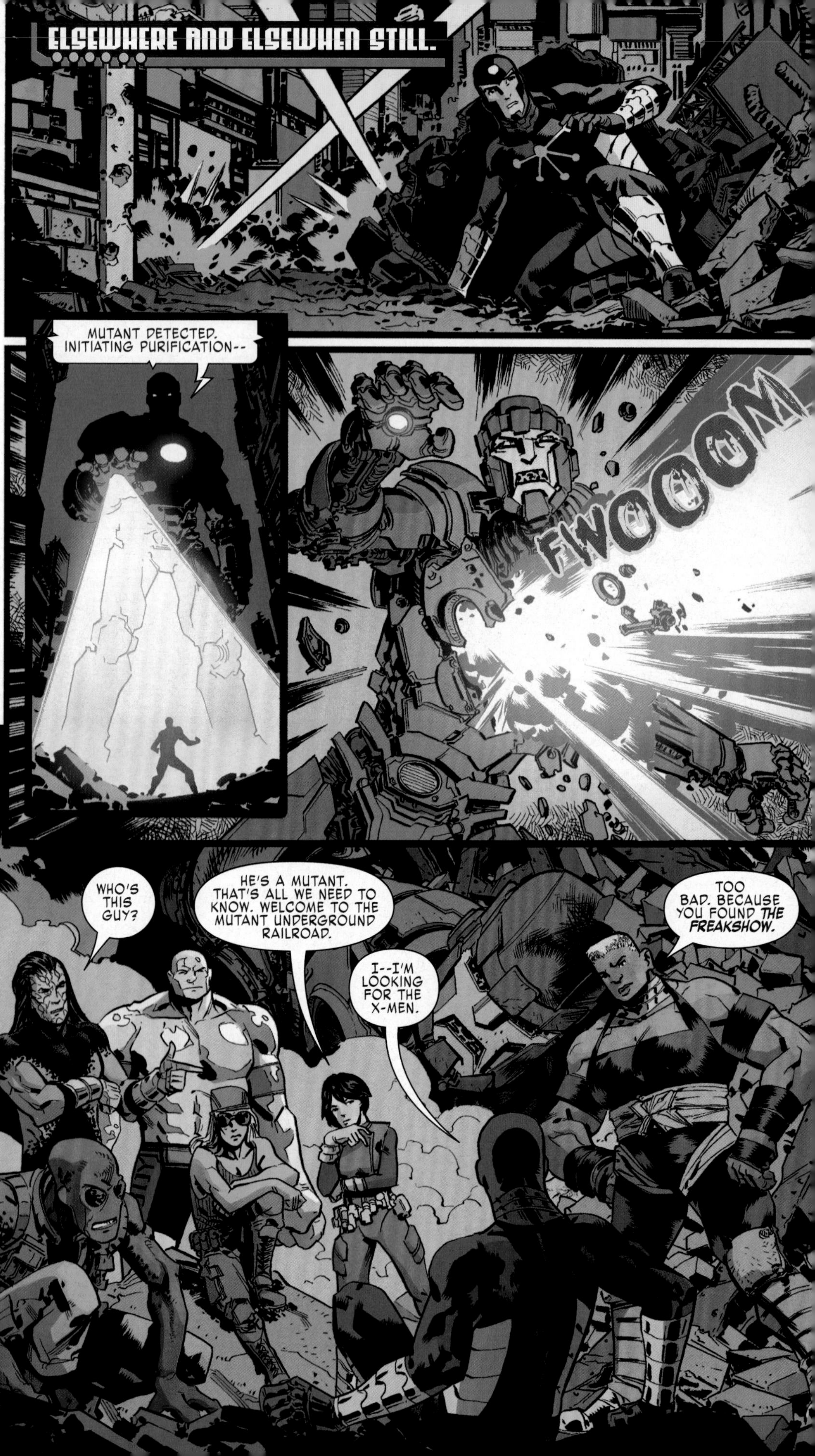
ELSEWHERE AND ELSEWHEN STILL.
MUTANT DETECTED. INITIATING PURIFICATION--
FWOOOOM
WHO'S THIS GUY?
HE'S A MUTANT. THAT'S ALL WE NEED TO KNOW. WELCOME TO THE MUTANT UNDERGROUND RAILROAD.
I--I'M LOOKING FOR THE X-MEN.
TOO BAD. BECAUSE YOU FOUND *THE FREAKSHOW.*

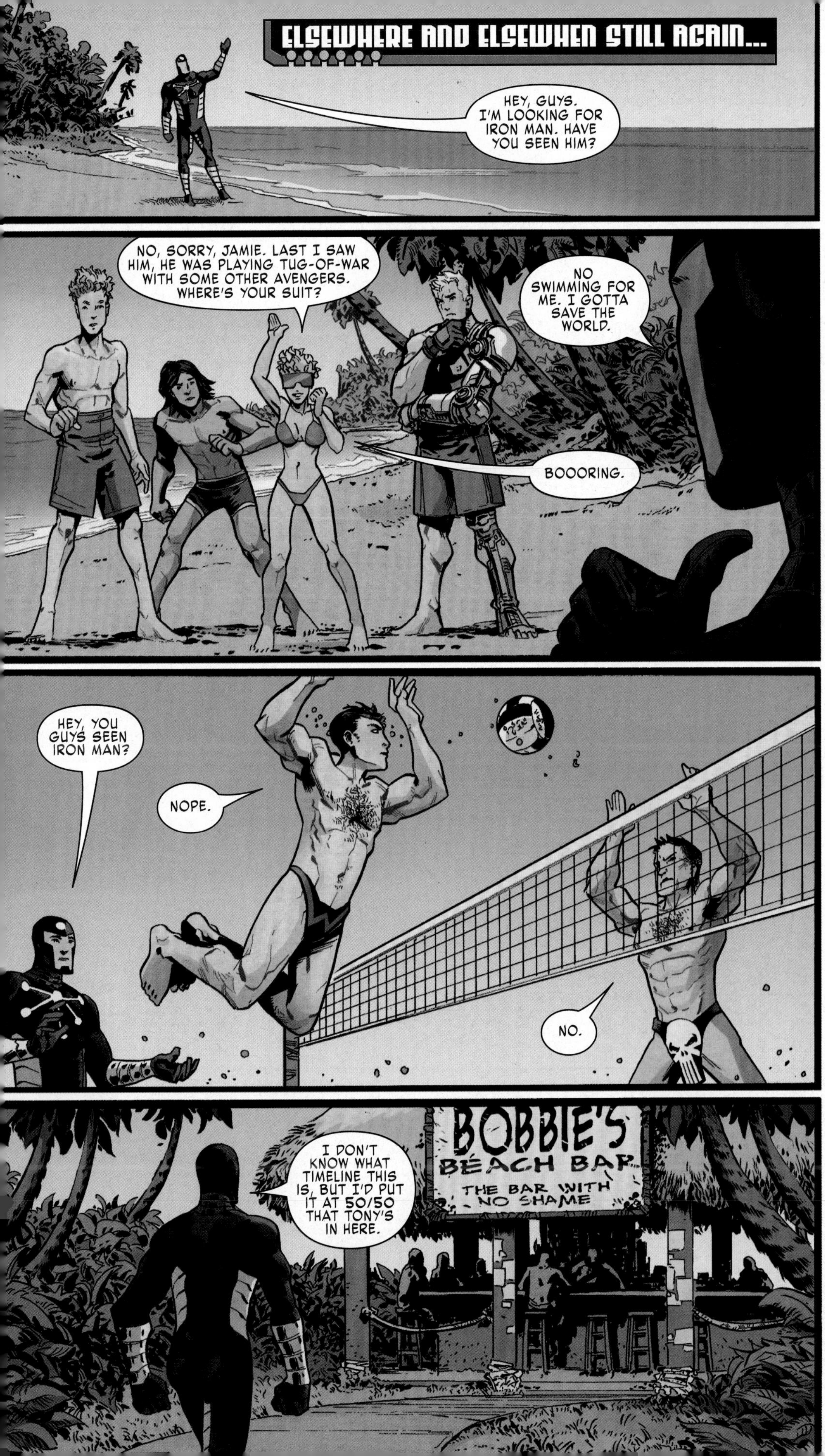

ELSEWHERE AND ELSEWHEN STILL AGAIN...
HEY, GUYS. I'M LOOKING FOR IRON MAN. HAVE YOU SEEN HIM?
NO, SORRY, JAMIE. LAST I SAW HIM, HE WAS PLAYING TUG-OF-WAR WITH SOME OTHER AVENGERS. WHERE'S YOUR SUIT?
NO SWIMMING FOR ME. I GOTTA SAVE THE WORLD.
BOOORING.
HEY, YOU GUYS SEEN IRON MAN?
NOPE.
NO.
BOBBIE'S BEACH BAR
THE BAR WITH NO SHAME
I DON'T KNOW WHAT TIMELINE THIS IS, BUT I'D PUT IT AT 50/50 THAT TONY'S IN HERE.

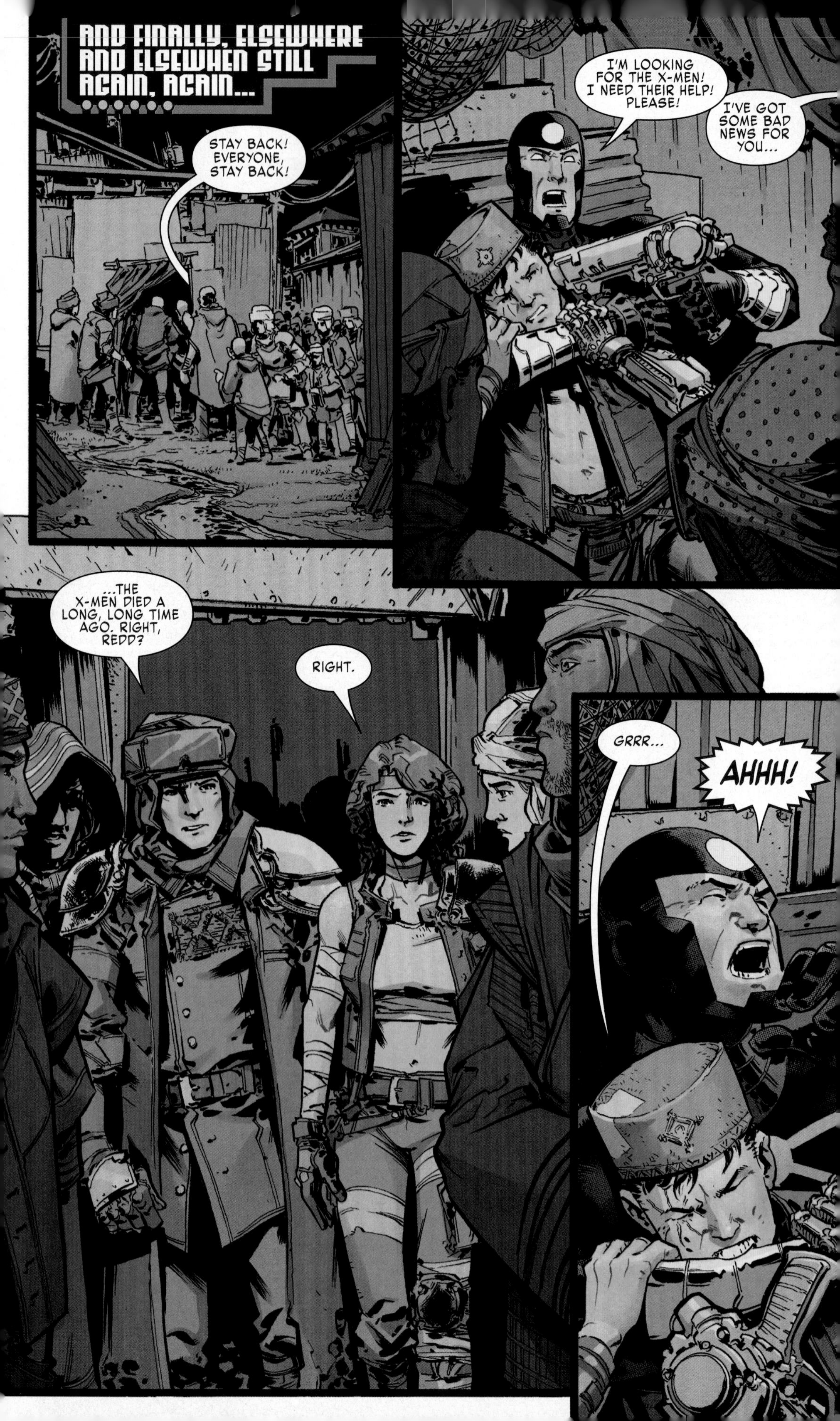

AND FINALLY, ELSEWHERE AND ELSEWHEN STILL AGAIN, AGAIN...
STAY BACK! EVERYONE, STAY BACK!
I'M LOOKING FOR THE X-MEN! I NEED THEIR HELP! PLEASE!
I'VE GOT SOME BAD NEWS FOR YOU...
...THE X-MEN DIED A LONG, LONG TIME AGO. RIGHT, REDD?
RIGHT.
GRRR...
AHHH!

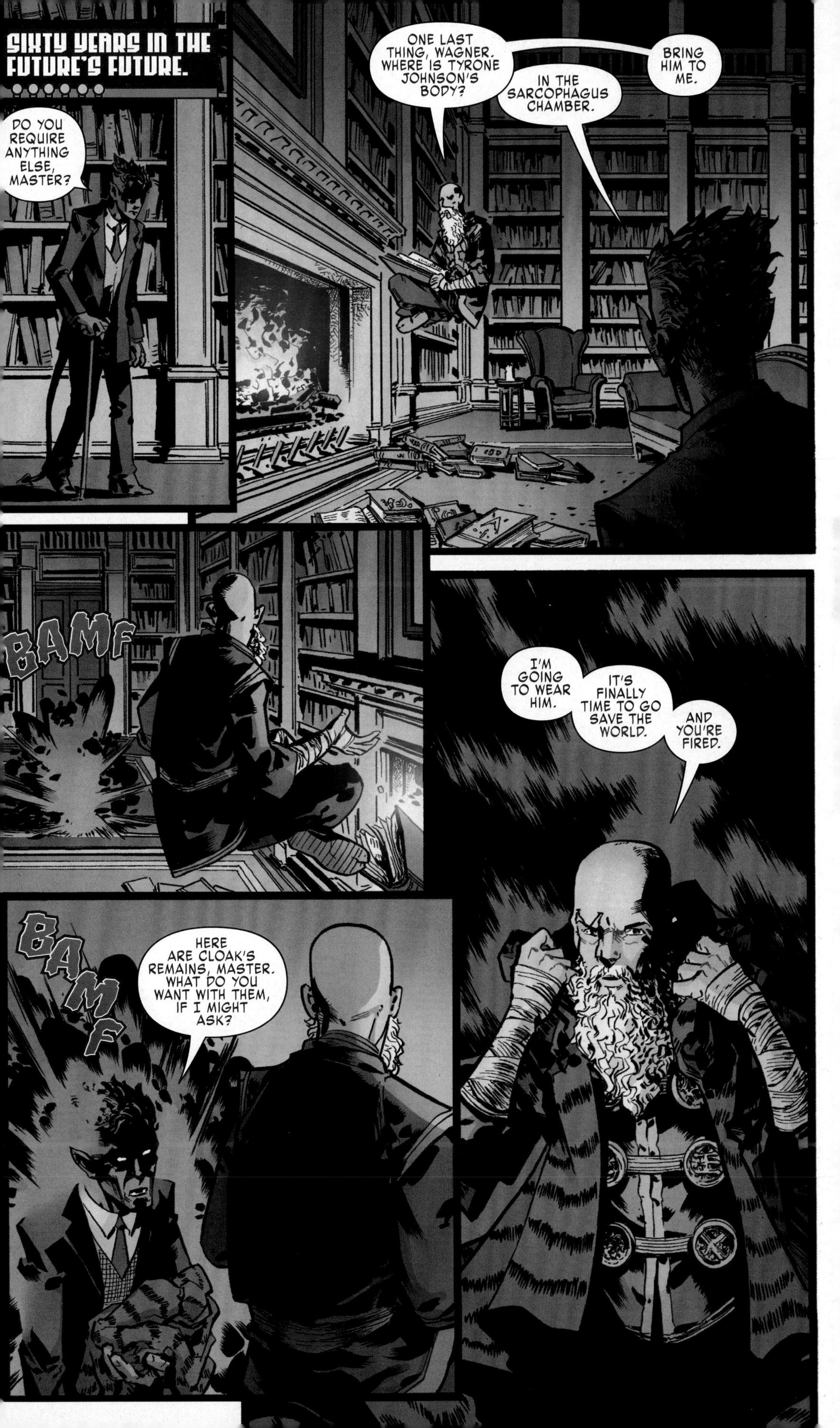
SIXTY YEARS IN THE FUTURE'S FUTURE.
DO YOU REQUIRE ANYTHING ELSE, MASTER?
ONE LAST THING, WAGNER. WHERE IS TYRONE JOHNSON'S BODY?
IN THE SARCOPHAGUS CHAMBER.
BRING HIM TO ME.
BAMF
BAMF
HERE ARE CLOAK'S REMAINS, MASTER. WHAT DO YOU WANT WITH THEM, IF I MIGHT ASK?
I'M GOING TO WEAR HIM.
IT'S FINALLY TIME TO GO SAVE THE WORLD.
AND YOU'RE FIRED.

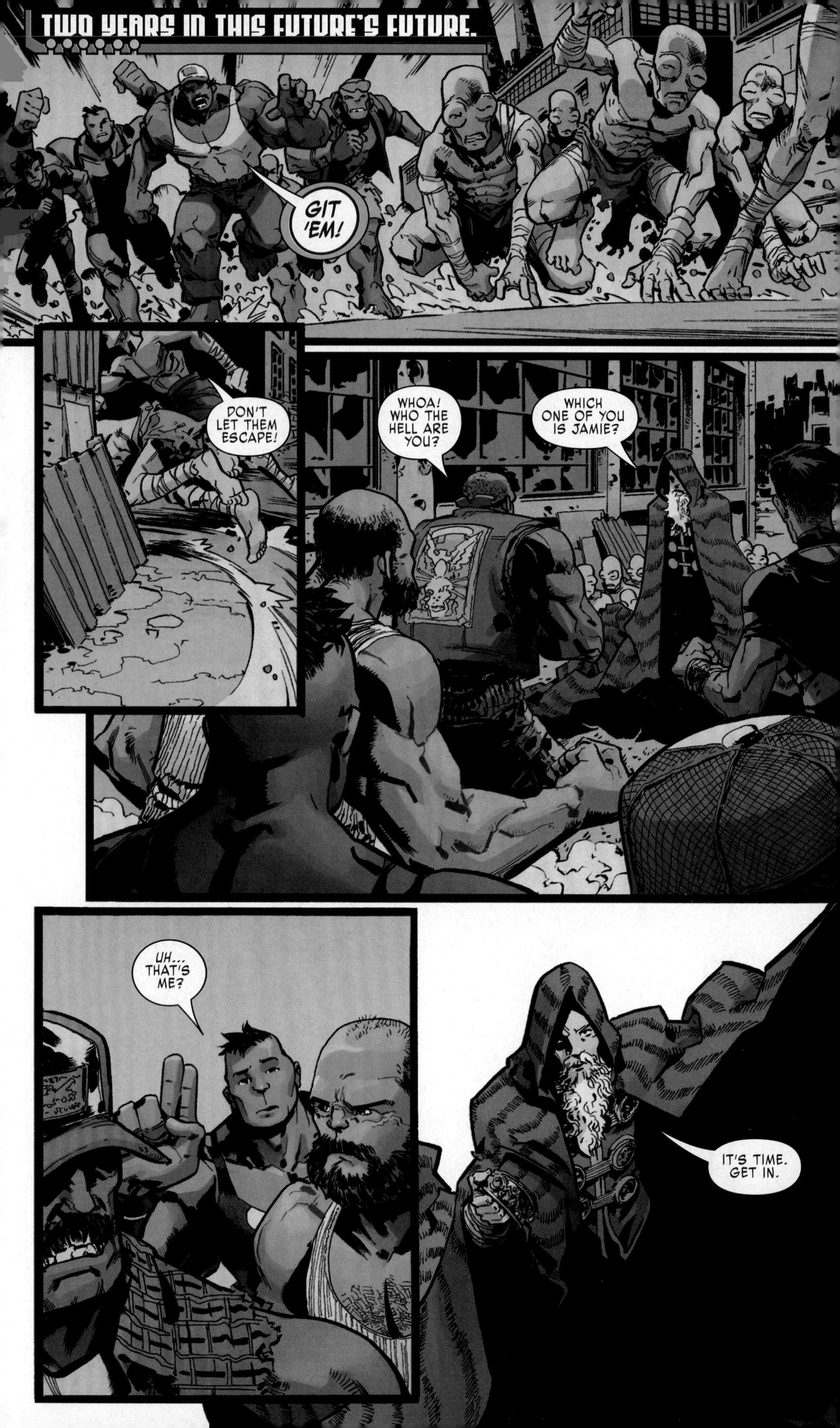
TWO YEARS IN THIS FUTURE'S FUTURE.
GIT 'EM!
DON'T LET THEM ESCAPE!
WHOA! WHO THE HELL ARE YOU?
WHICH ONE OF YOU IS JAMIE?
UH... THAT'S ME?
IT'S TIME. GET IN.

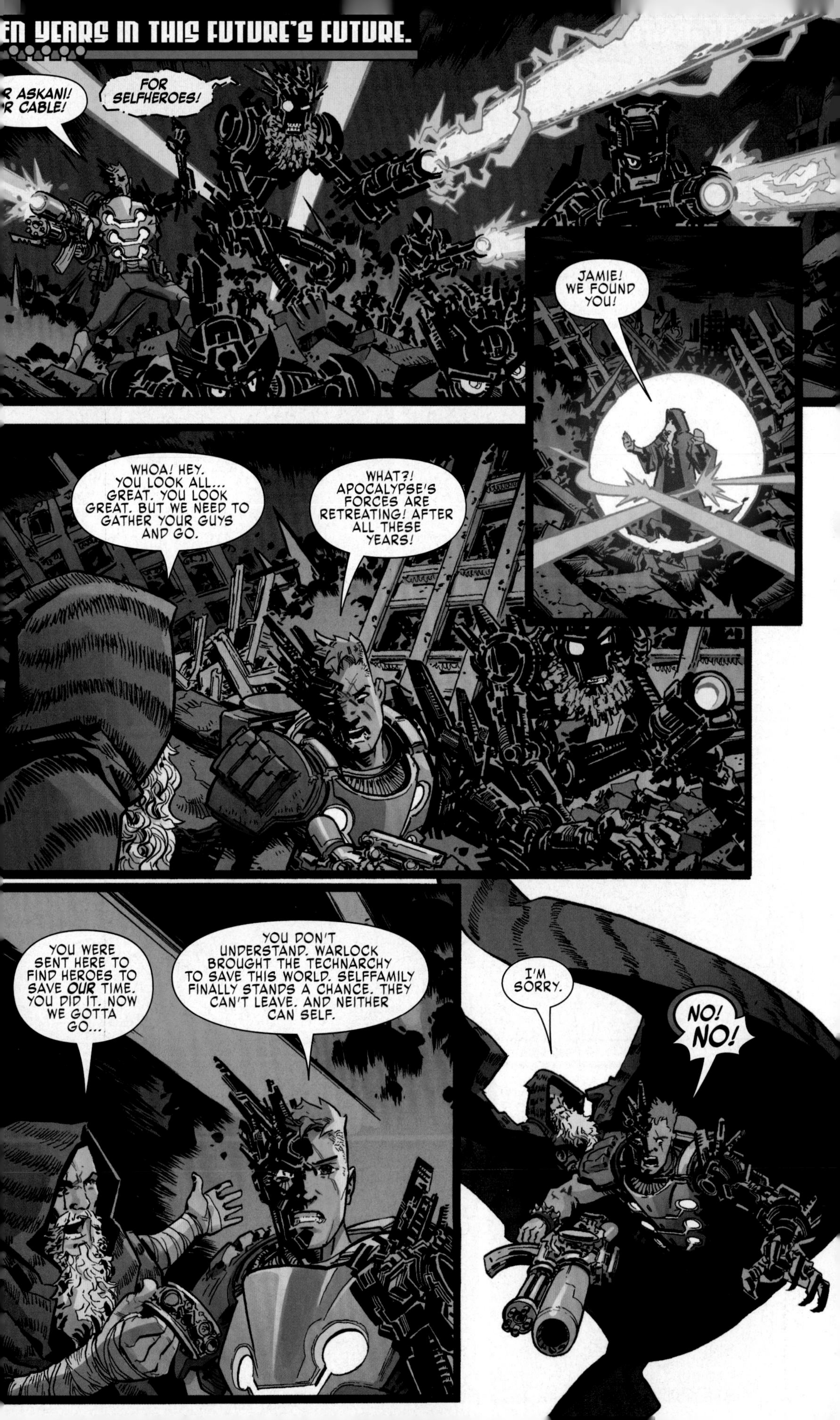
EN YEARS IN THIS FUTURE'S FUTURE.
R ASKANI! R CABLE!
FOR SELFHEROES!
JAMIE! WE FOUND YOU!
WHOA! HEY. YOU LOOK ALL... GREAT. YOU LOOK GREAT. BUT WE NEED TO GATHER YOUR GUYS AND GO.
WHAT?! APOCALYPSE'S FORCES ARE RETREATING! AFTER ALL THESE YEARS!
YOU WERE SENT HERE TO FIND HEROES TO SAVE *OUR* TIME. YOU DID IT. NOW WE GOTTA GO...
YOU DON'T UNDERSTAND. WARLOCK BROUGHT THE TECHNARCHY TO SAVE THIS WORLD. SELFFAMILY FINALLY STANDS A CHANCE. THEY CAN'T LEAVE. AND NEITHER CAN SELF.
I'M SORRY.
NO! NO!

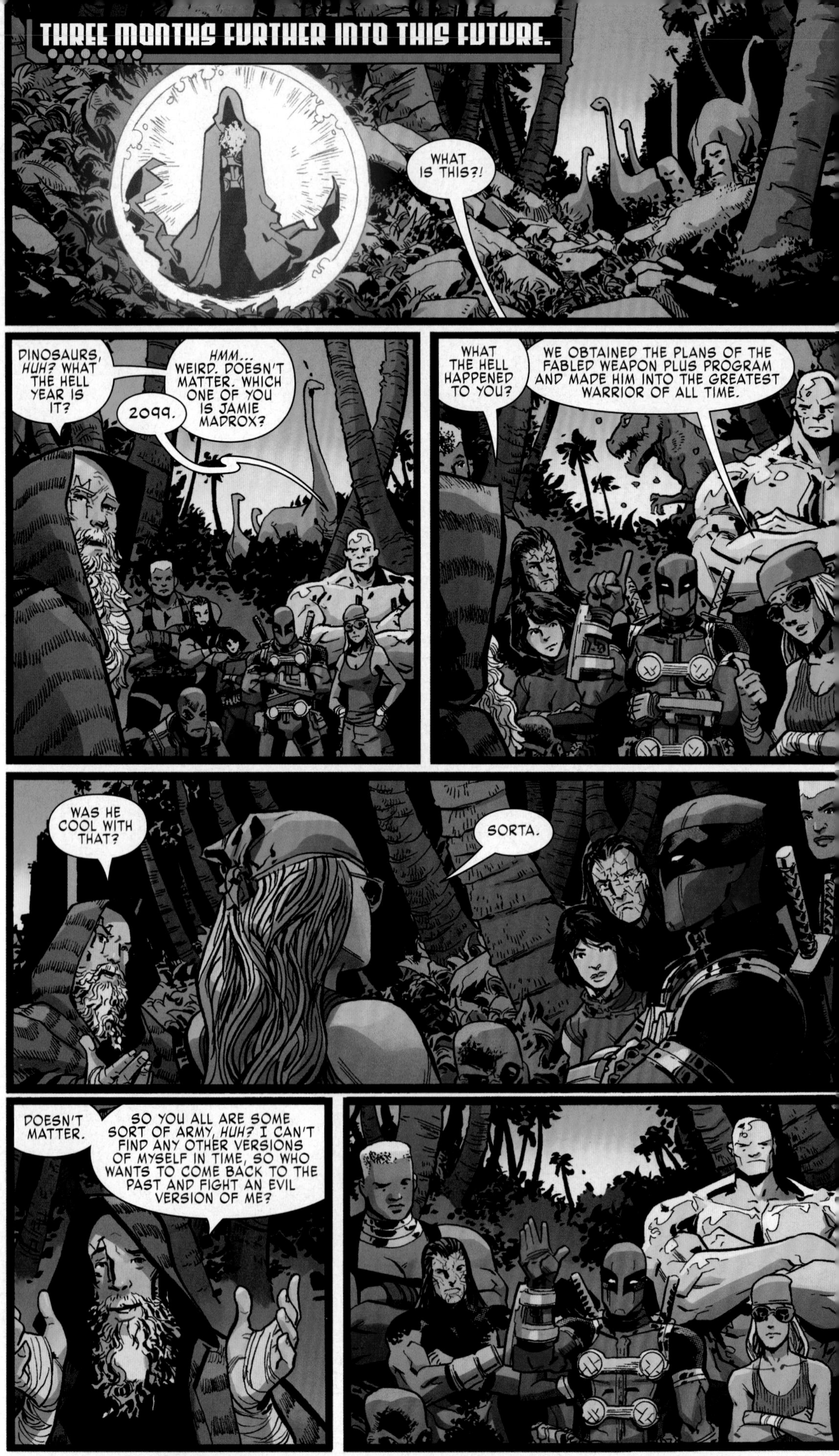
THREE MONTHS FURTHER INTO THIS FUTURE.
WHAT IS THIS?!
DINOSAURS, HUH? WHAT THE HELL YEAR IS IT?
2099.
HMM... WEIRD. DOESN'T MATTER. WHICH ONE OF YOU IS JAMIE MADROX?
WHAT THE HELL HAPPENED TO YOU?
WE OBTAINED THE PLANS OF THE FABLED WEAPON PLUS PROGRAM AND MADE HIM INTO THE GREATEST WARRIOR OF ALL TIME.
WAS HE COOL WITH THAT?
SORTA.
DOESN'T MATTER.
SO YOU ALL ARE SOME SORT OF ARMY, HUH? I CAN'T FIND ANY OTHER VERSIONS OF MYSELF IN TIME, SO WHO WANTS TO COME BACK TO THE PAST AND FIGHT AN EVIL VERSION OF ME?

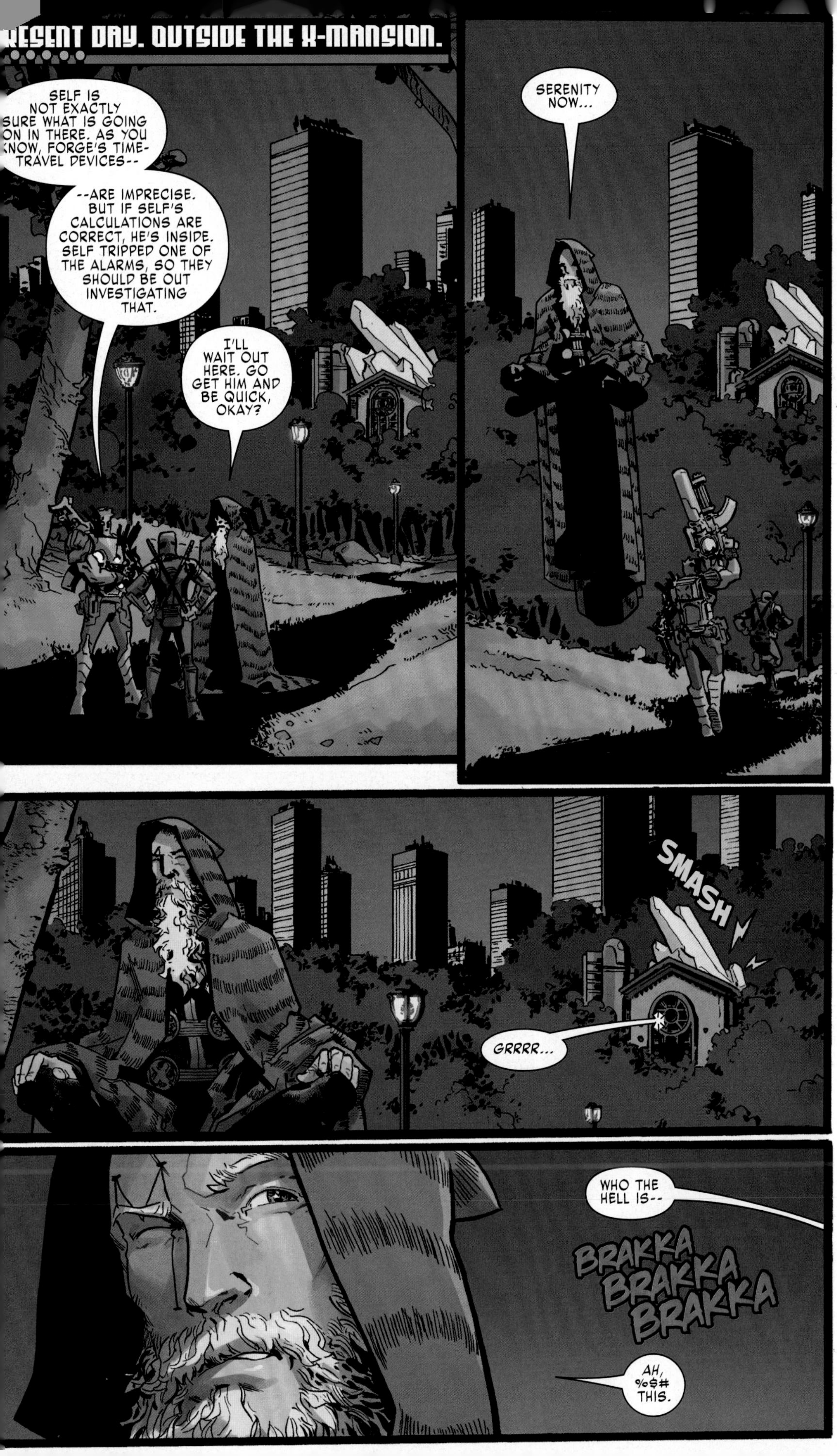
RESENT DAY. OUTSIDE THE X-MANSION.
SELF IS NOT EXACTLY SURE WHAT IS GOING ON IN THERE. AS YOU KNOW, FORGE'S TIME-TRAVEL DEVICES--
--ARE IMPRECISE. BUT IF SELF'S CALCULATIONS ARE CORRECT, HE'S INSIDE. SELF TRIPPED ONE OF THE ALARMS, SO THEY SHOULD BE OUT INVESTIGATING THAT.
I'LL WAIT OUT HERE. GO GET HIM AND BE QUICK, OKAY?
SERENITY NOW...
SMASH
GRRRR...
WHO THE HELL IS--
BRAKKA BRAKKA BRAKKA
AH, %$# THIS.

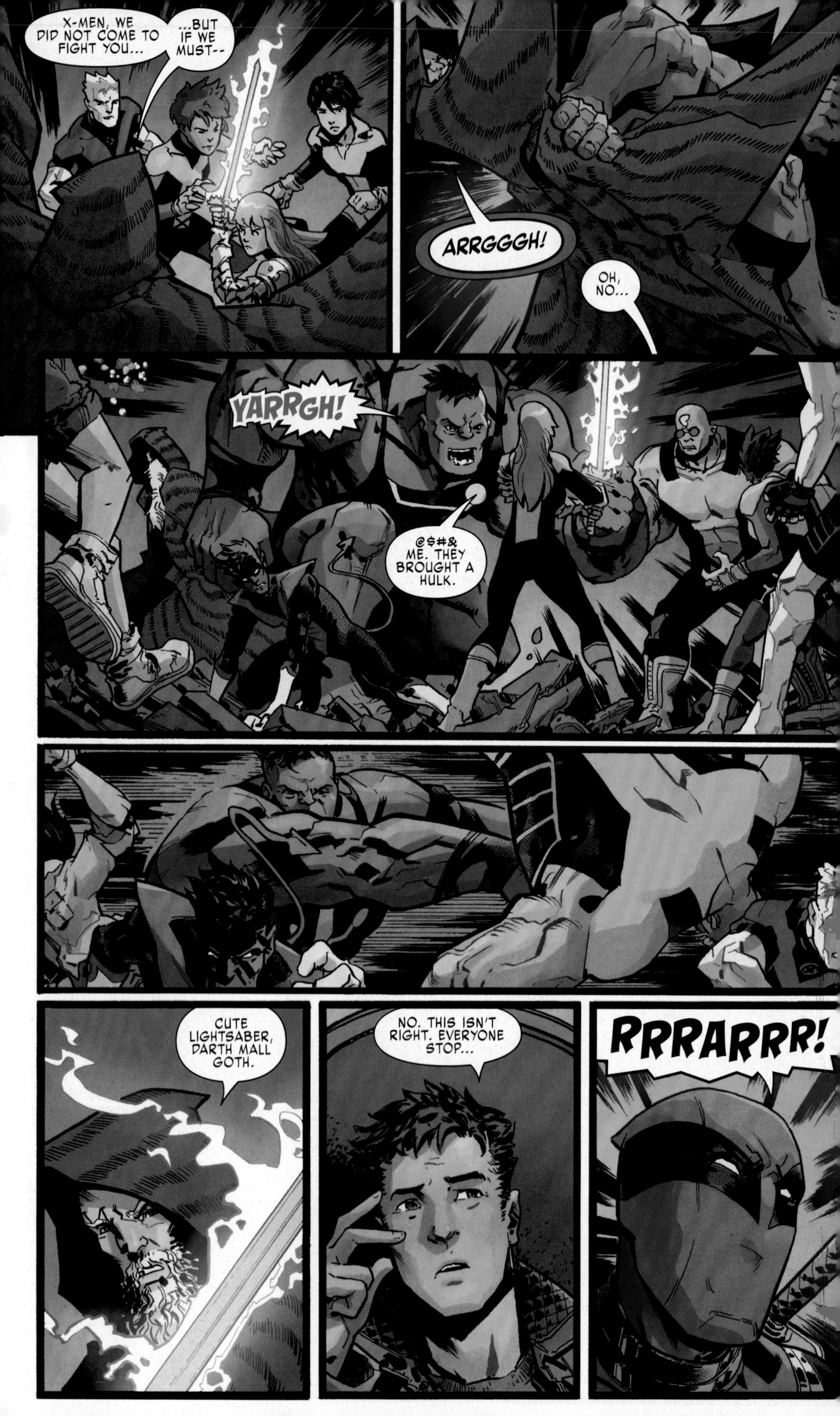
X-MEN, WE DID NOT COME TO FIGHT YOU...
...BUT IF WE MUST--
ARRGGGH!
OH, NO...
YARRGH!
@$#& ME. THEY BROUGHT A HULK.
CUTE LIGHTSABER, DARTH MALL GOTH.
NO. THIS ISN'T RIGHT. EVERYONE STOP...
RRRARRR!

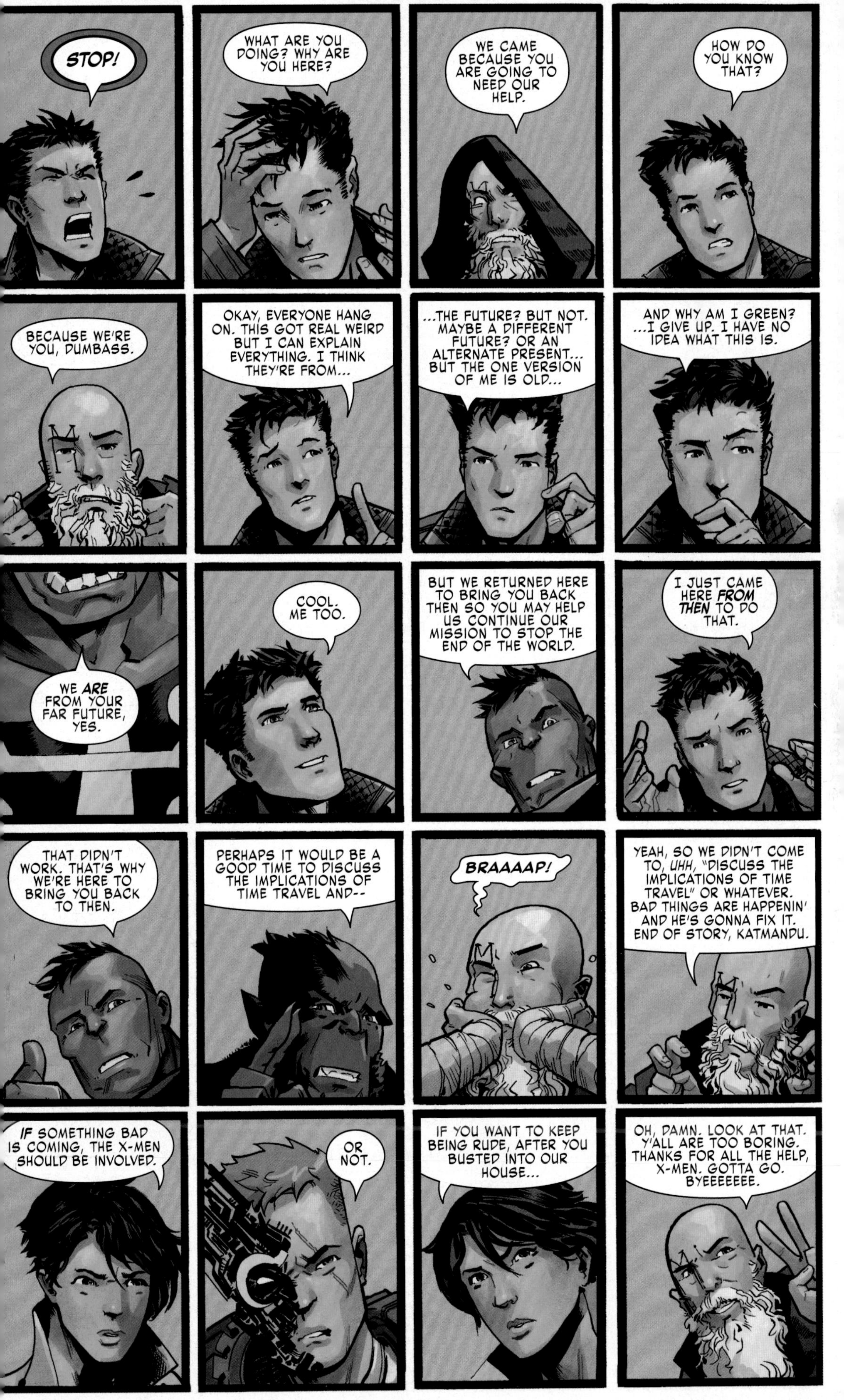
STOP!
WHAT ARE YOU DOING? WHY ARE YOU HERE?
WE CAME BECAUSE YOU ARE GOING TO NEED OUR HELP.
HOW DO YOU KNOW THAT?
BECAUSE WE'RE YOU, DUMBASS.
OKAY, EVERYONE HANG ON. THIS GOT REAL WEIRD BUT I CAN EXPLAIN EVERYTHING. I THINK THEY'RE FROM...
...THE FUTURE? BUT NOT. MAYBE A DIFFERENT FUTURE? OR AN ALTERNATE PRESENT... BUT THE ONE VERSION OF ME IS OLD...
AND WHY AM I GREEN? ...I GIVE UP. I HAVE NO IDEA WHAT THIS IS.
WE ARE FROM YOUR FAR FUTURE, YES.
COOL. ME TOO.
BUT WE RETURNED HERE TO BRING YOU BACK THEN SO YOU MAY HELP US CONTINUE OUR MISSION TO STOP THE END OF THE WORLD.
I JUST CAME HERE FROM THEN TO DO THAT.
THAT DIDN'T WORK. THAT'S WHY WE'RE HERE TO BRING YOU BACK TO THEN.
PERHAPS IT WOULD BE A GOOD TIME TO DISCUSS THE IMPLICATIONS OF TIME TRAVEL AND--
BRAAAAP!
YEAH, SO WE DIDN'T COME TO, UHH, "DISCUSS THE IMPLICATIONS OF TIME TRAVEL" OR WHATEVER. BAD THINGS ARE HAPPENIN' AND HE'S GONNA FIX IT. END OF STORY, KATMANDU.
IF SOMETHING BAD IS COMING, THE X-MEN SHOULD BE INVOLVED.
OR NOT.
IF YOU WANT TO KEEP BEING RUDE, AFTER YOU BUSTED INTO OUR HOUSE...
OH, DAMN. LOOK AT THAT. Y'ALL ARE TOO BORING. THANKS FOR ALL THE HELP, X-MEN. GOTTA GO. BYEEEEEEE.

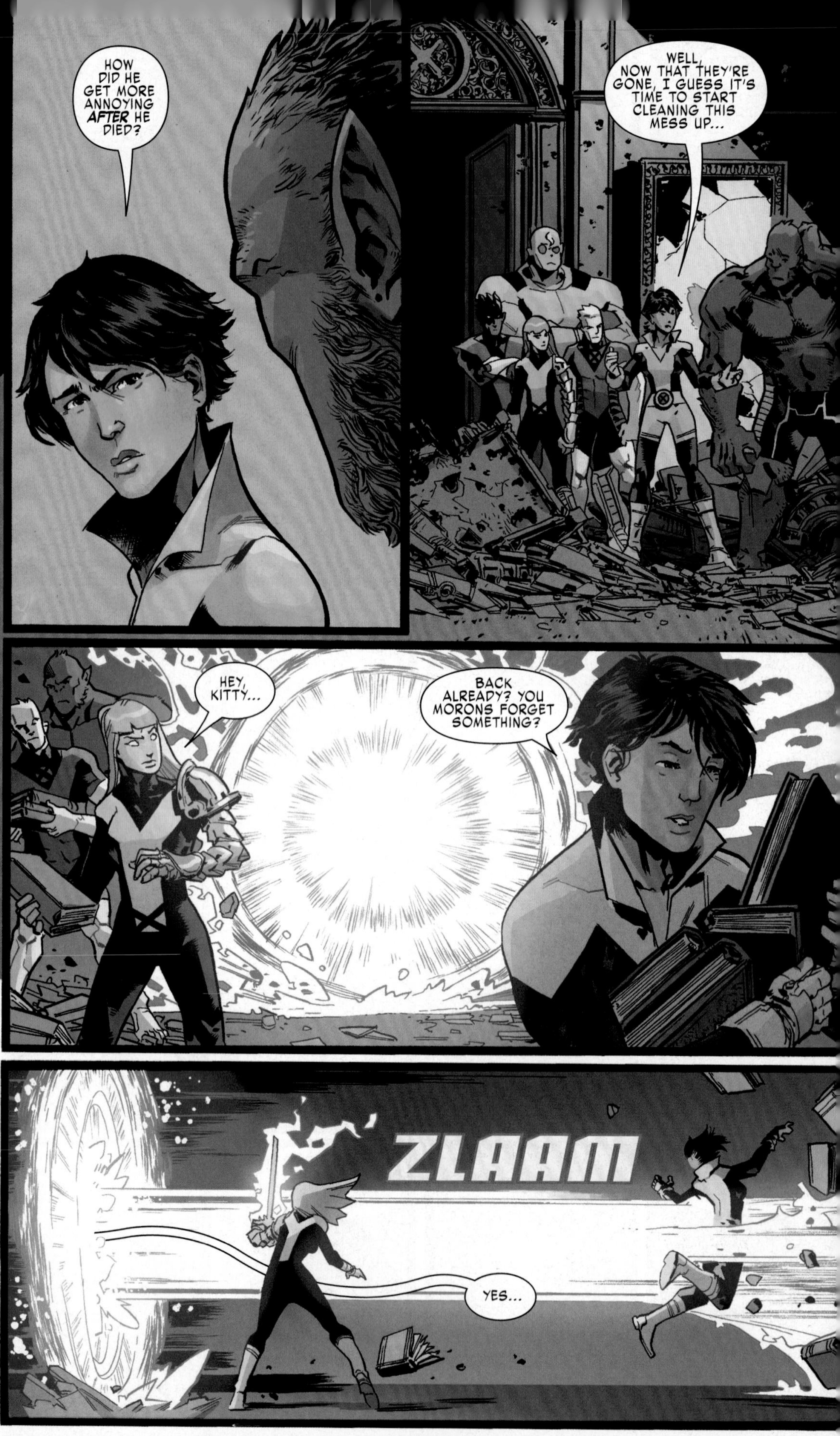
HOW DID HE GET MORE ANNOYING AFTER HE DIED?
WELL, NOW THAT THEY'RE GONE, I GUESS IT'S TIME TO START CLEANING THIS MESS UP...
HEY, KITTY...
BACK ALREADY? YOU MORONS FORGET SOMETHING?
ZLAAM
YES...

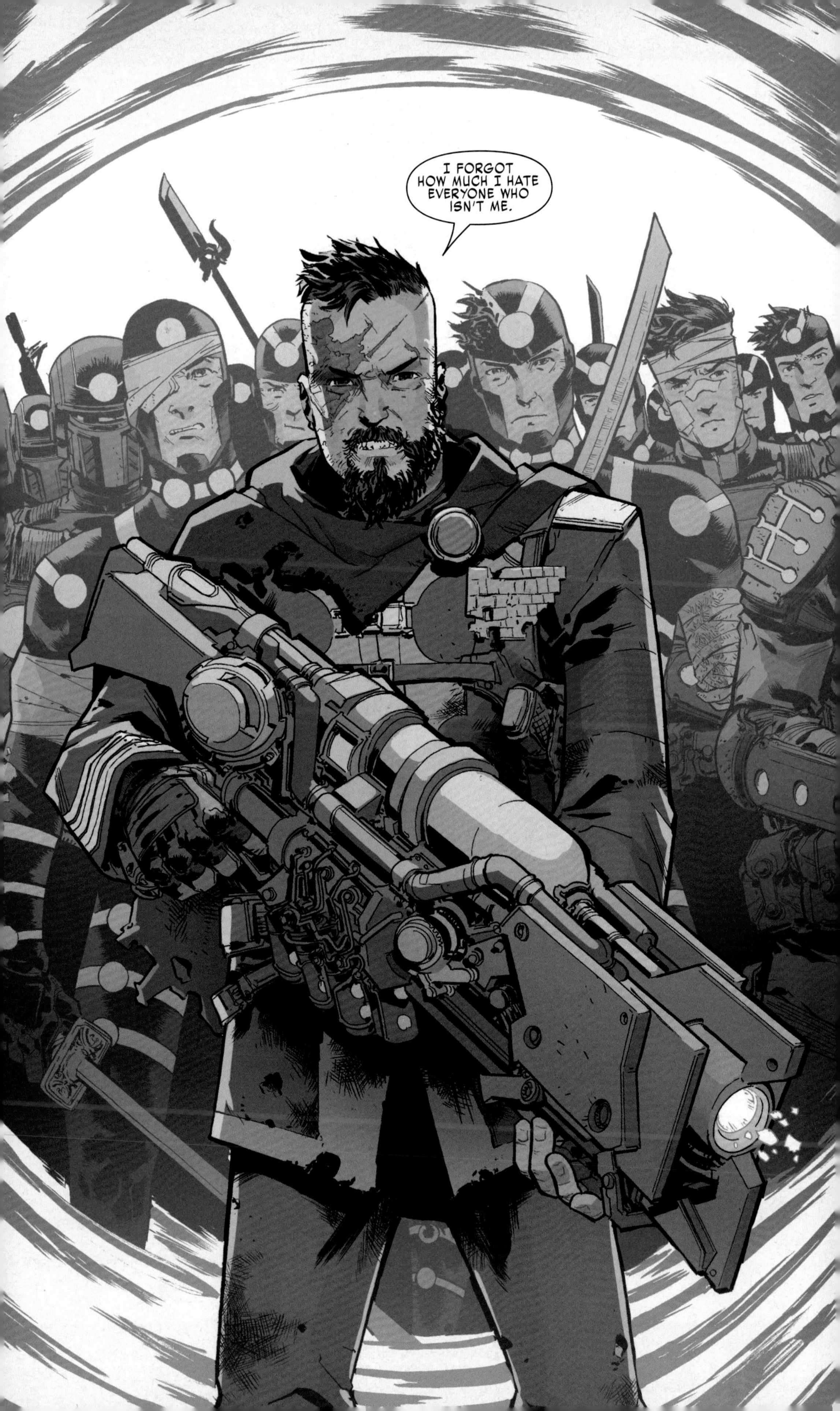
I FORGOT HOW MUCH I HATE EVERYONE WHO ISN'T ME.

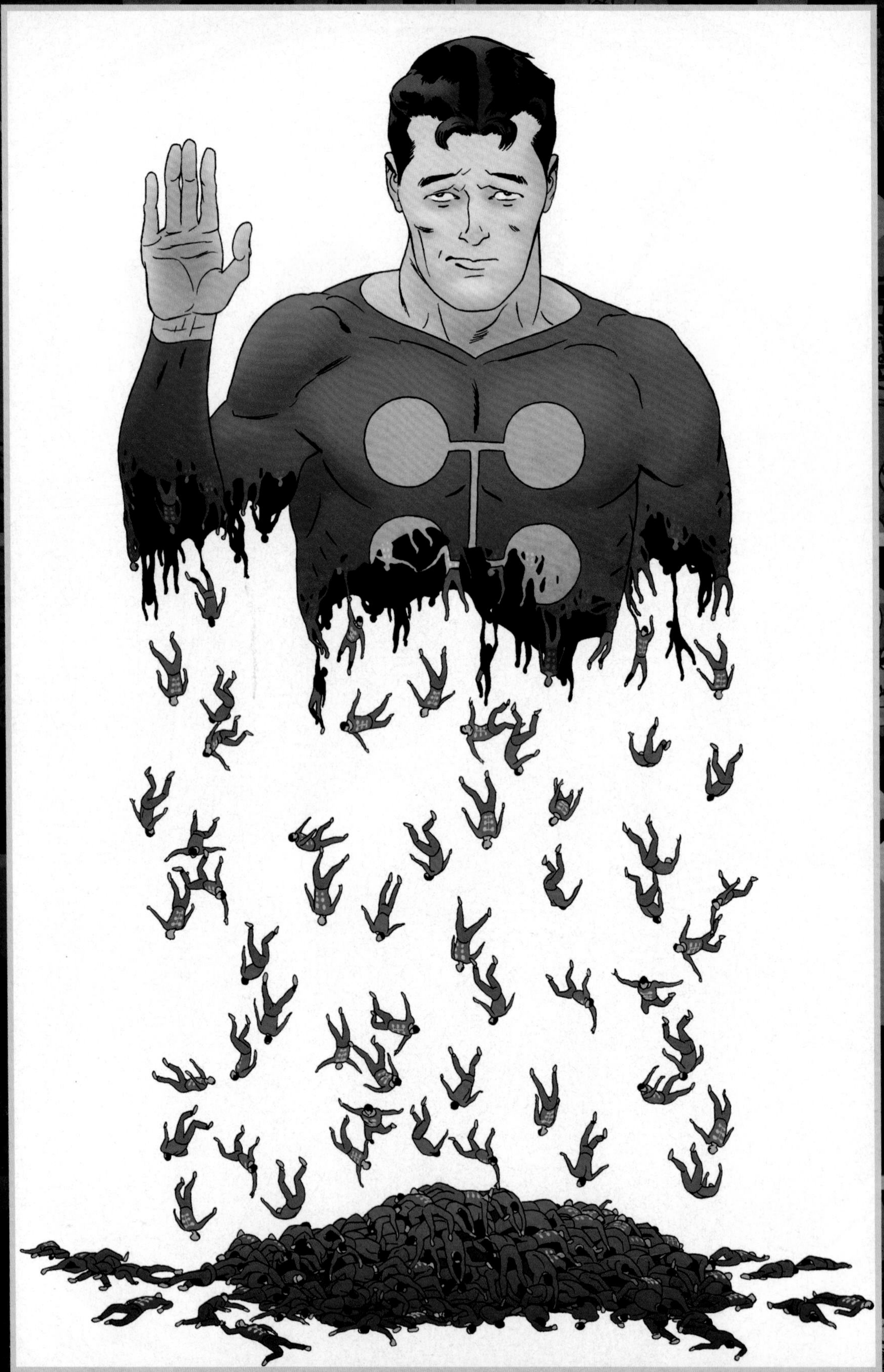

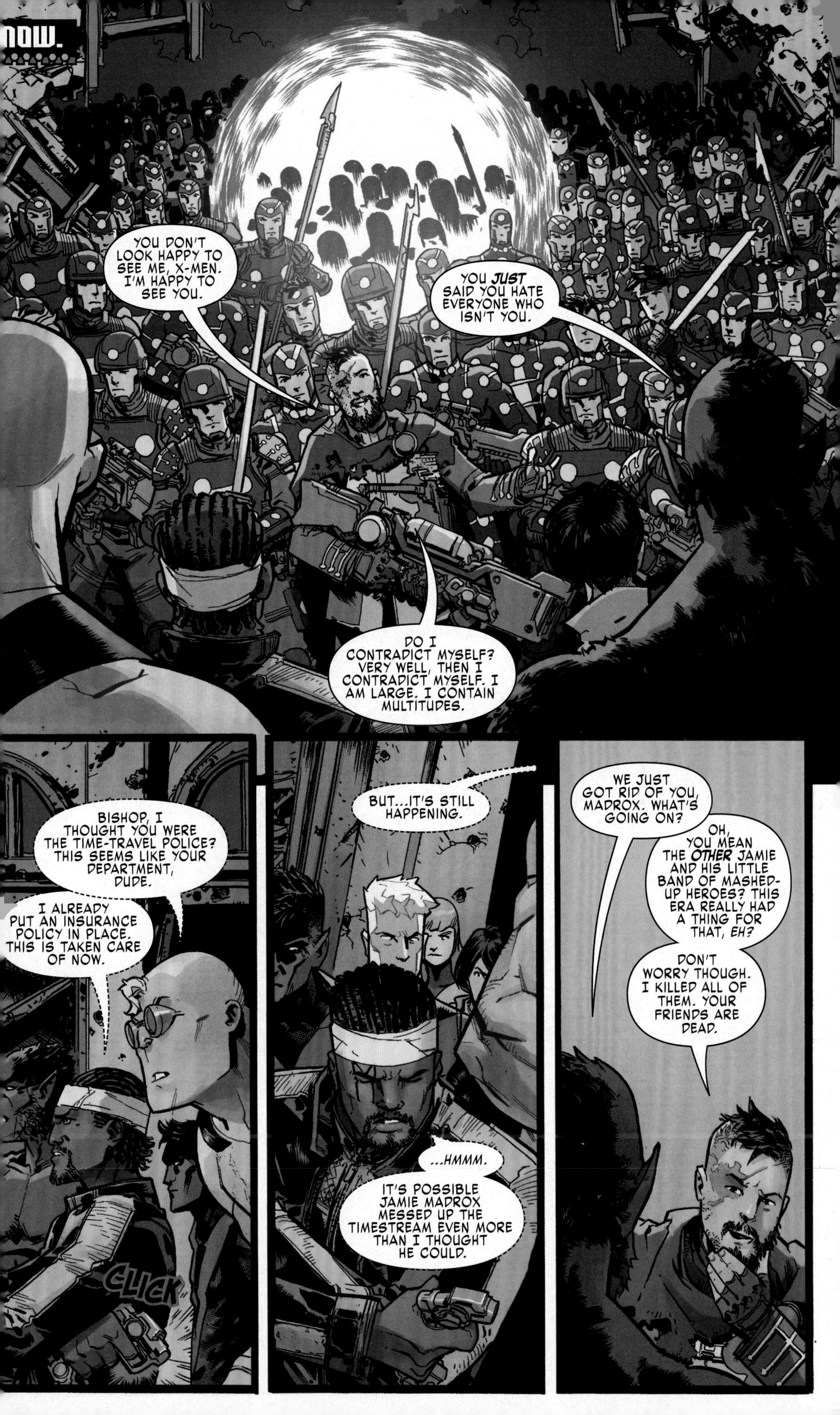
NOW.
YOU DON'T LOOK HAPPY TO SEE ME, X-MEN. I'M HAPPY TO SEE YOU.
YOU JUST SAID YOU HATE EVERYONE WHO ISN'T YOU.
DO I CONTRADICT MYSELF? VERY WELL, THEN I CONTRADICT MYSELF. I AM LARGE. I CONTAIN MULTITUDES.
BISHOP, I THOUGHT YOU WERE THE TIME-TRAVEL POLICE? THIS SEEMS LIKE YOUR DEPARTMENT, DUDE.
I ALREADY PUT AN INSURANCE POLICY IN PLACE. THIS IS TAKEN CARE OF NOW.
CLICK
BUT...IT'S STILL HAPPENING.
...HMMM.
IT'S POSSIBLE JAMIE MADROX MESSED UP THE TIMESTREAM EVEN MORE THAN I THOUGHT HE COULD.
WE JUST GOT RID OF YOU, MADROX. WHAT'S GOING ON?
OH, YOU MEAN THE OTHER JAMIE AND HIS LITTLE BAND OF MASHED-UP HEROES? THIS ERA REALLY HAD A THING FOR THAT, EH?
DON'T WORRY THOUGH. I KILLED ALL OF THEM. YOUR FRIENDS ARE DEAD.

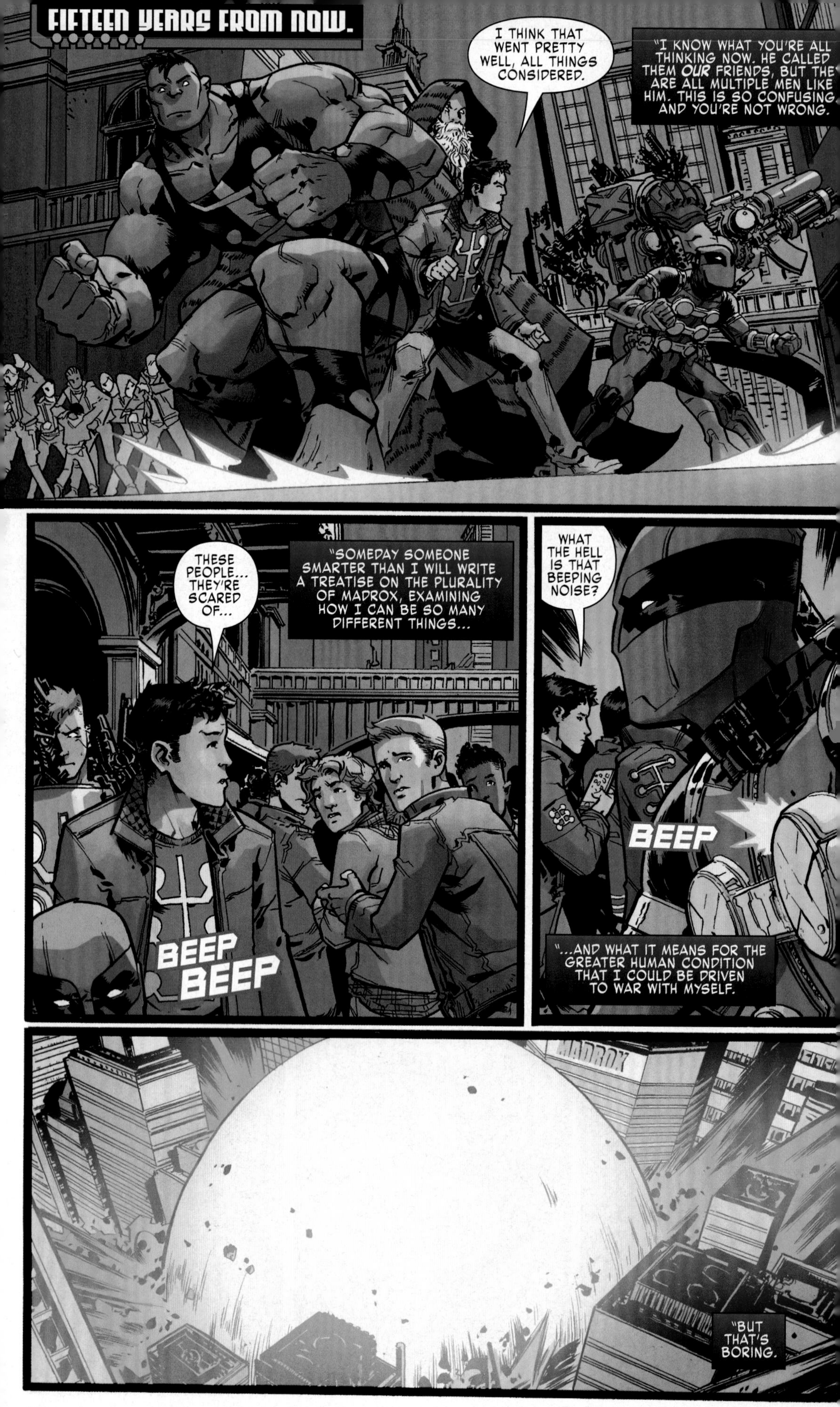
FIFTEEN YEARS FROM NOW.
I THINK THAT WENT PRETTY WELL, ALL THINGS CONSIDERED.
"I KNOW WHAT YOU'RE ALL THINKING NOW. HE CALLED THEM OUR FRIENDS, BUT THE ARE ALL MULTIPLE MEN LIKE HIM. THIS IS SO CONFUSING AND YOU'RE NOT WRONG.
THESE PEOPLE... THEY'RE SCARED OF...
"SOMEDAY SOMEONE SMARTER THAN I WILL WRITE A TREATISE ON THE PLURALITY OF MADROX, EXAMINING HOW I CAN BE SO MANY DIFFERENT THINGS...
BEEP BEEP
WHAT THE HELL IS THAT BEEPING NOISE?
BEEP
"...AND WHAT IT MEANS FOR THE GREATER HUMAN CONDITION THAT I COULD BE DRIVEN TO WAR WITH MYSELF.
MADROX
"BUT THAT'S BORING.

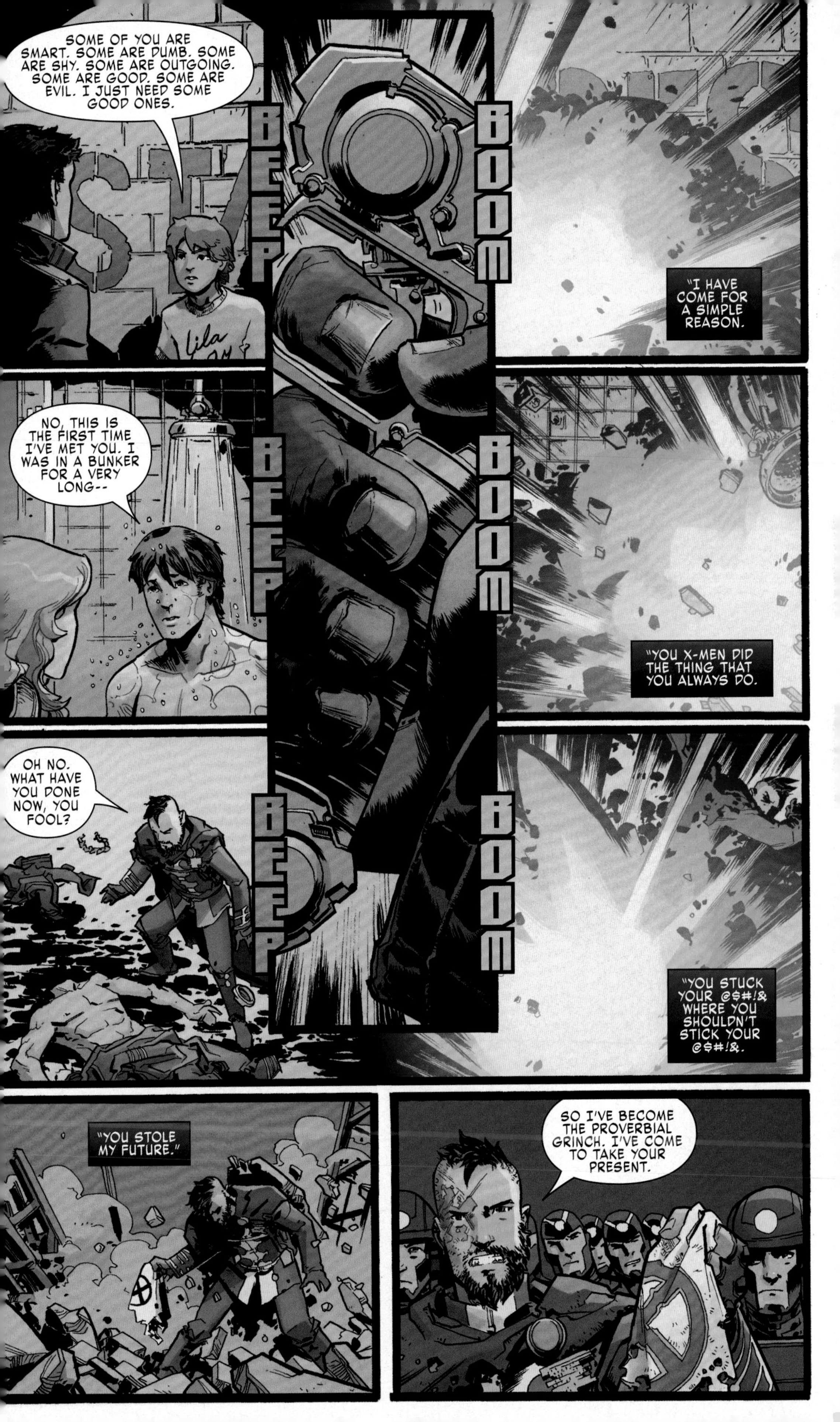
SOME OF YOU ARE SMART. SOME ARE DUMB. SOME ARE SHY. SOME ARE OUTGOING. SOME ARE GOOD. SOME ARE EVIL. I JUST NEED SOME GOOD ONES.
BEEP
BOOM
"I HAVE COME FOR A SIMPLE REASON.
NO, THIS IS THE FIRST TIME I'VE MET YOU. I WAS IN A BUNKER FOR A VERY LONG--
BEEP
BOOM
"YOU X-MEN DID THE THING THAT YOU ALWAYS DO.
OH NO. WHAT HAVE YOU DONE NOW, YOU FOOL?
BEEP
BOOM
"YOU STUCK YOUR @$#!& WHERE YOU SHOULDN'T STICK YOUR @$#!&.
"YOU STOLE MY FUTURE."
SO I'VE BECOME THE PROVERBIAL GRINCH. I'VE COME TO TAKE YOUR PRESENT.

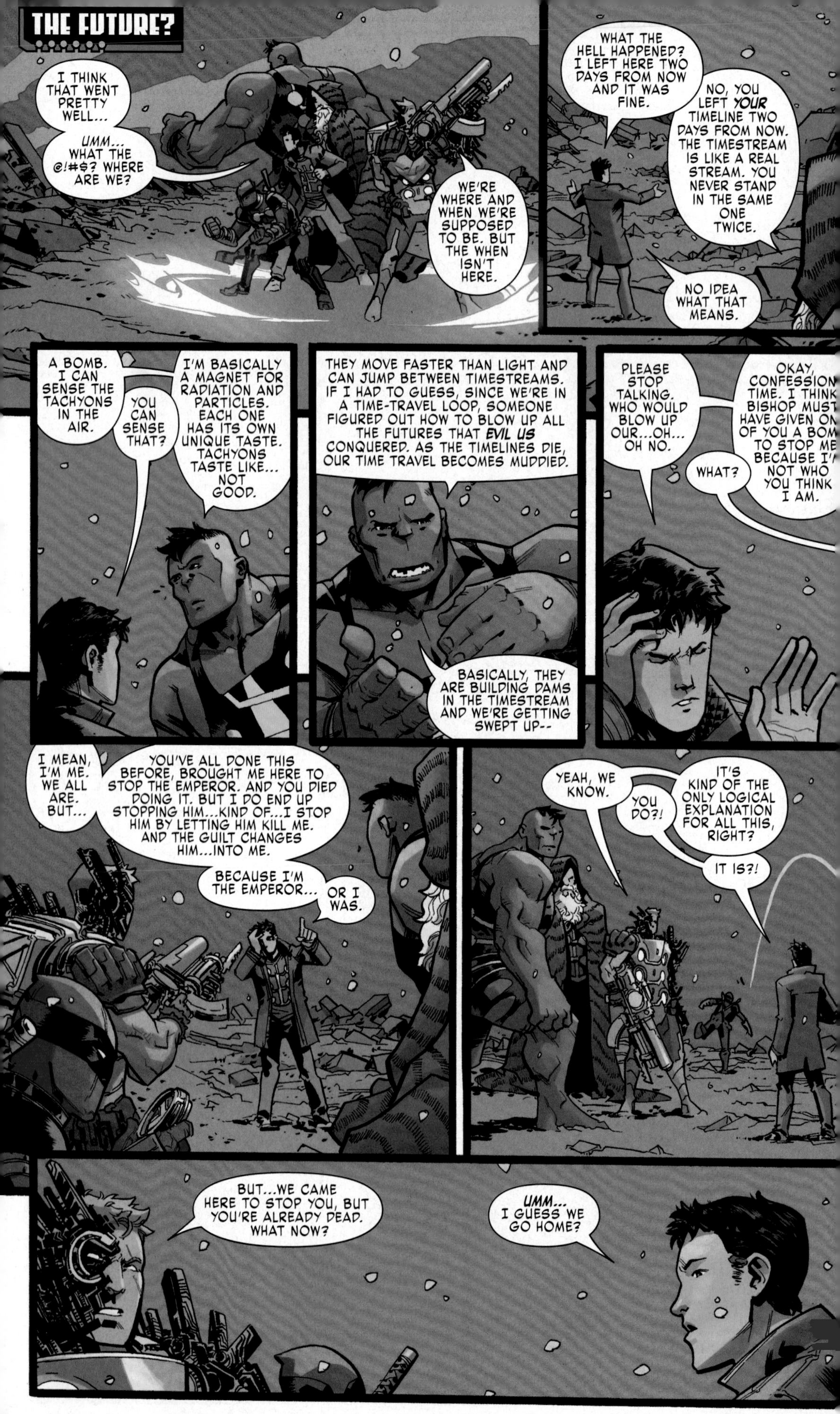
THE FUTURE?
I THINK THAT WENT PRETTY WELL...
UMM... WHAT THE @!#$? WHERE ARE WE?
WE'RE WHERE AND WHEN WE'RE SUPPOSED TO BE. BUT THE WHEN ISN'T HERE.
WHAT THE HELL HAPPENED? I LEFT HERE TWO DAYS FROM NOW AND IT WAS FINE.
NO, YOU LEFT YOUR TIMELINE TWO DAYS FROM NOW. THE TIMESTREAM IS LIKE A REAL STREAM. YOU NEVER STAND IN THE SAME ONE TWICE.
NO IDEA WHAT THAT MEANS.
A BOMB. I CAN SENSE THE TACHYONS IN THE AIR.
YOU CAN SENSE THAT?
I'M BASICALLY A MAGNET FOR RADIATION AND PARTICLES. EACH ONE HAS ITS OWN UNIQUE TASTE. TACHYONS TASTE LIKE... NOT GOOD.
THEY MOVE FASTER THAN LIGHT AND CAN JUMP BETWEEN TIMESTREAMS. IF I HAD TO GUESS, SINCE WE'RE IN A TIME-TRAVEL LOOP, SOMEONE FIGURED OUT HOW TO BLOW UP ALL THE FUTURES THAT EVIL US CONQUERED. AS THE TIMELINES DIE, OUR TIME TRAVEL BECOMES MUDDIED.
BASICALLY, THEY ARE BUILDING DAMS IN THE TIMESTREAM AND WE'RE GETTING SWEPT UP--
PLEASE STOP TALKING. WHO WOULD BLOW UP OUR...OH... OH NO.
OKAY, CONFESSION TIME. I THINK BISHOP MUST HAVE GIVEN ON OF YOU A BOM TO STOP ME BECAUSE I' NOT WHO YOU THINK I AM.
WHAT?
I MEAN, I'M ME. WE ALL ARE. BUT...
YOU'VE ALL DONE THIS BEFORE, BROUGHT ME HERE TO STOP THE EMPEROR. AND YOU DIED DOING IT. BUT I DO END UP STOPPING HIM...KIND OF...I STOP HIM BY LETTING HIM KILL ME. AND THE GUILT CHANGES HIM...INTO ME.
BECAUSE I'M THE EMPEROR...
OR I WAS.
YEAH, WE KNOW.
YOU DO?!
IT'S KIND OF THE ONLY LOGICAL EXPLANATION FOR ALL THIS, RIGHT?
IT IS?!
BUT...WE CAME HERE TO STOP YOU, BUT YOU'RE ALREADY DEAD. WHAT NOW?
UMM... I GUESS WE GO HOME?

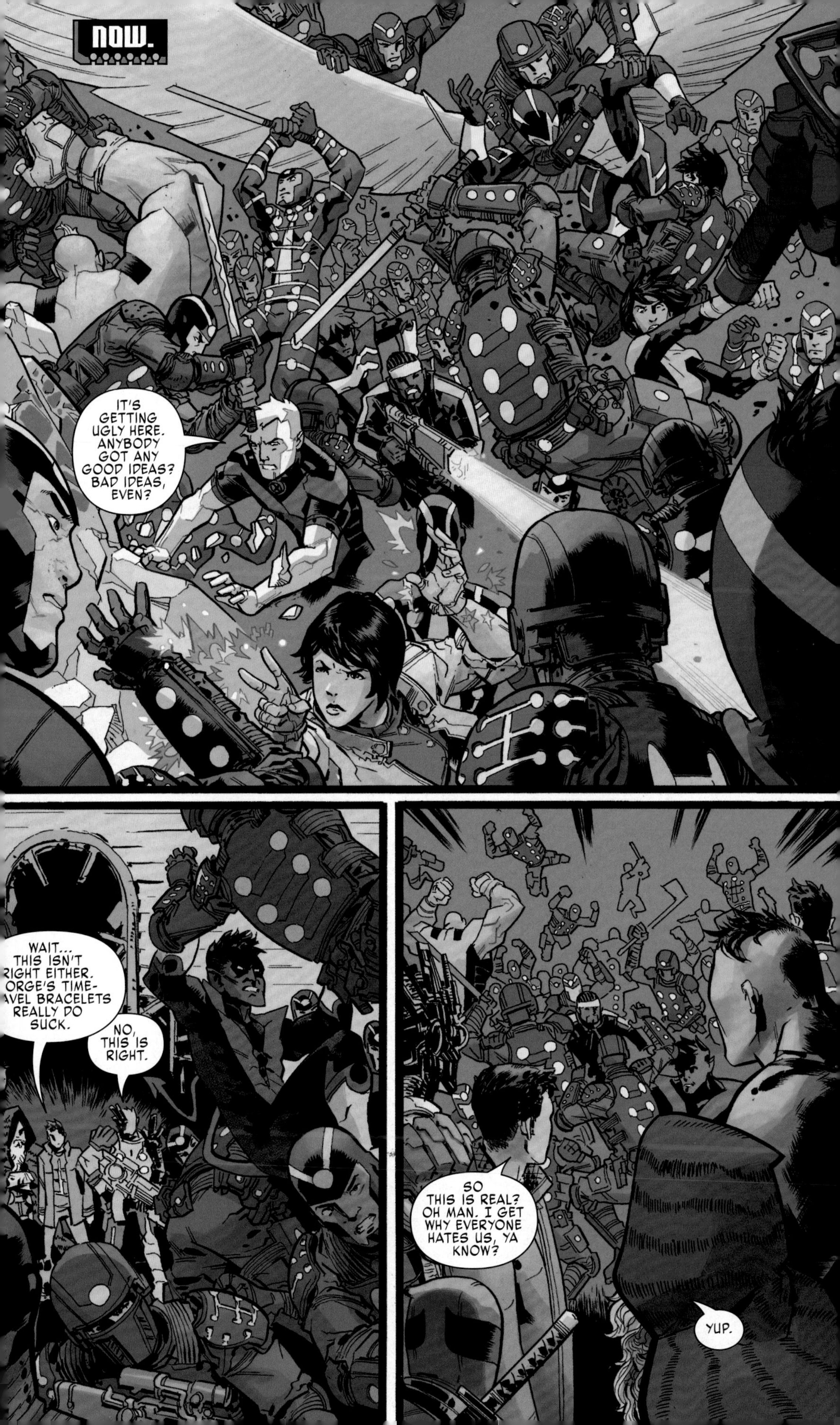
NOW.
IT'S GETTING UGLY HERE. ANYBODY GOT ANY GOOD IDEAS? BAD IDEAS, EVEN?
WAIT... THIS ISN'T IGHT EITHER. ORGE'S TIME-AVEL BRACELETS REALLY DO SUCK.
NO, THIS IS RIGHT.
SO THIS IS REAL? OH MAN. I GET WHY EVERYONE HATES US, YA KNOW?
YUP.

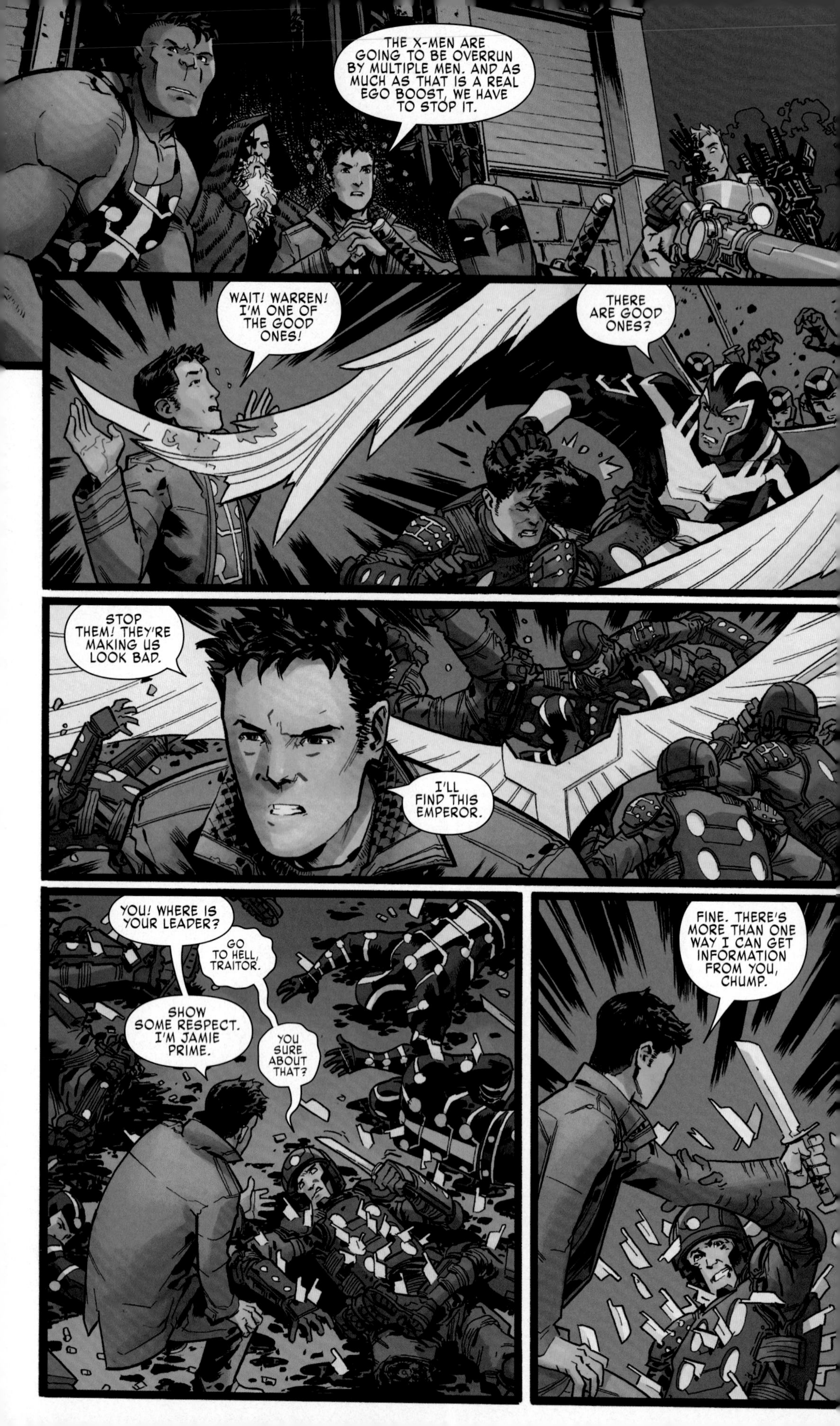
THE X-MEN ARE GOING TO BE OVERRUN BY MULTIPLE MEN. AND AS MUCH AS THAT IS A REAL EGO BOOST, WE HAVE TO STOP IT.
WAIT! WARREN! I'M ONE OF THE GOOD ONES!
THERE ARE GOOD ONES?
STOP THEM! THEY'RE MAKING US LOOK BAD.
I'LL FIND THIS EMPEROR.
YOU! WHERE IS YOUR LEADER?
GO TO HELL, TRAITOR.
SHOW SOME RESPECT. I'M JAMIE PRIME.
YOU SURE ABOUT THAT?
FINE. THERE'S MORE THAN ONE WAY I CAN GET INFORMATION FROM YOU, CHUMP.

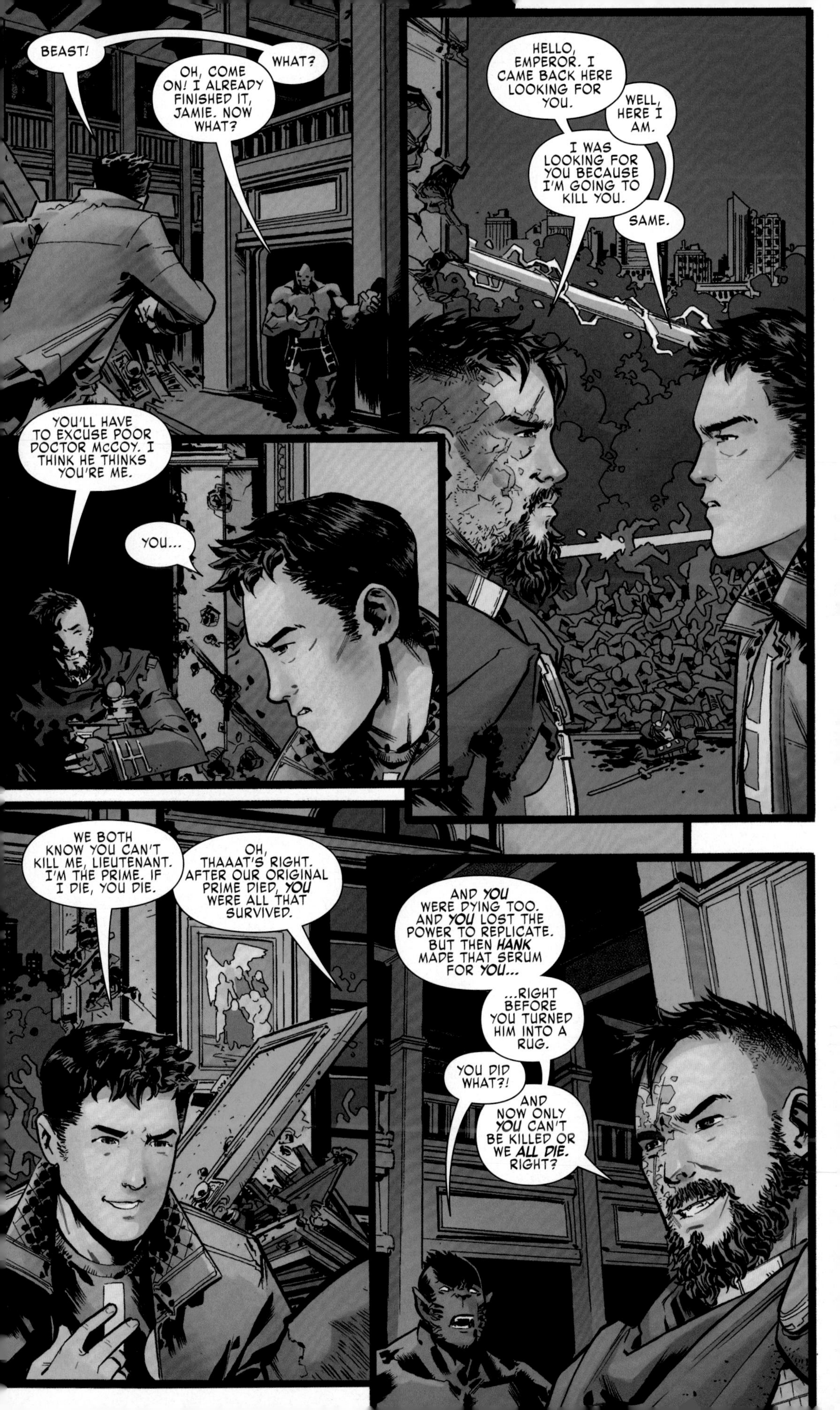
BEAST!
WHAT?
OH, COME ON! I ALREADY FINISHED IT, JAMIE. NOW WHAT?
HELLO, EMPEROR. I CAME BACK HERE LOOKING FOR YOU.
WELL, HERE I AM.
I WAS LOOKING FOR YOU BECAUSE I'M GOING TO KILL YOU.
SAME.
YOU'LL HAVE TO EXCUSE POOR DOCTOR McCOY. I THINK HE THINKS YOU'RE ME.
YOU...
WE BOTH KNOW YOU CAN'T KILL ME, LIEUTENANT. I'M THE PRIME. IF I DIE, YOU DIE.
OH, THAAAT'S RIGHT. AFTER OUR ORIGINAL PRIME DIED, YOU WERE ALL THAT SURVIVED.
AND YOU WERE DYING TOO. AND YOU LOST THE POWER TO REPLICATE. BUT THEN HANK MADE THAT SERUM FOR YOU...
...RIGHT BEFORE YOU TURNED HIM INTO A RUG.
YOU DID WHAT?!
AND NOW ONLY YOU CAN'T BE KILLED OR WE ALL DIE. RIGHT?

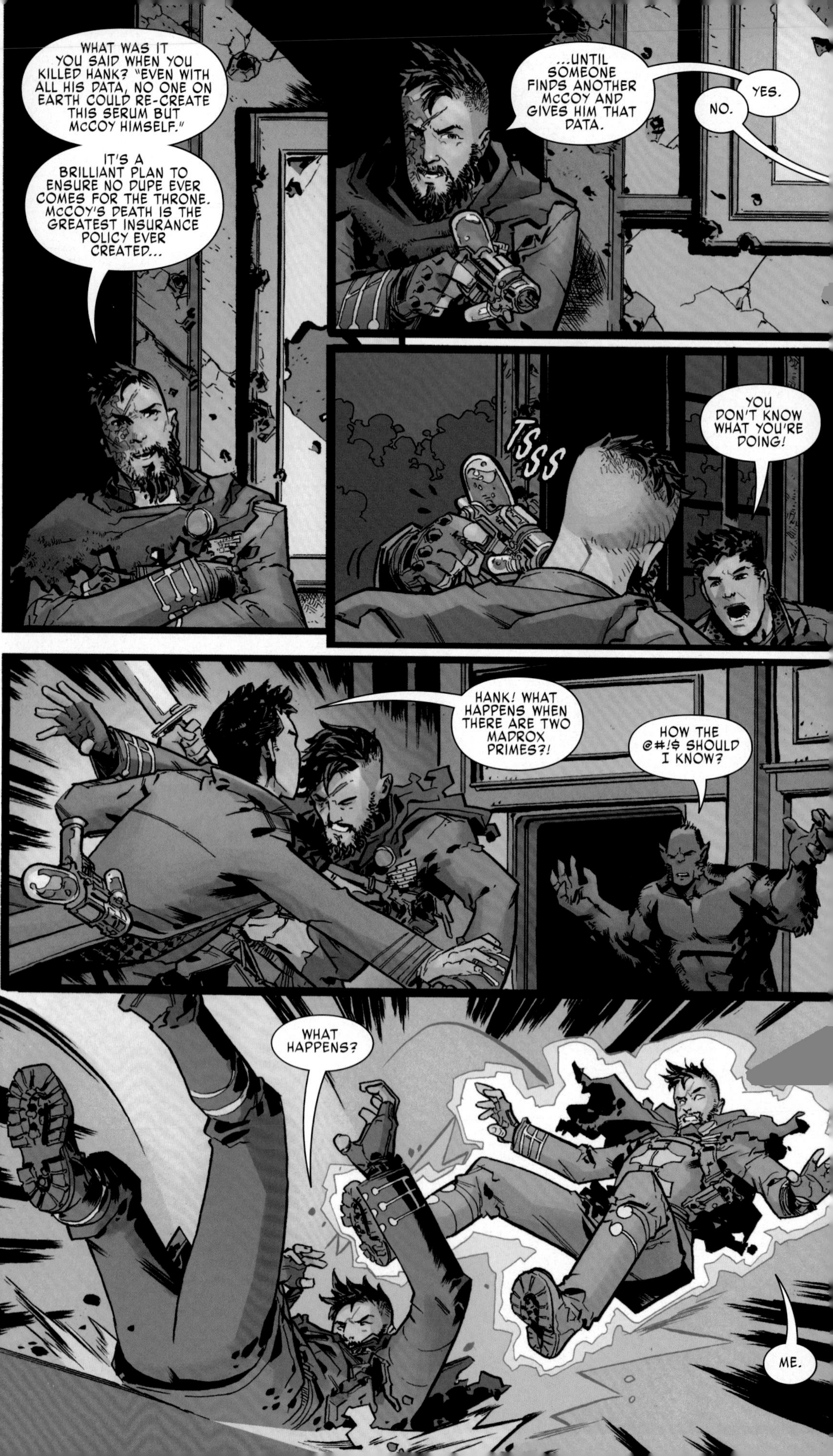
WHAT WAS IT YOU SAID WHEN YOU KILLED HANK? "EVEN WITH ALL HIS DATA, NO ONE ON EARTH COULD RE-CREATE THIS SERUM BUT McCOY HIMSELF."
IT'S A BRILLIANT PLAN TO ENSURE NO DUPE EVER COMES FOR THE THRONE. McCOY'S DEATH IS THE GREATEST INSURANCE POLICY EVER CREATED...
...UNTIL SOMEONE FINDS ANOTHER McCOY AND GIVES HIM THAT DATA.
YES.
NO.
TSSS
YOU DON'T KNOW WHAT YOU'RE DOING!
HANK! WHAT HAPPENS WHEN THERE ARE TWO MADROX PRIMES?!
HOW THE @#!$ SHOULD I KNOW?
WHAT HAPPENS?
ME.

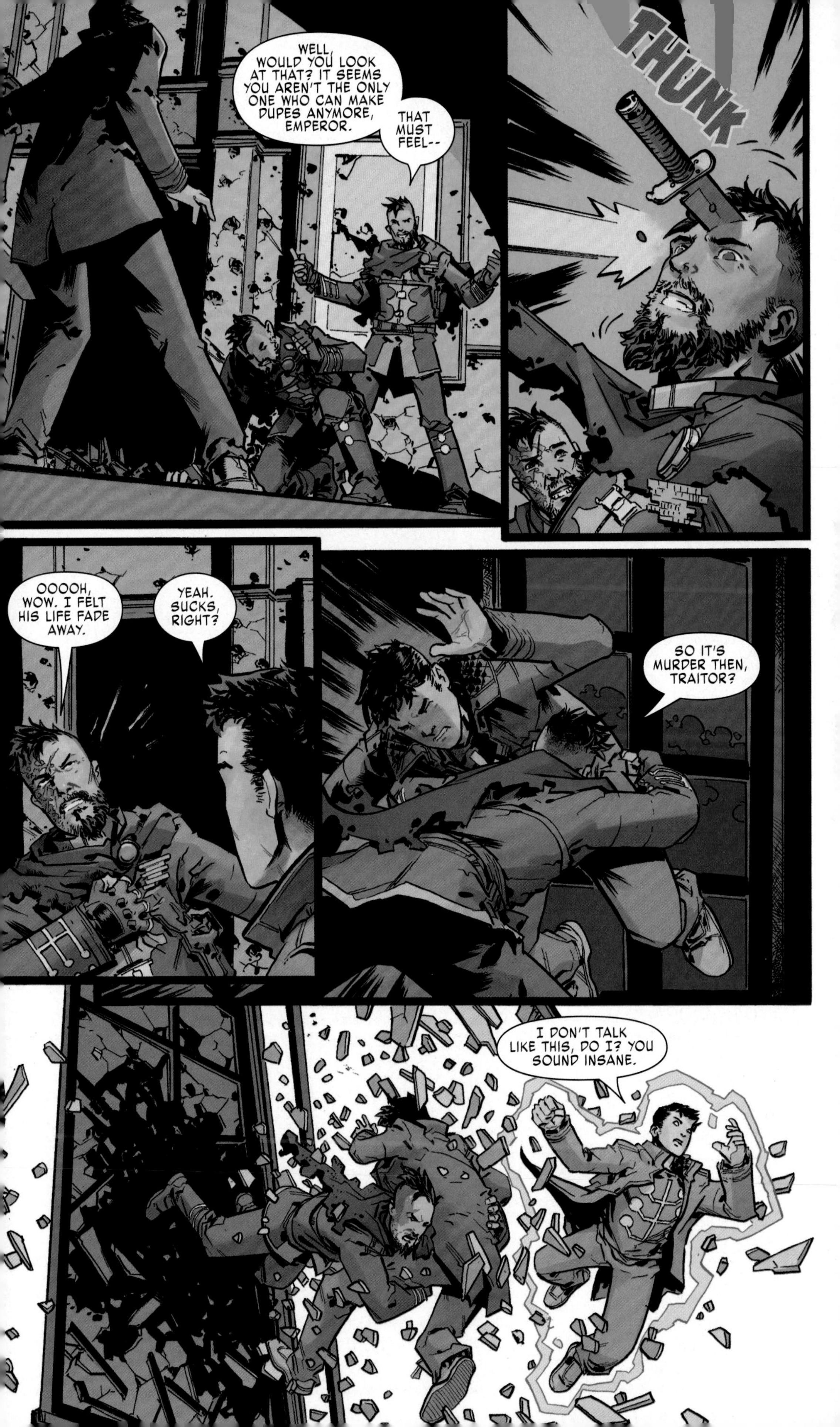
WELL, WOULD YOU LOOK AT THAT? IT SEEMS YOU AREN'T THE ONLY ONE WHO CAN MAKE DUPES ANYMORE, EMPEROR.
THAT MUST FEEL--
THUNK
OOOOH, WOW. I FELT HIS LIFE FADE AWAY.
YEAH. SUCKS, RIGHT?
SO IT'S MURDER THEN, TRAITOR?
I DON'T TALK LIKE THIS, DO I? YOU SOUND INSANE.

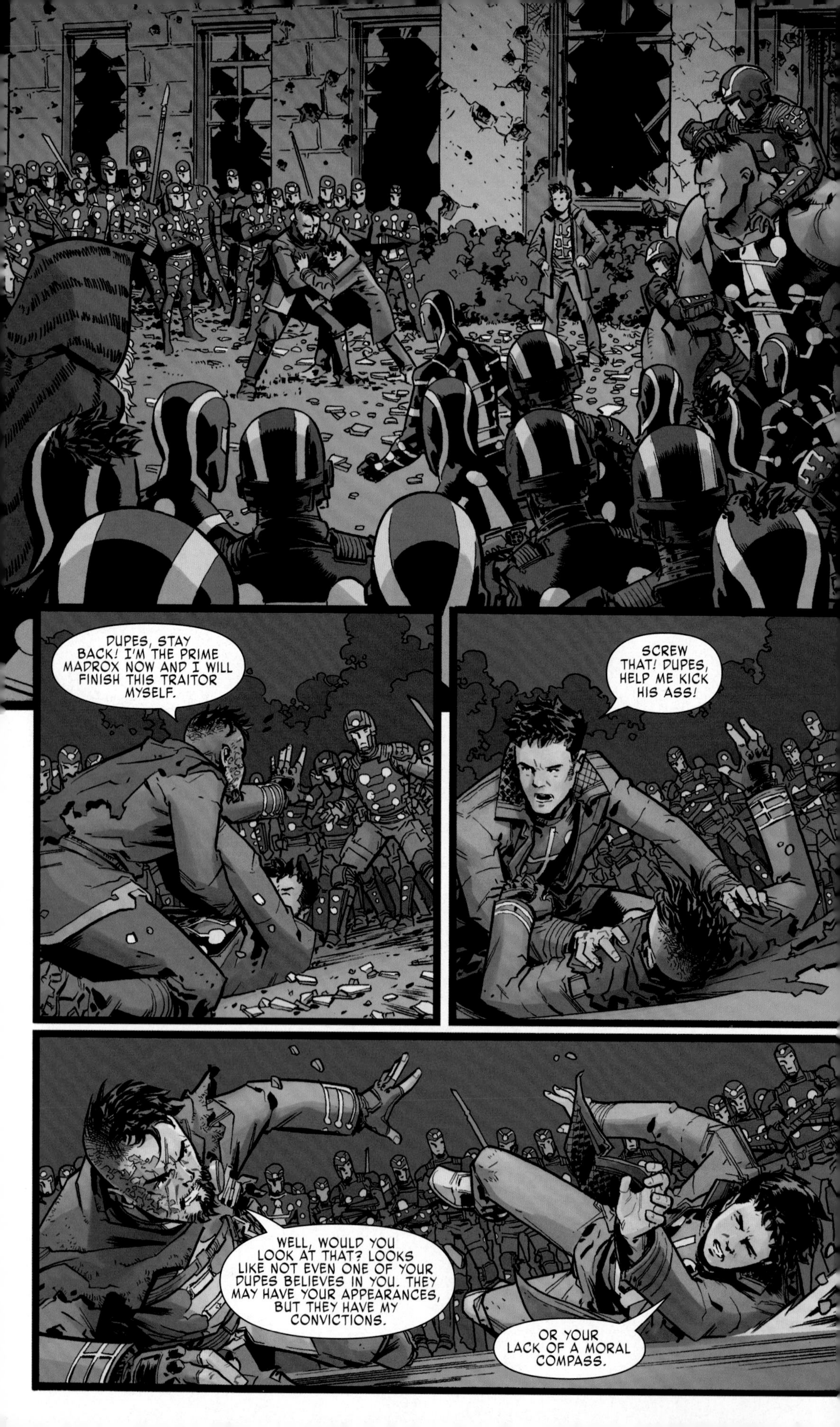
DUPES, STAY BACK! I'M THE PRIME MADROX NOW AND I WILL FINISH THIS TRAITOR MYSELF.
SCREW THAT! DUPES, HELP ME KICK HIS ASS!
WELL, WOULD YOU LOOK AT THAT? LOOKS LIKE NOT EVEN ONE OF YOUR DUPES BELIEVES IN YOU. THEY MAY HAVE YOUR APPEARANCES, BUT THEY HAVE MY CONVICTIONS.
OR YOUR LACK OF A MORAL COMPASS.

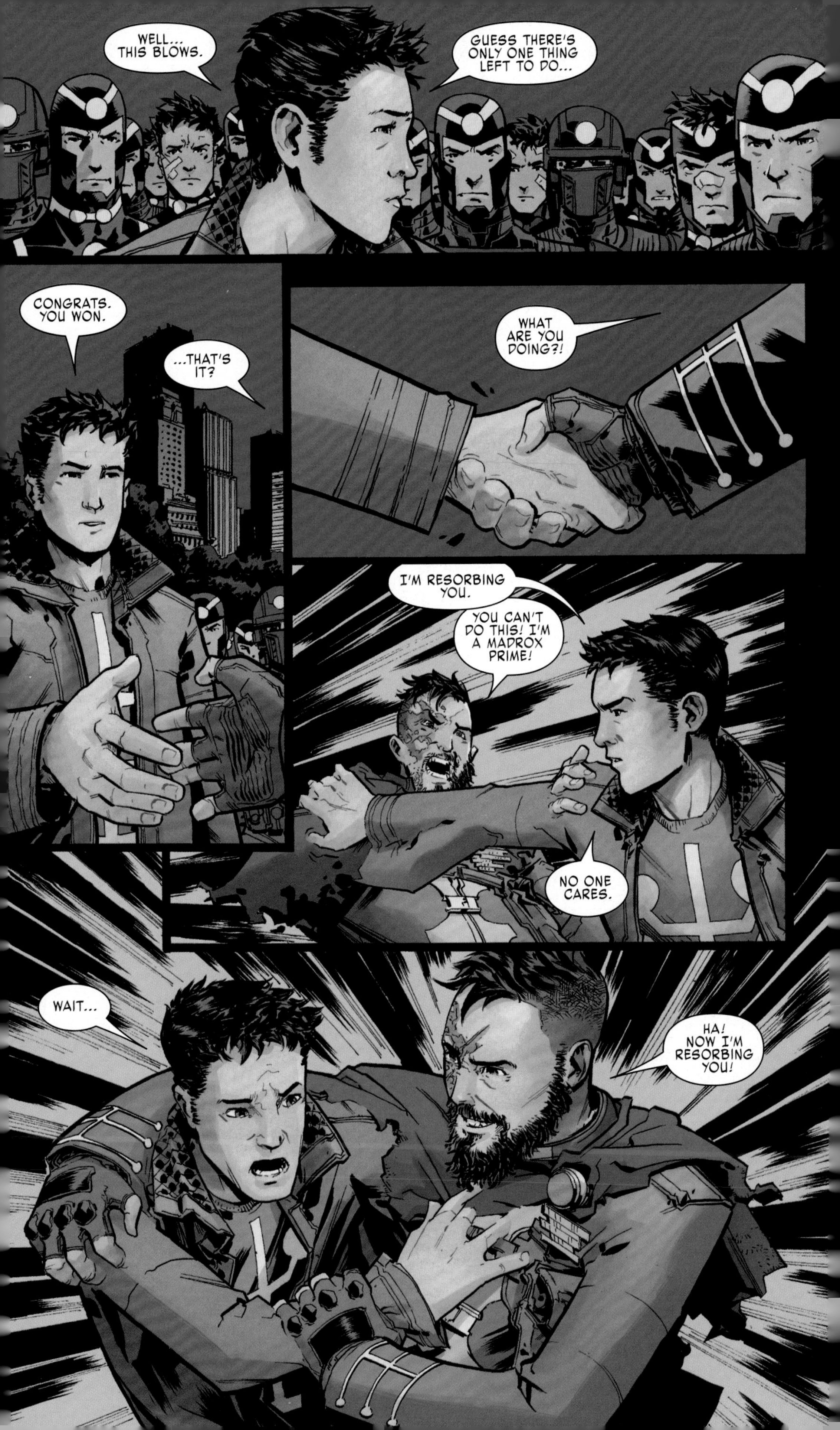
WELL... THIS BLOWS.
GUESS THERE'S ONLY ONE THING LEFT TO DO...
CONGRATS. YOU WON.
...THAT'S IT?
WHAT ARE YOU DOING?!
I'M RESORBING YOU.
YOU CAN'T DO THIS! I'M A MADROX PRIME!
NO ONE CARES.
WAIT...
HA! NOW I'M RESORBING YOU!

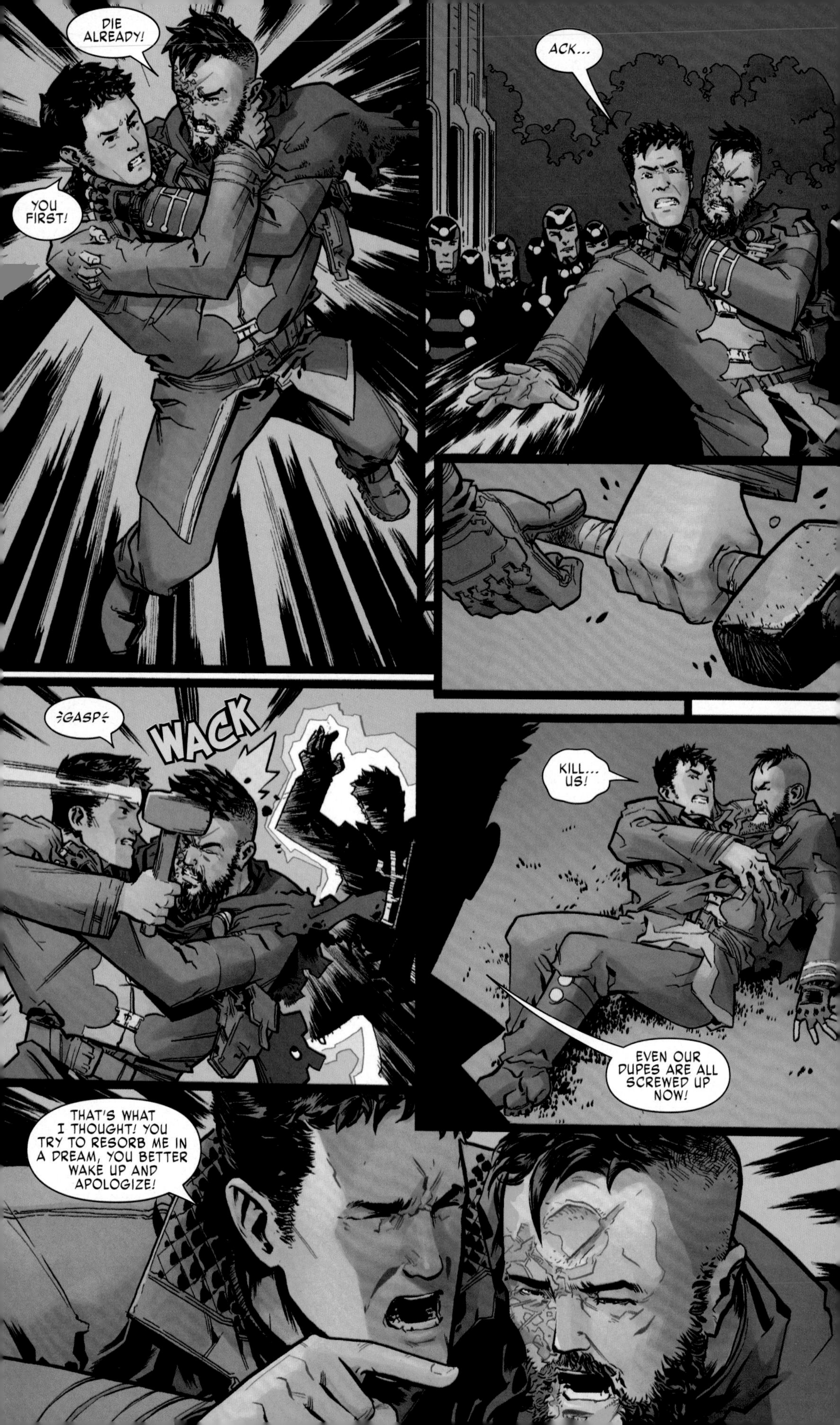
DIE ALREADY!
YOU FIRST!
ACK...
=GASP=
WACK
KILL... US!
EVEN OUR DUPES ARE ALL SCREWED UP NOW!
THAT'S WHAT I THOUGHT! YOU TRY TO RESORB ME IN A DREAM, YOU BETTER WAKE UP AND APOLOGIZE!

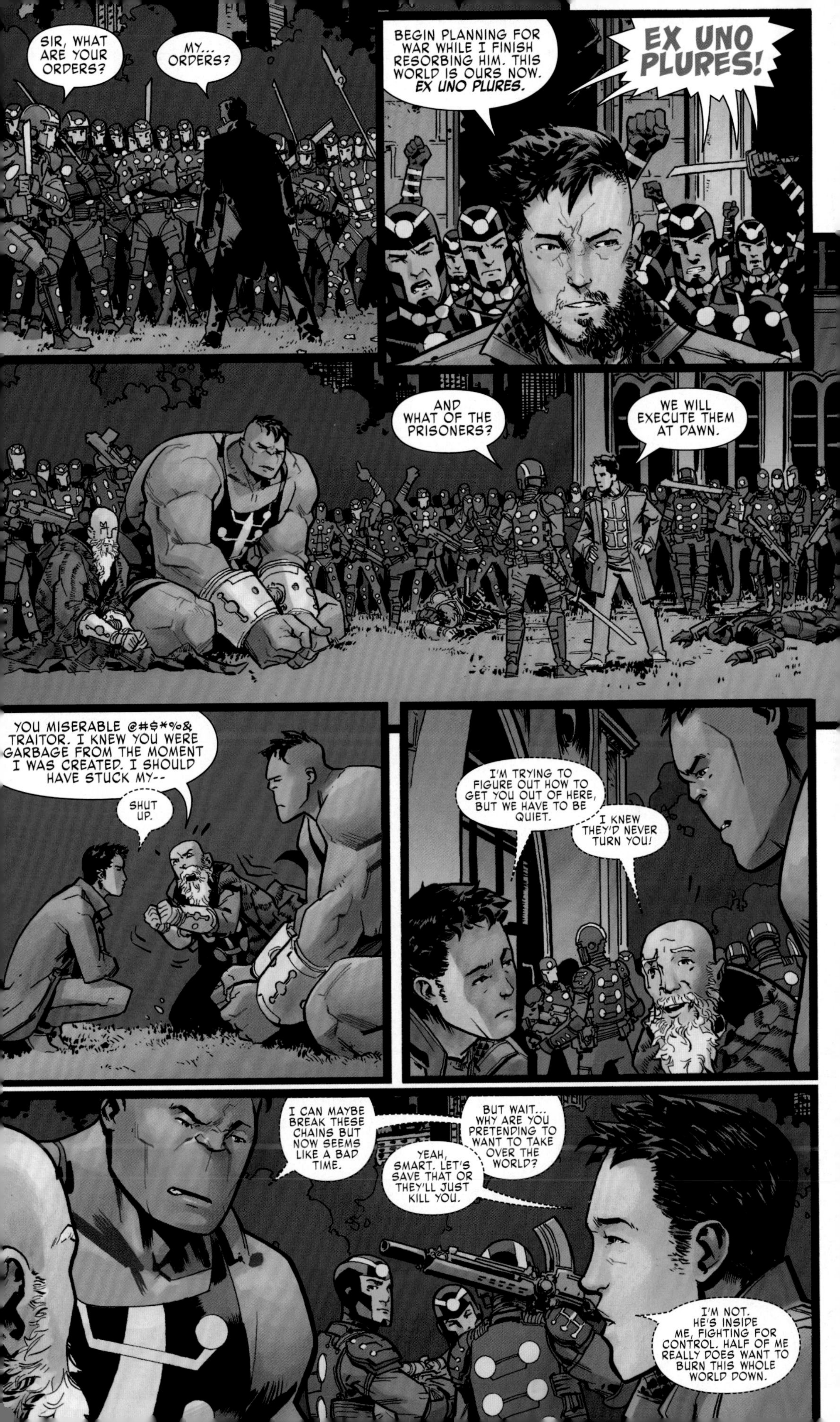

SIR, WHAT ARE YOUR ORDERS?
MY... ORDERS?
BEGIN PLANNING FOR WAR WHILE I FINISH RESORBING HIM. THIS WORLD IS OURS NOW. EX UNO PLURES.
EX UNO PLURES!
AND WHAT OF THE PRISONERS?
WE WILL EXECUTE THEM AT DAWN.
YOU MISERABLE @#$*%& TRAITOR. I KNEW YOU WERE GARBAGE FROM THE MOMENT I WAS CREATED. I SHOULD HAVE STUCK MY--
SHUT UP.
I'M TRYING TO FIGURE OUT HOW TO GET YOU OUT OF HERE, BUT WE HAVE TO BE QUIET.
I KNEW THEY'D NEVER TURN YOU!
I CAN MAYBE BREAK THESE CHAINS BUT NOW SEEMS LIKE A BAD TIME.
BUT WAIT... WHY ARE YOU PRETENDING TO WANT TO TAKE OVER THE WORLD?
YEAH, SMART. LET'S SAVE THAT OR THEY'LL JUST KILL YOU.
I'M NOT. HE'S INSIDE ME, FIGHTING FOR CONTROL. HALF OF ME REALLY DOES WANT TO BURN THIS WHOLE WORLD DOWN.

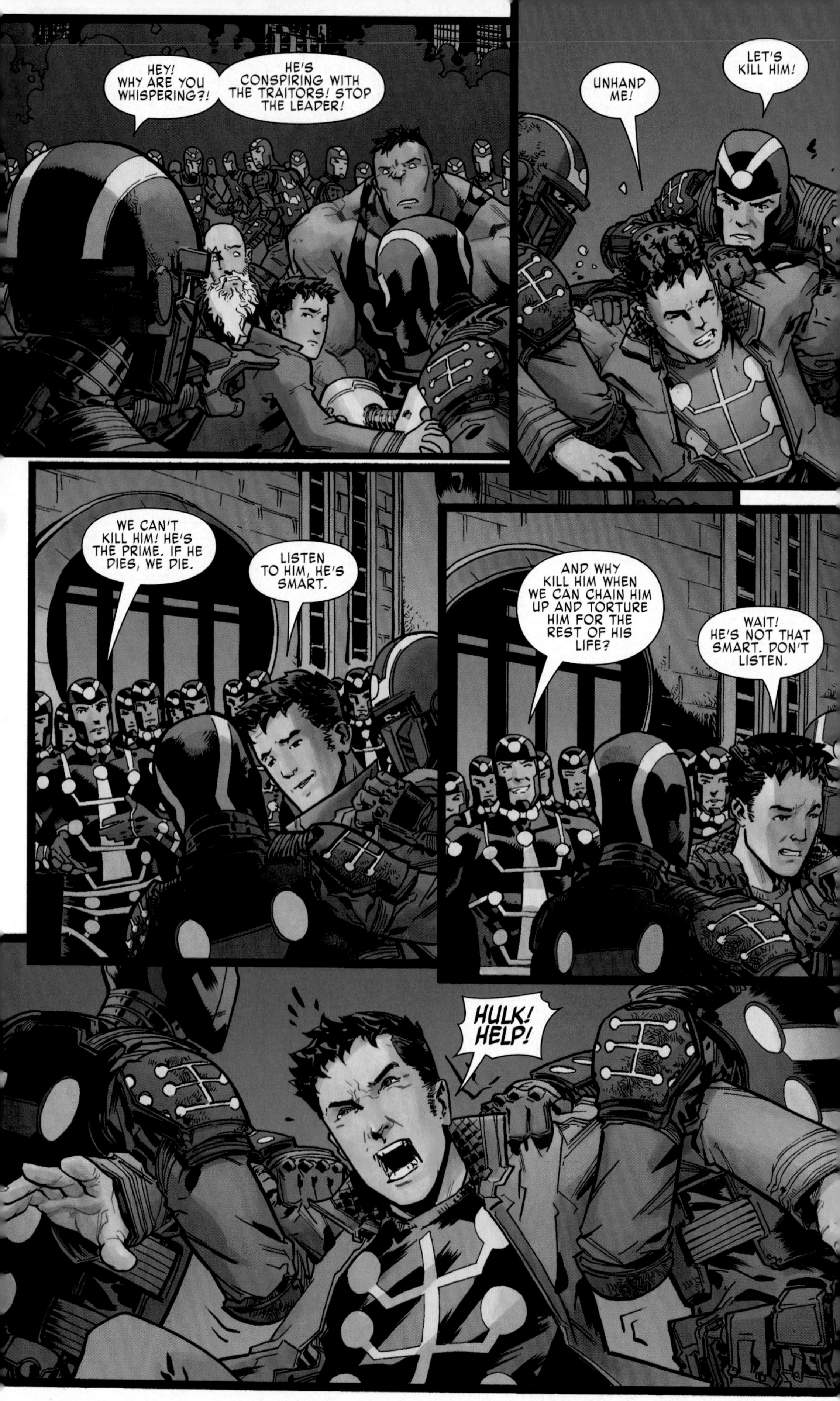
HEY! WHY ARE YOU WHISPERING?!
HE'S CONSPIRING WITH THE TRAITORS! STOP THE LEADER!
UNHAND ME!
LET'S KILL HIM!
WE CAN'T KILL HIM! HE'S THE PRIME. IF HE DIES, WE DIE.
LISTEN TO HIM, HE'S SMART.
AND WHY KILL HIM WHEN WE CAN CHAIN HIM UP AND TORTURE HIM FOR THE REST OF HIS LIFE?
WAIT! HE'S NOT THAT SMART. DON'T LISTEN.
HULK! HELP!

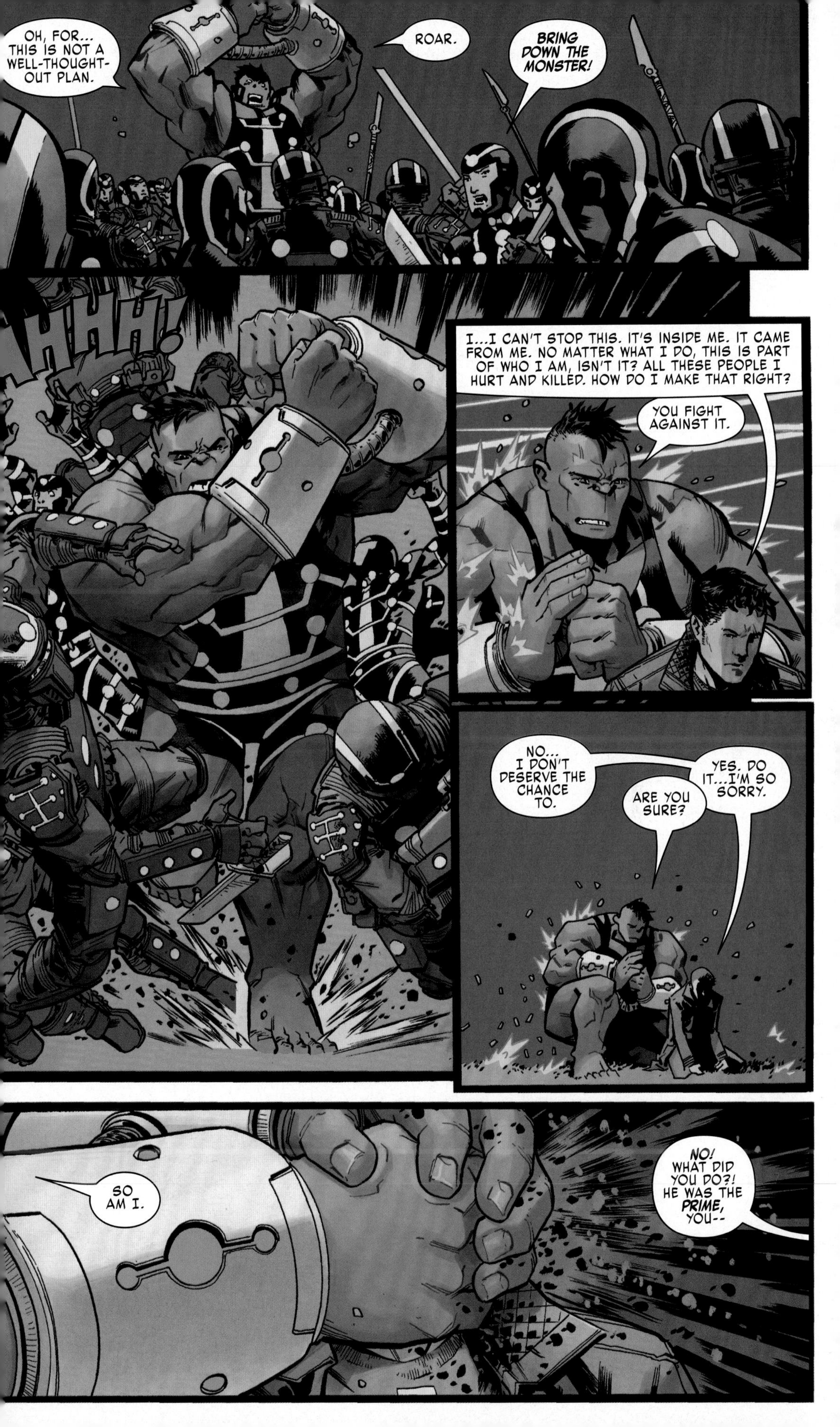
OH, FOR... THIS IS NOT A WELL-THOUGHT-OUT PLAN.
ROAR.
BRING DOWN THE MONSTER!
HHH!
I...I CAN'T STOP THIS. IT'S INSIDE ME. IT CAME FROM ME. NO MATTER WHAT I DO, THIS IS PART OF WHO I AM, ISN'T IT? ALL THESE PEOPLE I HURT AND KILLED. HOW DO I MAKE THAT RIGHT?
YOU FIGHT AGAINST IT.
NO... I DON'T DESERVE THE CHANCE TO.
ARE YOU SURE?
YES. DO IT...I'M SO SORRY.
SO AM I.
NO! WHAT DID YOU DO?! HE WAS THE PRIME, YOU--

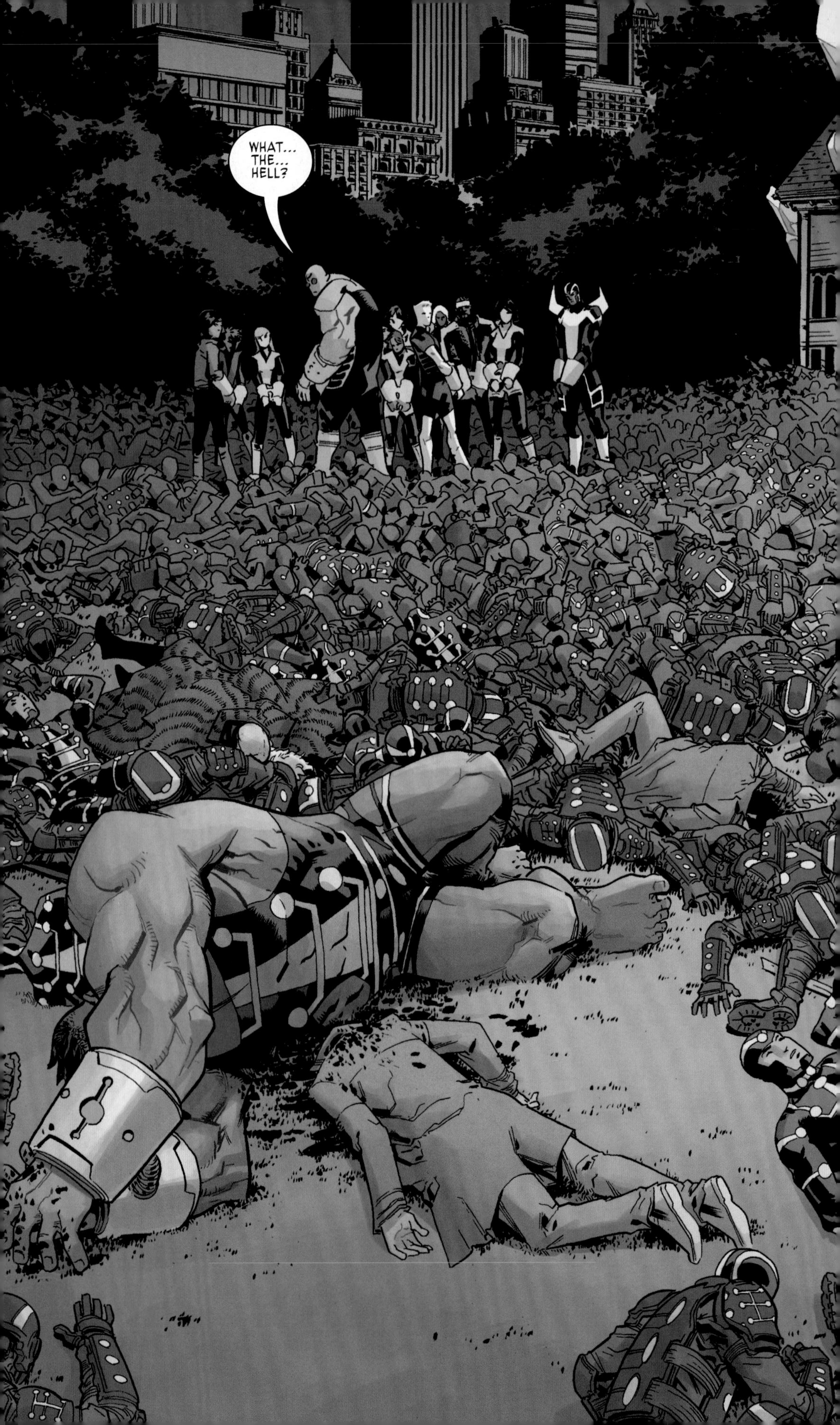
WHAT... THE... HELL?

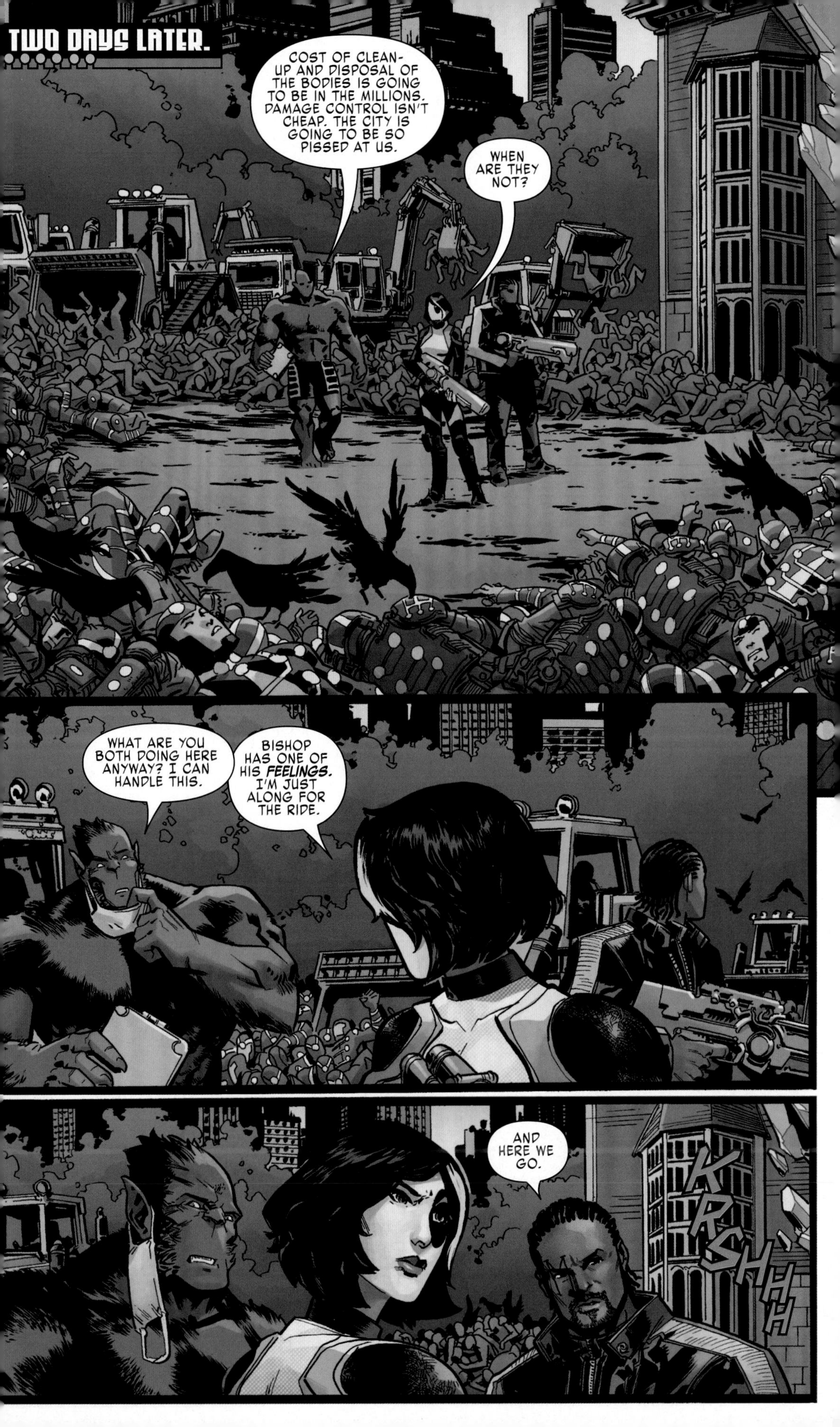
TWO DAYS LATER.
COST OF CLEAN-UP AND DISPOSAL OF THE BODIES IS GOING TO BE IN THE MILLIONS. DAMAGE CONTROL ISN'T CHEAP. THE CITY IS GOING TO BE SO PISSED AT US.
WHEN ARE THEY NOT?
WHAT ARE YOU BOTH DOING HERE ANYWAY? I CAN HANDLE THIS.
BISHOP HAS ONE OF HIS *FEELINGS.* I'M JUST ALONG FOR THE RIDE.
AND HERE WE GO.
KRSHHH

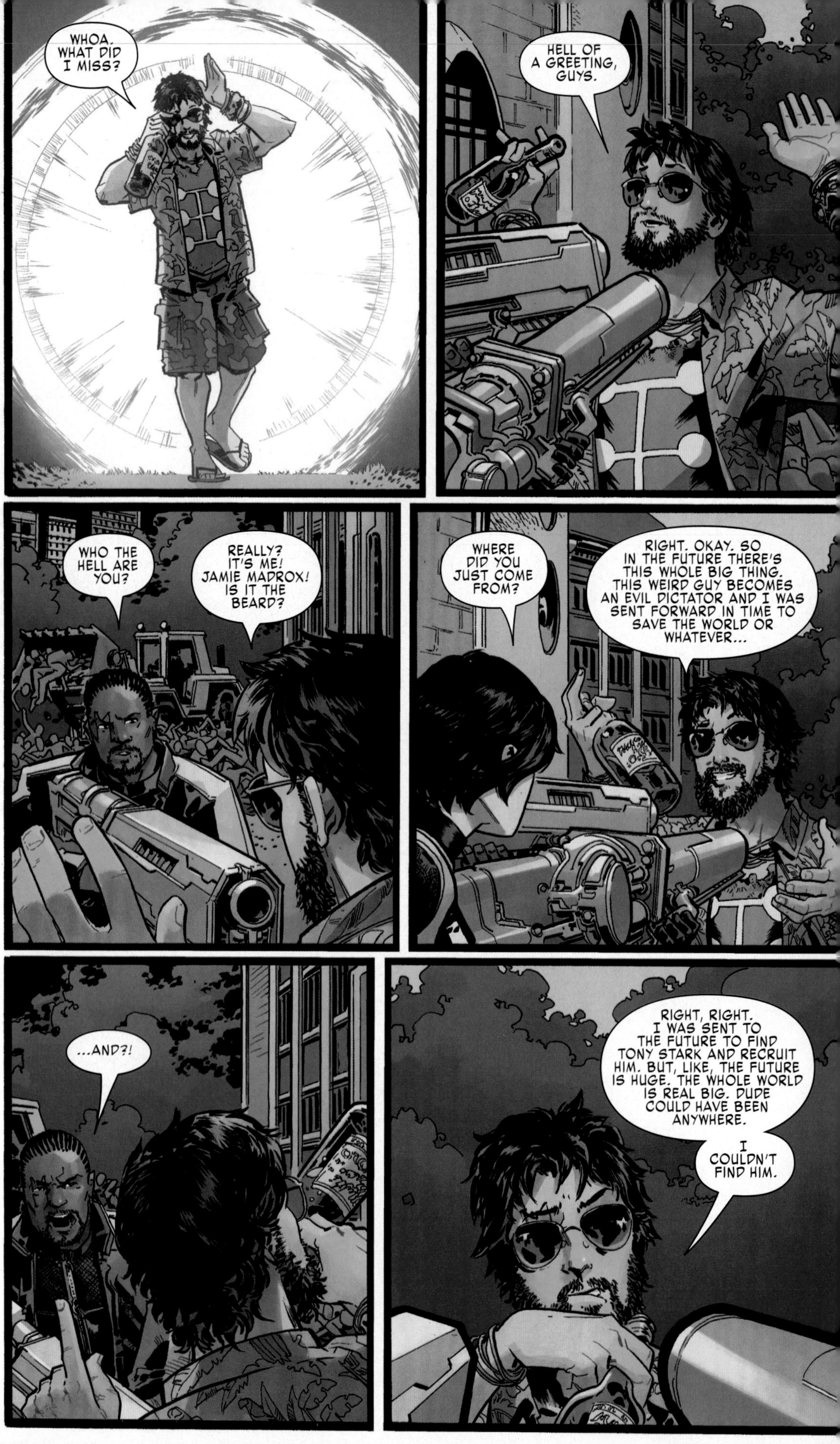
WHOA. WHAT DID I MISS?
HELL OF A GREETING, GUYS.
WHO THE HELL ARE YOU?
REALLY? IT'S ME! JAMIE MADROX! IS IT THE BEARD?
WHERE DID YOU JUST COME FROM?
RIGHT. OKAY. SO IN THE FUTURE THERE'S THIS WHOLE BIG THING. THIS WEIRD GUY BECOMES AN EVIL DICTATOR AND I WAS SENT FORWARD IN TIME TO SAVE THE WORLD OR WHATEVER...
...AND?!
RIGHT, RIGHT. I WAS SENT TO THE FUTURE TO FIND TONY STARK AND RECRUIT HIM. BUT, LIKE, THE FUTURE IS HUGE. THE WHOLE WORLD IS REAL BIG. DUDE COULD HAVE BEEN ANYWHERE.
I COULDN'T FIND HIM.

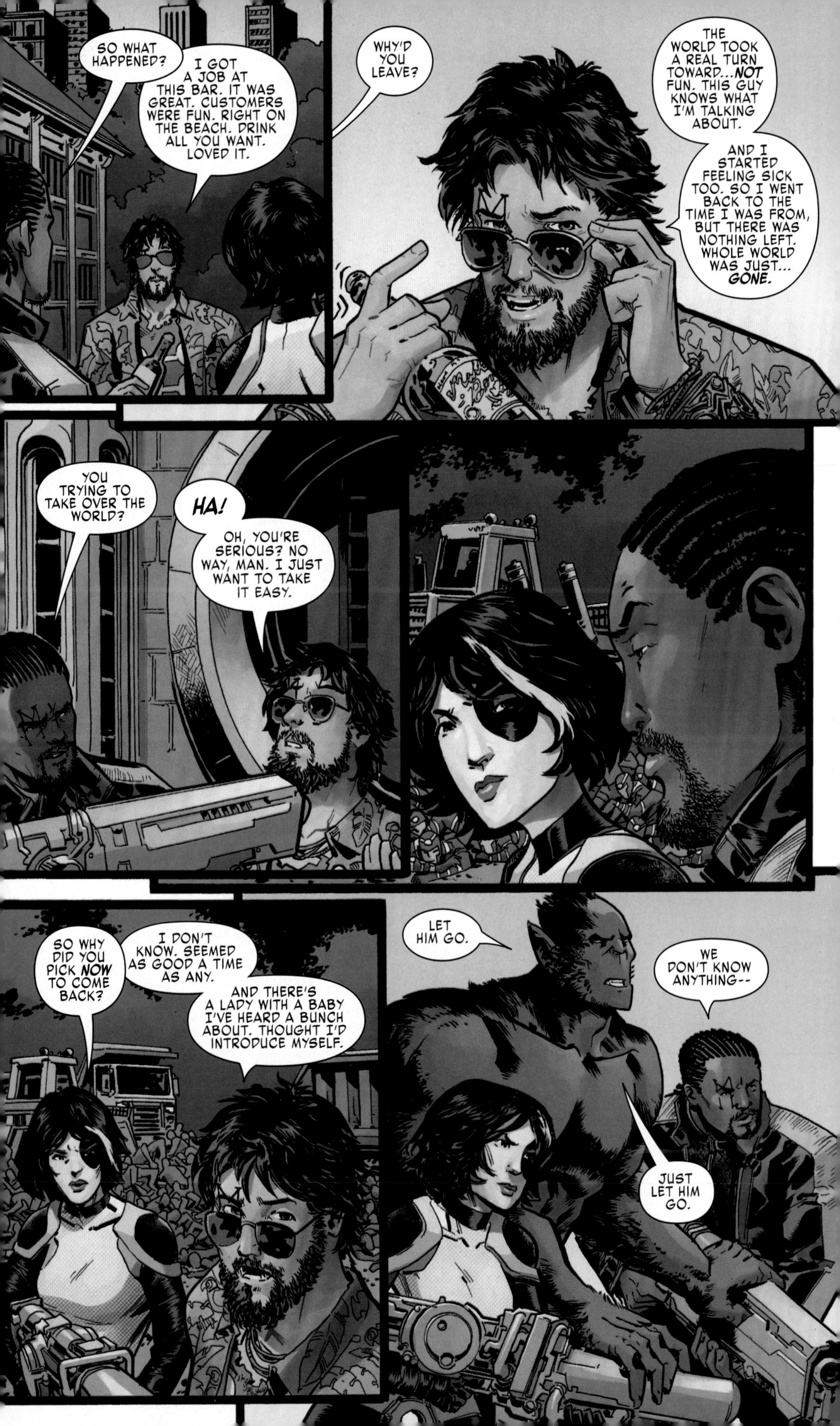
SO WHAT HAPPENED?
I GOT A JOB AT THIS BAR. IT WAS GREAT. CUSTOMERS WERE FUN. RIGHT ON THE BEACH. DRINK ALL YOU WANT. LOVED IT.
WHY'D YOU LEAVE?
THE WORLD TOOK A REAL TURN TOWARD...**NOT** FUN. THIS GUY KNOWS WHAT I'M TALKING ABOUT.
AND I STARTED FEELING SICK TOO. SO I WENT BACK TO THE TIME I WAS FROM, BUT THERE WAS NOTHING LEFT. WHOLE WORLD WAS JUST... **GONE.**
YOU TRYING TO TAKE OVER THE WORLD?
HA!
OH, YOU'RE SERIOUS? NO WAY, MAN. I JUST WANT TO TAKE IT EASY.
SO WHY DID YOU PICK **NOW** TO COME BACK?
I DON'T KNOW. SEEMED AS GOOD A TIME AS ANY.
AND THERE'S A LADY WITH A BABY I'VE HEARD A BUNCH ABOUT. THOUGHT I'D INTRODUCE MYSELF.
LET HIM GO.
WE DON'T KNOW ANYTHING--
JUST LET HIM GO.

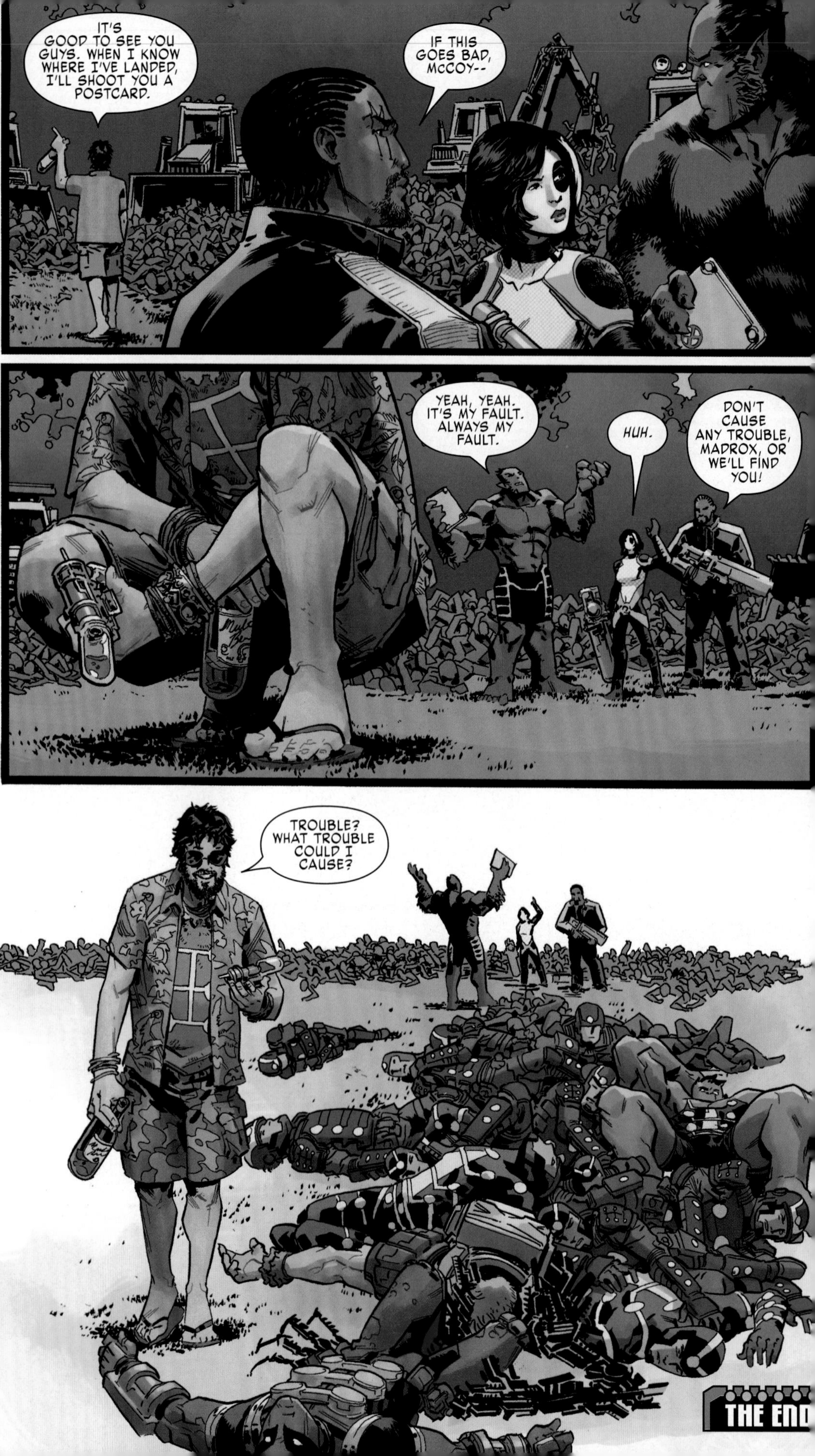
IT'S GOOD TO SEE YOU GUYS. WHEN I KNOW WHERE I'VE LANDED, I'LL SHOOT YOU A POSTCARD.
IF THIS GOES BAD, McCOY--
YEAH, YEAH. IT'S MY FAULT. ALWAYS MY FAULT.
HUH.
DON'T CAUSE ANY TROUBLE, MADROX, OR WE'LL FIND YOU!
TROUBLE? WHAT TROUBLE COULD I CAUSE?
THE END

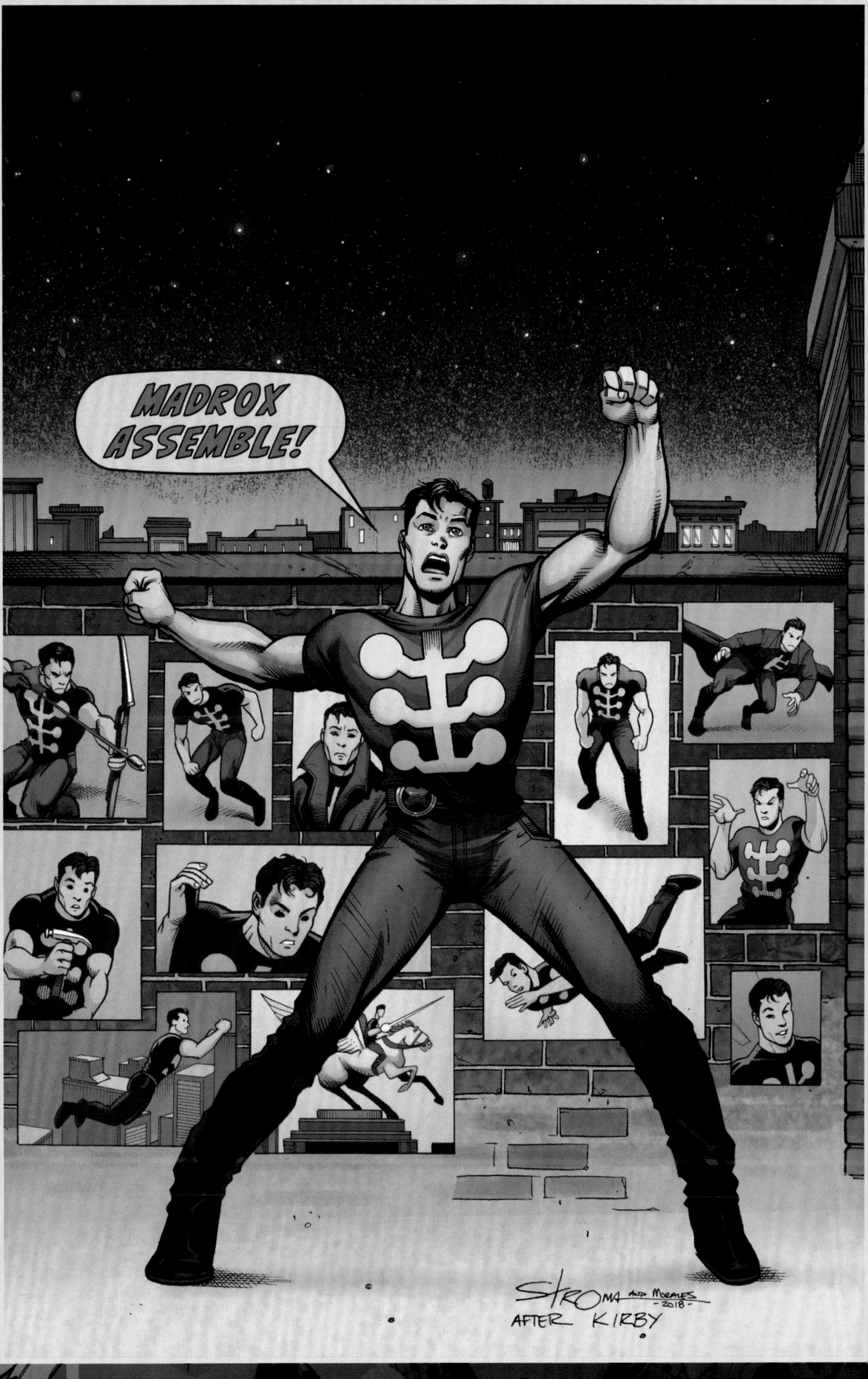
MADROX ASSEMBLE!
STROMAN AND MORALES -2018-
AFTER KIRBY

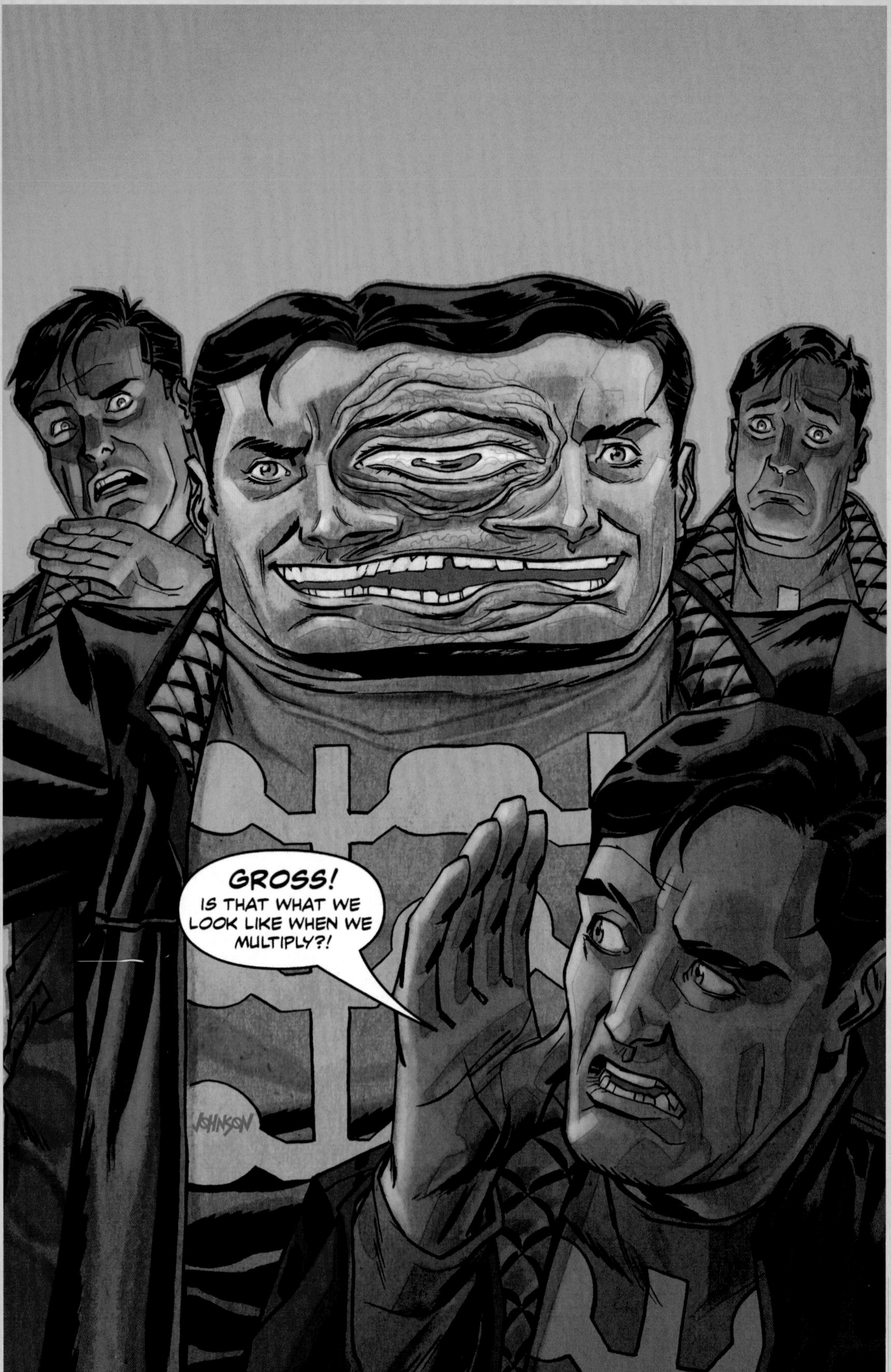
GROSS!
IS THAT WHAT WE LOOK LIKE WHEN WE MULTIPLY?!
JOHNSON

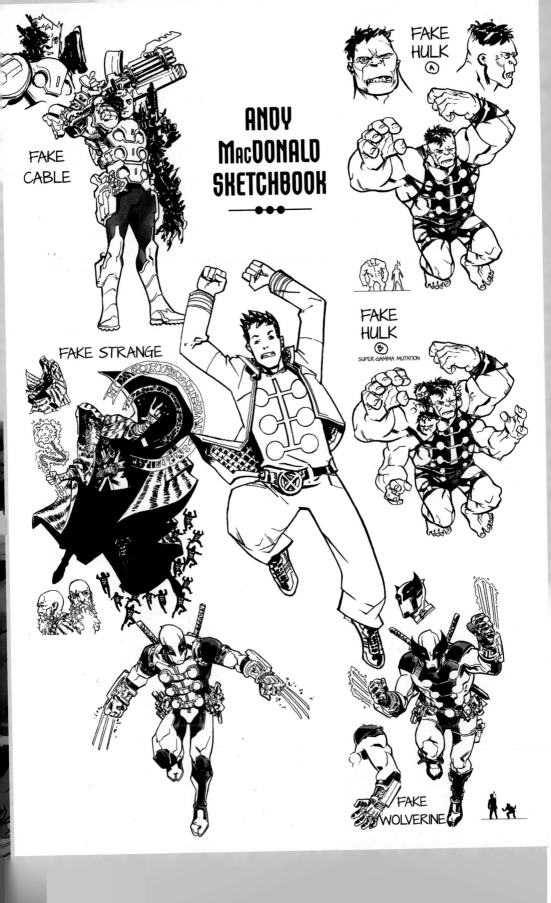

ANDY MacDONALD SKETCHBOOK

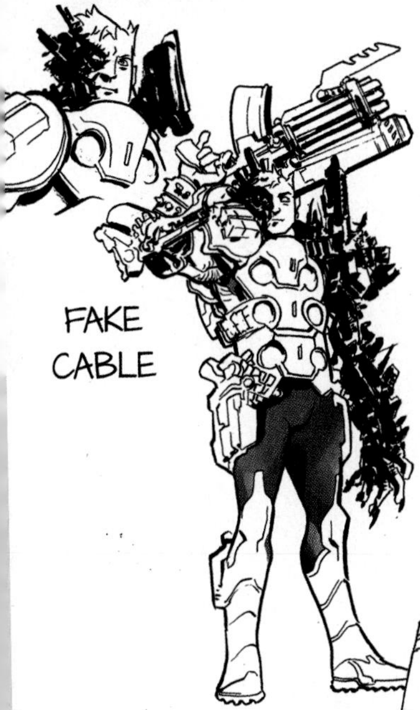
FAKE
CABLE

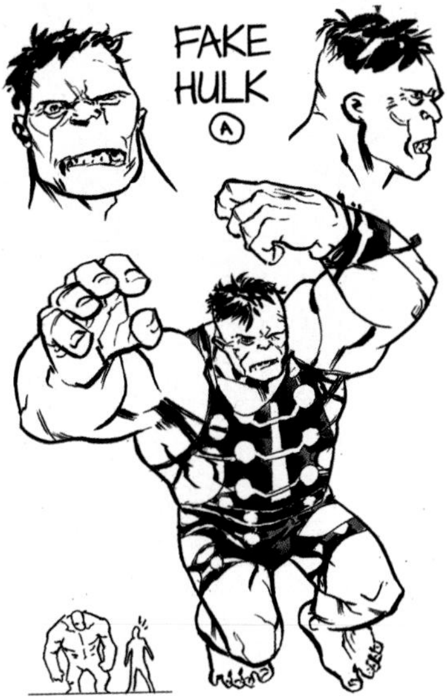
FAKE
HULK
A

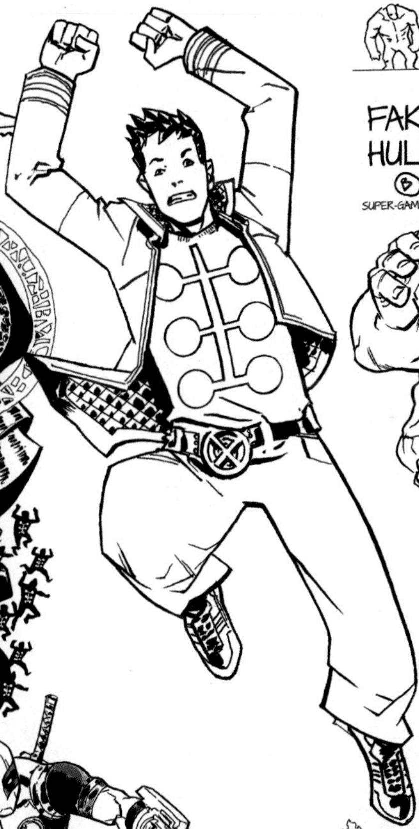

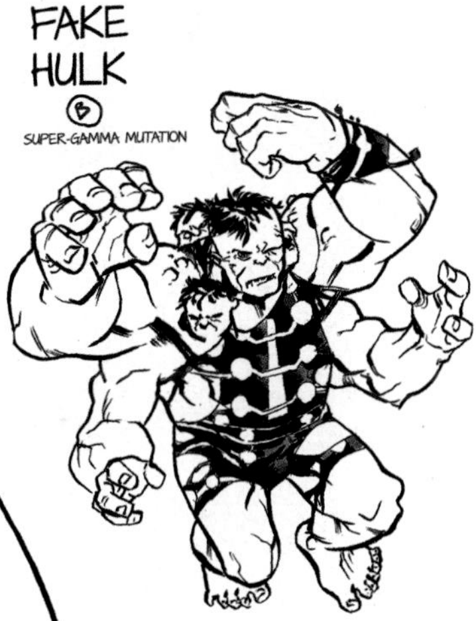
FAKE
HULK
B
SUPER-GAMMA MUTATION

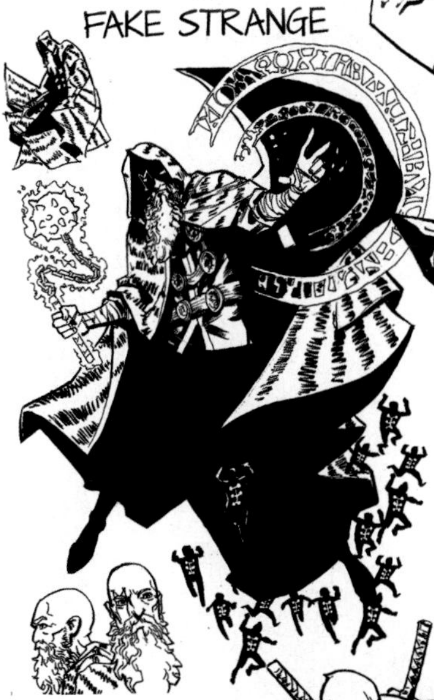
FAKE STRANGE

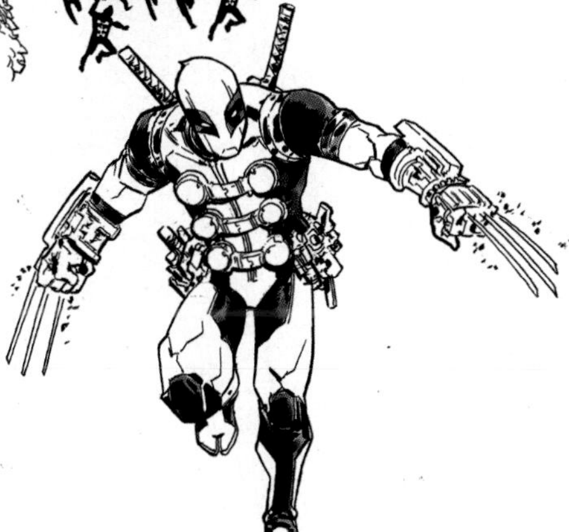

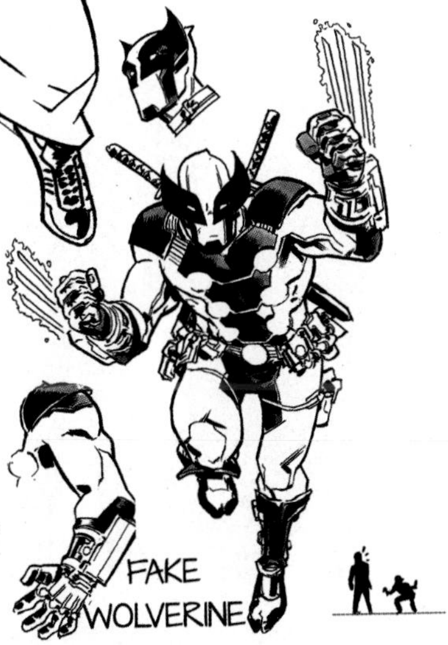
FAKE
WOLVERINE

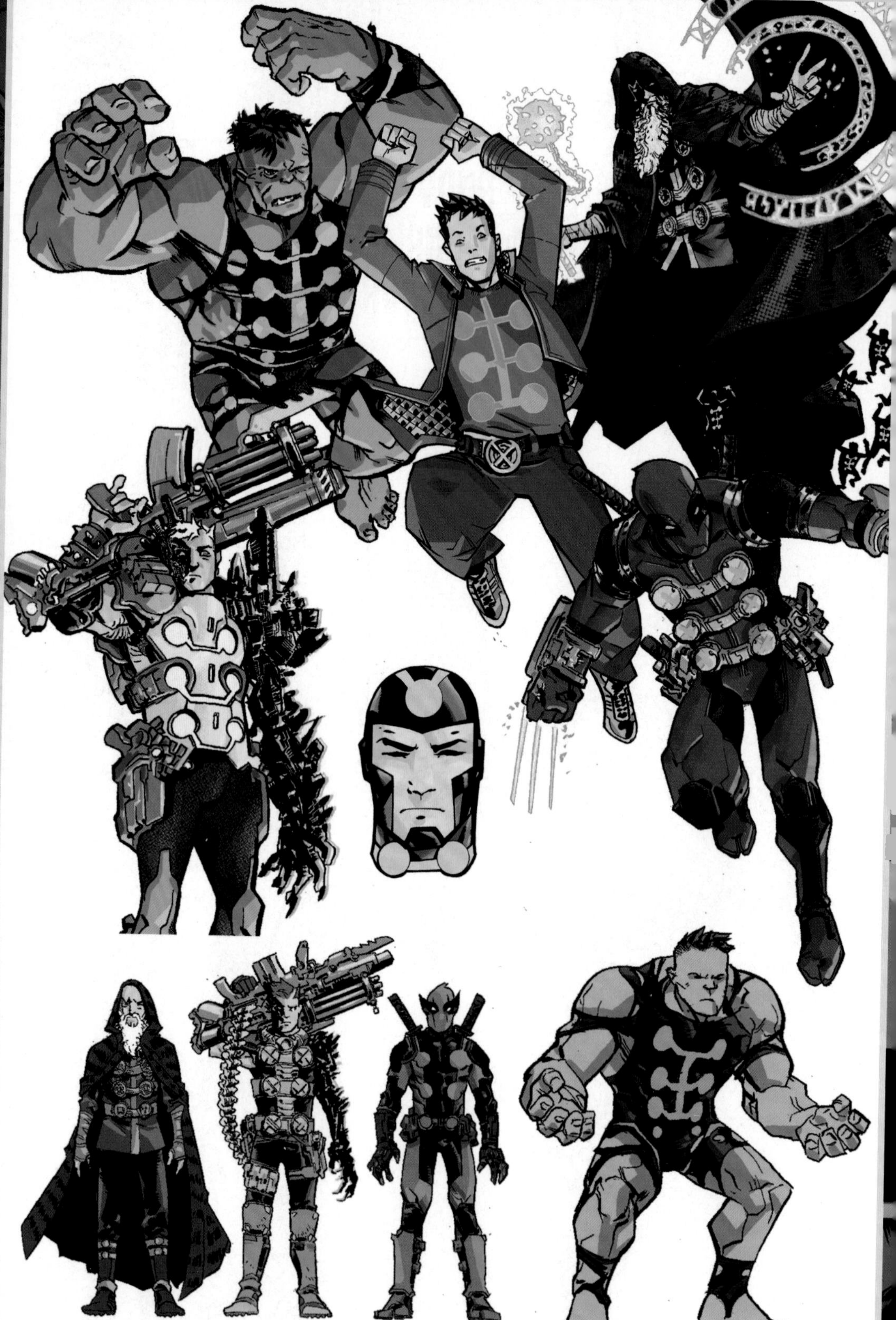